Interior Design Illustrated

Interior Design Illustrated

Marker and Watercolor Techniques

Christina M. Scalise

Fairchild Books, Inc.

New York

Director of Sales and Acquisitions:
Dana Meltzer-Berkowitz

Executive Editor: Olga T. Kontzias

Senior Development Editor: Jennifer Crane

Development Editor: Michelle Levy

Assistant Development Editor: Blake Royer

Art Director: Adam B. Bohannon

Production Director: Ginger Hillman

Production Editor: Jessica Rozler

Associate Art Director: Erin Fitzsimmons

Photo Research: Beth Cohen

Design: Robert L. Wiser

Cover Art: Christina M. Scalise

Cover Design: Adam B. Bohannon

All illustrations are copyright © 2008 by Christina M. Scalise, except where otherwise noted (see page 413).

Third Printing, 2011
Second Printing, 2010
Copyright © 2008 Fairchild Books,
A Division of Condé Nast Publications.

A catalog record for this book is held in the Library of Congress.

ISBN-13: 978-1-56367-531-7

ISBN-10: 1-56367-531-5

GST R 133004424

Printed in China

Title page: Floral wall art and Walter Gropius's Fagus factory armchair (1911) (watercolor and marker)

Contents

Preface

*"The visual image is a
kind of tripwire for the emotions."*

Diane Ackerman (b. 1948)

Interior designers use visual images to explain spatial relationships among a setting, its contents, and the people who use them. In any design presentation, renderings are one of the most powerful sales tools. We render for client appeal. Illustrations invite participation by the client and provoke a personal emotional interaction.

Although computer graphics are an invaluable aid to an interior designer—particularly because they allow quick revisions to drawings—a designer must balance computer and manual graphic skills. To illustrate an interior using a computer takes an enormous amount of time. Combining a computer-generated base perspective with hand refinement and illustration is a more sensible and pleasing approach. Hand skills are especially important to concept development in the interior design profession, and ideation flows rapidly when drawing manually. The ability to express your creativity in freehand drawing will set you apart from other designers. You will be far more valuable to an employer, make a personal connection to your design work, and have more fun by bringing strong eye-hand visual communication skills that do not rely on a computer.

Because few textbooks concentrate on the subject of interior illustration, *Interior Design Illustrated: Marker and Watercolor Techniques* has been written to fill that void. It serves as an introductory and intermediate text for studio courses on interior design illustration, concentrating on the elements and subjects of interior spaces and focusing on marker and watercolor techniques. The book is organized around step-by-step illustrations and instructions.

The lessons are uncomplicated, structured with small tasks, and include a comprehensive range of interior design elements and materials. A limited palette is used for the illustrations, making unnecessary a full palette of markers or paint. This approach takes less class time to mix colors and is more practical in budgeting supplies.

Chapters 1 through 3 discuss the creative tools, techniques, and symbols used for interior illustration, showing how to develop your ability to see, interpret, and synthesize interior subjects. Some of the best examples of professional illustrators from the present and the past are presented. In these and the subsequent chapters, practice exercises presented throughout the chapter are supplemented with additional assignments, found at the end of each chapter.

Louis Ghost chairs (Philippe Starck) and a coffee table (Marcel Wanders) (marker)

Several examples of uncomplicated interior vignettes are shown in chapter 4 to encourage study and experimentation on your own. These simple vignettes will help you see how rendered elements come together in an interior illustration. The subjects include residential, office, hospitality, and retail interiors in styles from minimalism to more complex and traditional.

Chapters 5 through 8 include detailed step-by-step instructions on illustrating interior architectural features, wall and floor finishes, and furniture. They focus on how to indicate various materials on many different surfaces. Addressed first are overall color application and how to indicate the texture of materials. Later steps bring the material and surface to life with definition and detail. Chapter 9 covers a variety of design enhancements, including the artwork, plants, tabletops, bedding, and sizzle that make illustrations come alive. Included in chapter 10 are additional materials and textures such as glass and metal, while the challenge of illustrating patterns is addressed in chapter 11.

The first item in the appendix is a selection of sample drawings to trace or copy for practice and specific assignments; instances in which the drawings in this tracing file will be helpful are cited in the text. The appendix also provides a checklist for self-evaluation of your work. Use it often during the process of learning, because feedback in the form of a critique is one of a designer's greatest tools for refining concepts. Critiques are used regularly in interior design offices throughout the design process. The more you evaluate your own work, the more you will welcome and understand the value of studio critiques from an instructor or an employer.

Independent research on the subject of illustration is also essential. As you work through each chapter, make it an ongoing project to gather additional resources related to specific topics in creation files (discussed in chapter 3).

Take full advantage of classes to learn by doing, using them to assess your work alongside your instructor and classmates. But be prepared for your studio time—it is disruptive to your learning process to stop and look for a tool or a material. Interruptions and distractions keep you from producing your best work. I encourage spontaneity, which can be lost in repetitious step-by-step procedures. Repeat the exercises presented, using a quicker pace and free-spirited gestures.

All the best on your new flight.

Christina M. Scalise

Acknowledgments

First and foremost, I thank my family and feel blessed to be the recipient of such support and kindness. The special character of my parents has been a great inspiration all through my life.

A very particular thank you goes to Guy Romagna for sharing his talent by letting me include a number of his fine-art paintings and illustrations in this book. I greatly appreciate this contribution and am honored to have him participate as a guest illustrator.

What a joy to have such enthusiastic colleagues and friends. Gregory Hoffman fortuitously planted a seed in my mind that gave this book its unique impetus. Virginia Tanner contributed her review and useful suggestions. Bina Abling offered insightful critiques. Maryse, Ruth, Sherry, and Mary—thank you for the comments, critiques, and encouragement. With excitement and humor, my friends Guy, Beatriz Tarajano, Cheryl, and Bina were frequently standing by. A huge thank you for the rally rounds.

I value the gems of experience imparted by Olga Kontzias, the executive editor of Fairchild Books. She is a grand lady and a perceptive editor whose passion, encouragement, and motivation have a huge positive impact on interior design education. Thanks to Jennifer Crane for her serenity and flexibility in a project such as this one. And a big hand for Adam Bohannon, Erin Fitzsimmons, Michelle Levy, Blake Royer, and Jessica Rozler, the very dedicated design, development, and production staff at Fairchild whose expertise brought it all together.

Thank you Donald S. Bozek, marketing manager, Strathmore™ Artist Papers; Mike Travers, Letraset Limited; and Robert Toth, vice president for marketing, Canson, Inc., for such extraordinary industry support. It is a delight to work with world-class products and organizations.

These reviewers have been very generous with their time and thoughtful suggestions: Katrina Lewis of Kansas State University and Sherwood Myers of the International Academy of Design and Technology–Florida.

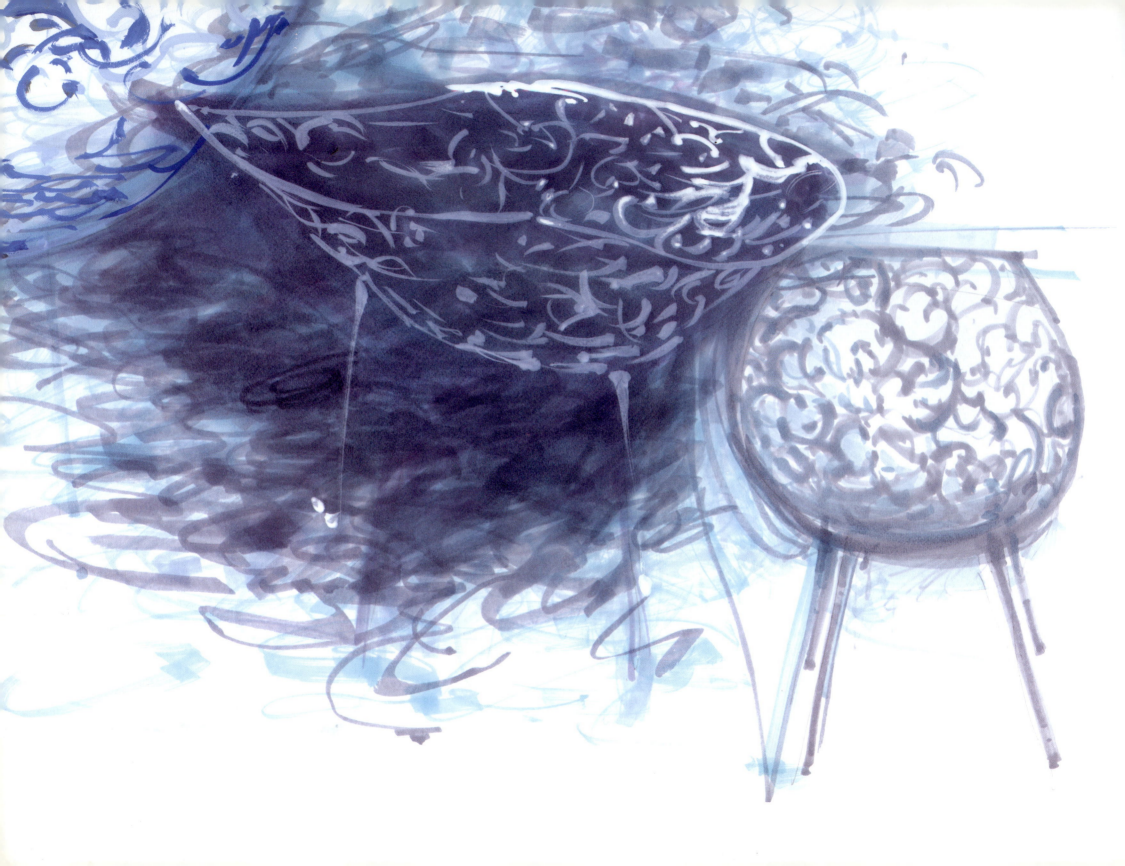

1

Creative Tools

Before you start any project, it is vital to have a comfortable studio area set up with proper lighting, a drawing table, a chair or a stool, and a parallel bar or a T-square. Because establishing a studio with the proper equipment, materials, and tools will cost hundreds of dollars, you may want to make the purchases over time. Yet keep in mind that the right tools for drawing and design thinking will help bring you closer to finding your own potential.

Miss Lacy chair (Philippe Starck) (marker and gouache)

Drawing Tools

An investment in proper drawing tools will produce great results. Make your purchases based on what you know to be your favorites from previous use and what is affordable. The materials presented below represent my own favorites, including items used to prepare the illustrations for this book:

- **Sketch roll.** 8-pound canary paper.

- **Staedtler Mars Lumograph pencils.** These drawing pencils are created in different leads designated with a B or an H. The B to 8B (softest) range creates soft drawing lines, while the H to 6H (hardest) range creates hard lines used in drafting. Sketch with a 2B pencil.

- **Staedtler Mars nonprint pencil (#108-40) and a blue nonphoto pencil.** These pencils will create lines that do not have to be erased. A nonprint pencil produces a purple line that does not reproduce on a blueprint machine, while a nonphoto pencil creates a line that does not reproduce on a photocopier.

- **Set of colored pencils.** These are needed because neither markers nor paint is used exclusively in an illustration. Watercolor pencils, which produce a softer and richer line, are useful if your budget allows. For a wider line, try color pencil sticks by Prismacolor. Using a watercolor crayon, such as Caran d'Ache, can produce some interesting strokes that look like crayon, oil paint, or watercolor.

- **Staedtler permanent black ink pigment liner pens.** These pens are available in a set that includes one each in 0.1, 0.3, 0.5, and 0.7 mm sizes.

- **Calligraphy markers.** These markers are my favorite for lettering and creating interesting line work. Try the double-ended Staedtler duo markers in black with a chisel tip, which have two chisel points; the water-based pigment ink is fade resistant and waterproof. A "painter's" calligraphy opaque paint marker is a great substitute for white gouache line work.

- **Variously sized transparent triangles (30/60 and 45/90) with inking edges.** Please resist the temptation to use them as cutting edges!

- **Large triangle or see-through ruler.** This can help relocate vanishing points and the horizon line within a perspective line drawing or a photograph.

- **Ship curves, flex curves, French curves, other form curves, and ellipse templates.** These tools, fabricated from clear plastic, are used to draw arcs and curves. A set contains curves of the following sizes: 24" (two), 13", 15½", 12½", and 6¾". I use ship curves far more often than the others.

- **Cork-backed stainless-steel ruler or no-slip inking rule.** Such rules are useful for cutting frisket film.

- **Drafting tape in ½", ¾", or 1" size.** Drafting tape is repositionable, acid free, and easily removed.

- **Mars plastic eraser.** This brand is better than most because it erases graphite cleanly and completely without damage to the paper surface.

- **Polished stainless-steel erasing shield.** An erasing shield will help control erasures of small areas on a drawing. Unless you are rendering a very light color over the lines, it is usually not necessary to remove all unwanted marks; they may disappear after color is applied.

- **Pounce cleaning powder.** This material removes dirt and smudges from tracing vellum without irritating the surface; it also prepares the paper surface to take ink more readily.

- **Drafting brush.** A drafting brush will gently remove eraser remains, dust, and lint from paper. It is better to use a brush, rather than your hand, so that you do not transfer moisture or oils to the paper surface.

- **Utility knife and X-Acto #1 knife.** Use the utility knife for cutting heavy-ply paper and board. An X-Acto #1 knife is better for detailed cutting of frisket and lightweight bond papers or patches on drawings.

Tip! Use a nonphoto or nonprint pencil for a baseline drawing. It can be drawn over with a pigment liner or a pencil before or after completing an illustration.

Markers and Paper

You will learn quickly if you approach illustration with a willingness to spend the time—and invest in enormous amounts of paper. It is important to begin by practicing and experimenting with any new medium. You will gain know-how by testing your markers on different papers.

Markers

Markers are quicker and easier to use than paint, but they are expensive and have a short shelf life. It is thus important to select a paper that will not be too absorbent and unnecessarily use up ink. The exercises that follow will help you understand the properties of different tips, pressures, paper surfaces, bleeding control, color mixing, saturation, and fluidity. By twisting, twirling, and varying the pressure when color is applied, a wide variety of line quality and coverage is achievable with various nibs. You will need a full range of gray-value markers. Each brand has a wide selection of such

ULTRA FINE   FINE   BROAD CHISEL

BRUSH TIP

1.1. Various marker nibs— ultra fine, fine, broad chisel, and brush tip—are available for producing different line widths and variations.

Tip! *Before placing drafting tape on paper to mask an area, you can reduce the tack even more by first sticking it on your clothing. Doing this eliminates damage to the paper when removing the tape.*

3

markers, including cool, warm, French, and ice gray versions. Gray markers are noted in the text using manufacturers' color names—for example, Cool Gray 03 or 30% Gray.

Marker brands include Copic, Letraset Pantone and Tria, Prismacolor, and Chartpak. Take a look at Lucile Loona's "Marker Brand Comparisons" at Manga Revolution (www.mangarevolution.com/tutorial_display.php?tutorial_id=77) for some good information on different marker types. I use all brands and still love the old Magic Markers because their tips are soft. Most marker illustrations in this book were completed using Letraset Tria markers with a broad nib in color system numbers ending with a "T," unless otherwise noted.

Color charts can be used to compare marker colors, but a printed color is not an exact match. Manufacturers' color charts with names or numbers are available from art supply stores and catalogs, manufacturers' web sites, and art supply web sites (www.copicmarker.com, www.prisma-color.com, www.letraset.com, www.chartpak.com/kohinoor/1drawing/admarker_sets.html#). A sheet correlating Tria pens with the Pantone Matching System is available at O'Sullivan Graphics (http://www.osullivangraphics.com/p/tria.pdf). However, it is best to go to your local art store to view marker colors on paper swatches.

Pantone Cool Gray 03

Pantone Warm Gray 03

458T

4655T

182T

264T

304T

358T

1.2. To save time when selecting marker colors for an illustration, a chart can be made using various colors layered to create new combinations. This color matrix is composed of eight marker colors.

1.3. Tria marker pen colors, as shown in this Letraset chart, correlate with the Pantone Matching System colors.

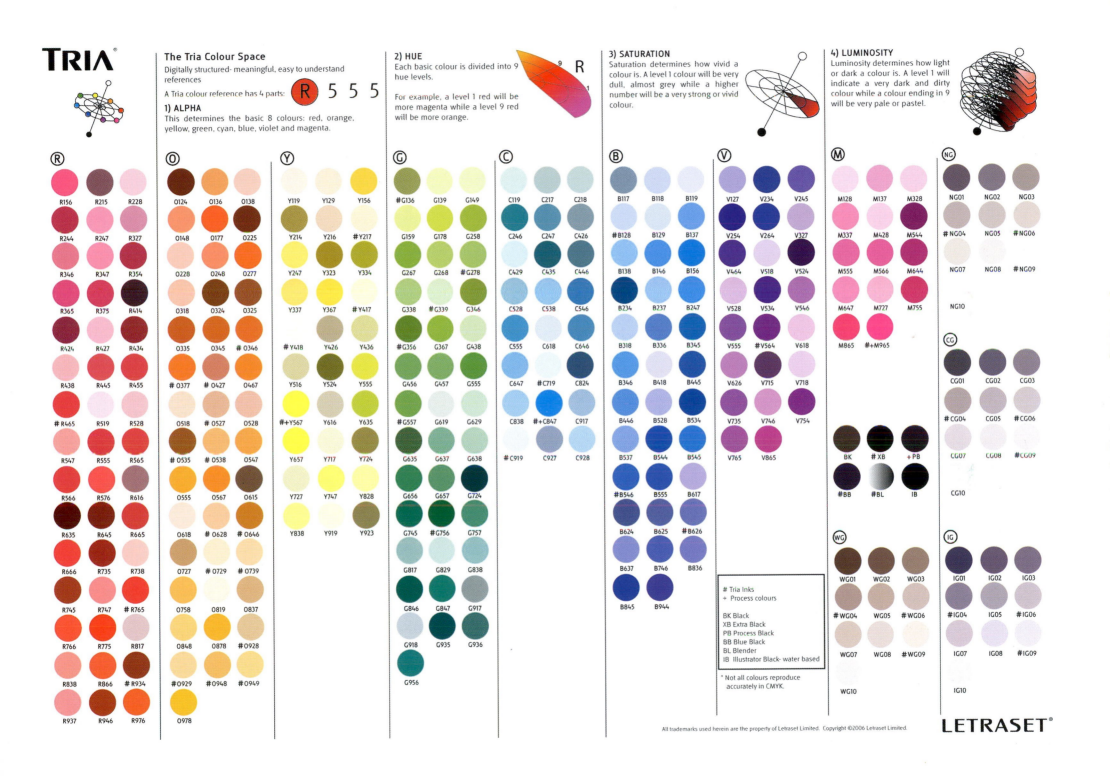

TRIA®

The Tria Colour Space
Digitally structured- meaningful, easy to understand references

A Tria colour reference has 4 parts: **R 5 5 5**

1) ALPHA
This determines the basic 8 colours: red, orange, yellow, green, cyan, blue, violet and magenta.

2) HUE
Each basic colour is divided into 9 hue levels.

For example, a level 1 red will be more magenta while a level 9 red will be more orange.

3) SATURATION
Saturation determines how vivid a colour is. A level 1 colour will be very dull, almost grey while a higher number will be a very strong or vivid colour.

4) LUMINOSITY
Luminosity determines how light or dark a colour is. A level 1 will indicate a very dark and dirty colour while a colour ending in 9 will be very pale or pastel.

Tria Inks
+ Process colours

BK Black
XB Extra Black
PB Process Black
BB Blue Black
BL Blender
IB Illustrator Black- water based

* Not all colours reproduce accurately in CMYK.

All trademarks used herein are the property of Letraset Limited. Copyright ©2006 Letraset Limited.

LETRASET®

1.4. *Demonstrating the effect of different paper stocks, marker color 4505T is used on the following paper types: (a) bond paper for markers, (b) bond paper for photocopiers and printers, (c) bond paper for laser printers, (d) smooth Bristol paper, (e) Bienfang #528P tracing sketch roll (canary), (f) tracing paper from a pad, (g) Strathmore™ tracing sketch roll (light canary), and (h) drafting vellum.*

1.5. *Marker lines applied in 30% Gray and 80% Gray show the variations achieved by using cardboard guides: (a) vertical strokes, (b) vertical strokes with an oblique layer on top, (c) horizontal strokes, (d) strokes going to the vanishing point, and (e) bleeding from an oversaturated cardboard guide.*

Marker Paper

Use any type of paper that will capture the mood of a space and enhance the presentation—it is fun to see the results on sepia paper, vellum, tissue, and lighter papers. Because marker papers vary, you must test each for absorbency and bleeding. Borden & Riley has a tablet with numerous types of paper that would be a good way to start your test.

Until you have mastered the use of markers, avoid papers that can be penetrated and bleed easily. Some do not absorb well, preventing easy color mixing. Bristol and illustration board are good to use but time consuming for the transfer of line work. I have used blueprint paper, copy paper, and the like, but they have a tendency to drag and rapidly dry out the markers.

My preference is layout bond paper that has been treated for markers because of its good color rendition; its transparency makes it easy to trace a block-out sketch. This paper will also absorb many layers of marker before the color begins to sit on top of the surface. For most of the marker illustrations in this book, I used these two bond paper tablets: Letraset Bleedproof marker pad and Borden & Riley 100s Smooth Comp marker paper. These are recommended for your practice studies because you will be happier with the results and the bond paper is relatively inexpensive.

1.6. Key materials used when working with markers include frisket film, drafting tape for masking, and a cardboard guide.

Remember that every paper has a front or drawing surface—the correct side is the one facing out when the tablet is opened. Using the back of the paper will produce different results. Test these different marker papers with your brand of markers to understand how each paper absorbs color and when it will bleed color if too much is applied.

Bond paper is best dry mounted to illustration board before adding any paint for enhancements. Dry mounting produces a sturdy, flat rendering surface. The paper is then ready to take light amounts of water for spattering or fine line work with paint. A removable dry-mounting tissue makes it easy to cut and patch any mistakes.

A marker guide is a long, narrow piece of heavy-ply illustration board. It is used as a guide for applying straight strokes of marker color. A white or light-colored board is best because you can see when the strip is too saturated to use any longer. This happens quickly and leaves undesirable results on the paper; therefore, precut a large supply of marker guides before beginning any marker rendering. Each must be cut with clean, crisp edges. A width of approximately 1½" works well. I use leftover dry-mounting board, but scrap pieces of mat board also work well. A guide that does not absorb ink—a plastic triangle or a ruler, for example—will allow the marker to build up and leave unwanted color marks on the paper as well as destroy the guide's edge.

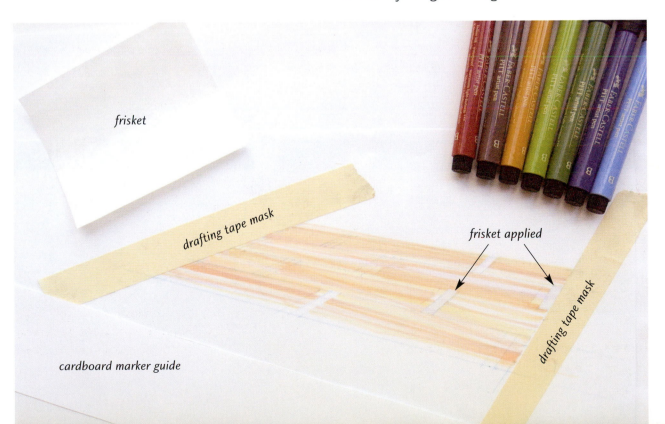

frisket

drafting tape mask

frisket applied

cardboard marker guide

drafting tape mask

Watercolor Paint and Paper

You can read forever about how to work in water-color, but you will learn only by trying the medium to get the feel of it. You will fall in love with water-color or dislike it because the learning process creates both treasures and disappointments. Several helpful watercolor books are listed in Resources.

Following are the tools you will need to create magic with watercolor. Here again, be prepared to use a tremendous amount of paper.

Watercolor Paint

Watercolor pigments vary in coverage from transparent and opaque colors to staining and nonstaining colors to granulating colors.

1.7. Watercolor paints are manufactured by a number of companies, such as Van Gogh, one of whose color charts is shown here. The company makes a starter set of a dozen colors in 10 ml tubes.

Tip! "A thin diluted application of Indigo (an opaque paint) is more transparent than a thick layer of Prussian Blue (transparent paint)." Frank Webb

Transparent colors

Aureolin
Gamboge Genuine
Indian Yellow
Quinacridone Red
Permanent Alizarin Crimson
Permanent Carmine
Rose Madder Genuine
Quinacridone Magenta
Purple Madder
Permanent Magenta
Thioindigo Violet
Winsor Violet (Dioxazine)
Ultramarine (Green Shade)
Winsor Blue (Red Shade)
Antwerp Blue
Prussian Blue
Viridian
Winsor Green (Yellow Shade)
Hooker's Green
Permanent Sap Green
Olive Green
Green Gold
Raw Sienna
Quinacridone Gold
Burnt Umber

Opaque colors

Lemon Yellow (Nickel Titanate)
Cadmium Yellows
Cadmium Orange and Reds
Cerulean Blue
Chromium Oxide Green
Vermilion
Winsor Emerald
Cobalt Green (Yellow Shade)
Naples Yellow
Naples Yellow Deep
Light Red
Venetian Red
Indian Red
Sepia
Indigo
Neutral Tint
Blue Black
Ivory Black
Lamp Black
Titanium White

Cadmium paints such as Cerulean Blue and Chromium Oxide Green are naturally opaque, so they have more covering power than most watercolors. They are tricky to use under a glaze or a layer because they may lift, deaden, or counteract the next layer.

Nonstaining colors

Emerald Green
Permanent Rose
Manganese Blue
Aureolin
Cobalt Violet

Heavy staining colors

Phthalocyanine Blue
Phthalocyanine Green
Phthalocyanine Violet
Dioxazine Purple (Winsor Violet)
Alizarin Crimson
Scarlet Lake
Sap Green
Hooker's Green

Light staining colors

Gold Ochre
Raw Umber
Cadmium Orange
Cobalt Blue
Gamboge Yellow
Cerulean Blue
Magenta

Staining colors such as Phthalo and Prussian Blue; Alizarin Crimson; and Winsor Red, Yellow, and Blue are difficult to remove, because the pigment is much finer and penetrates the paper fibers.

Granulating colors

Cadmium Red
Cadmium Red Deep
Rose Madder Genuine
Cobalt Violet
Permanent Mauve
Ultramarine Violet
Cobalt Blue Deep
French Ultramarine
Cobalt Blue
Cerulean Blue
Manganese Blue
Cobalt Green
Viridian
Raw Sienna
Raw Umber
Ivory Black

Granulation is a natural property of certain pigments, such as Cerulean Blue, French Ultramarine, Manganese Blue, and Raw Sienna. All such colors can get muddy if overworked.

Cobalt Violet

Raw Sienna

Cerulean Blue

Cerulean Blue

1.8. These granulating watercolors, painted on 140-pound Sennelier hot-pressed watercolor paper, leave a very fine and grainy sediment on the paper after drying, an effect useful for enhancing numerous surface textures.

Start with a small set of watercolors. Maintain a palette of twelve colors and add to it for your specific requirements. Brands include Van Gogh, Winsor & Newton, Cotman, Daler-Rowney Holbein, M. Graham & Company, MaimeriBlu, American Journey, and Sennelier. Van Gogh makes a set containing twelve 10 ml tubes of Permanent Red Light, Madder Lake Deep, Permanent Lemon Yellow, Azo Yellow Medium, Yellow Ochre, Cobalt Blue, Ultramarine Deep, Permanent Green, Viridian, Payne's Gray, Burnt Sienna, and Chinese White. The set also includes a #6 pointed round nylon brush and a sponge. This brand and American Journey are well priced and also available in large (37 ml) tubes.

I use the following colors made by Van Gogh: Thioindigo Violet, Cadmium Red Light, Cobalt Violet, Manganese Blue, Quinacridone Rose, Phthalo Green, Raw Sienna, Ultramarine Blue, Aureolin, Alizarin Crimson, Cadmium Orange, Cobalt Blue, Hansa Yellow Light, Payne's Gray, Raw Umber, Sepia, Yellow Ochre, Quinacridone Burnt Orange, Quinacridone Violet, Burnt Sienna, Cerulean Blue, Viridian Green, Cadmium Yellow Lemon, Gamboge, Prussian Blue, and Peach Black. In addition, you will need Designers Gouache in Permanent White.

Watercolor Paper

Experiment! The best way to understand the results of paint on paper is to experiment with many brands and grades of paper. Papers with a 100% rag content are high quality. Rag refers to the fibers, which are made into a souplike consistency and then transformed into paper. Cheaper papers are created with a combination of rag and wood pulp. (Construction paper is 100% wood pulp.) Watercolor papers are made with various surface qualities, including hot pressed (a smooth, hard surface), cold pressed (a medium or rough surface), and rough (a rugged texture). These papers are available in pound weights (based on the weight of a ream, or 500 sheets), connoting the thickness. Choices include 72-pound, 140-pound, and 300-pound paper. The heaviest is the thickest and the most expensive.

Look for hot-pressed or cold-pressed paper with a smooth surface for your illustrations. It is difficult to lay down a wash on rough paper. Very light paper wrinkles, holds water puddles and causes backwash rings, and must be taped to a painting board. However, a smooth surface is good for large painted areas, to which you can return and add brushwork and pen or pencil lines. A hard, smooth surface can take many media because it does not allow the paint to sink into or be absorbed by the paper as much as other types. Even so, a second wash of color may pick up the first layer of dried color; this can happen if you are too aggressive in applying the second wash.

For the illustrations in this book, I used several types of Strathmore™ paper: (1) 500 series illustration board, heavyweight plate, 240-022; (2) 500 series Bristol; (3) 400 series smooth art board, heavyweight, 478-15; and (4) 400 series Bristol. Another brand worth trying is Lenox 100 percent cotton, neutral pH. I used Bristol board for the small watercolor studies because it is inexpensive and the studies are small enough that the paper does not buckle too much from the moisture content.

Practice on a small pad of Bristol board before you spend too much money on better papers. Its drawback is puddle marks. Some papers may have a sizing or starch on the surface that creates tiny little white spots when paint is applied. By gently washing the surface with a soft, damp sponge and letting it dry, the sizing can be removed. After a bit of practice on the less expensive stock, try other watercolor boards to determine what works best for you.

Crescent cold-pressed illustration boards have a slightly textured surface and are used primarily for watercolor, gouache, acrylic, tempera, pen and ink, charcoal, and pencil illustration. Crescent #100 illustration board is a heavyweight, professional-grade board with a high rag content and a medium surface. The company recommends watercolor board as a surface for illustrations that will be scanned and transferred to digital media (it is not acid free, so it is not suitable for permanent artwork). Crescent watercolor board—used for watercolor, illustration, and airbrush—is a 100 percent cotton rag paper mounted on one side to an extra-heavy, ⅛"-thick (40-ply) board to eliminate the need for stretching. The paper is 140 pounds and is available in hot-press and cold-press surfaces.

You could also try Arches 140-pound hot-pressed watercolor paper. This stock, used more by fine artists than by illustrators, is of superior quality and suitable for all techniques in watercolor, acrylic, ink, alkyds (faster-dying oil paint), pencil (watercolor, color, and graphite), gouache, charcoal, and airbrush. It withstands rigorous scrubbing, scratching, and erasing but must be securely adhered to a board to keep it flat while working. Cold-pressed and rough-surface papers generally have too much texture for interior illustrations. Stay away from the tablets of machine-made synthetic watercolor paper, because the paint merely sits on the surface.

To transfer a drawing to illustration board or watercolor paper, you will need transfer paper that is waxless and greaseless and does not bleed through paint. Be sure that it is smudge proof and erasable as well. Do not use fixative spray on any line drawing for watercolor illustration, because the paint may not adhere; instead use fixative on the back of the transfer paper to reduce smudging.

Presenting an illustration with rippled paper is unprofessional and reflects poorly on your craftsmanship. Damaged paper can be flattened with a dry-mounting machine or a stack of heavy books to get rid of the ripples. Lightweight papers can be stretched before rendering to diminish some of the rippling.

Brushes and Additional Supplies

Choosing brushes is always a challenge. Test a brush before you purchase it by placing it in your hand and imagine painting on a sturdy surface. Also develop an eye for less obvious painting tools. Anything from quill pens to pastry cutters could some day help you achieve an unusual texture or effect.

Tip! Long-hair brushes are good to use when working on dry paper because they have a great capacity to carry water. Short-hair brushes work well on wet paper. And remember to wash brushes in soapy water immediately after use.

Brushes

Sable brushes are the top of the line; the finest fiber used for making brushes is Kolinsky sable. Synthetic fiber brushes can be substituted, however. I like to use the Aquarelle Flat, a top-quality synthetic brush, because it has a clear acrylic handle cut on an angle, which is good for scraping paint. The brush comes in ¼", ½", ¾", and 1" sizes and is an excellent tool for scraping and scribbling lines through color (see figure 2.25). Princeton Art & Brush Company manufactures a good synthetic sable blend (4050 series).

Here are some basic requirements for brushes:

- **Angled flat brushes.** Make sure that you have at least one of these, as they are great for tight spaces. Because of the angle, such a brush will feel familiar to you, like a broad-nib marker.

- **Watercolor wash brush.** Synthetic is okay. I use a 1½"-angle wash brush (#4050afw) by Princeton Art & Brush Company. The Pure Siberian Kazan Squirrel wash brush is soft and has a high water capacity for large watercolor washes and a short, flat handle for maximum control.

- **Flat brushes.** Have ½", ¾", and 1" sizes for various tasks.

- **Round brushes.** Purchase #10, #12, and #14 brushes.

- **Fan brush.** You will love to use a fan brush for indicating wood grain, deep carpet pile, and numerous other surface textures and patterns. An alternative is to split open the bristles of a damp flat brush with your fingers before or after loading it with paint.

- **Rigger brush.** Traditionally used for calligraphy type lines, this brush has long bristles that hold a lot of water and paint. It is useful for fine-line detailing and many interesting curvilinear brush strokes.

- **Sponges.** For creating textures, keep handy some natural sponges, such as small elephant ear and medium sea silk sponges.

Additional Supplies

You are not done yet! Some additional artist's supplies—some obvious and others less so—will prove useful as you embark on your illustration projects.

- **Palette.** A slotted palette works well to keep the paints from bleeding into each other. The palette should be white, with wide enough slots for a brush. I like to use porcelain palettes that look like old butcher trays. Arrange your colors in the palette in a way that is easiest for you to remember where they are. Label the slots if that helps, and arrange the paint by warm colors, cool colors, and earth tones.

- **Painting panel.** Panels of Masonite, a resilient surface that will stand up to years of use, can be put to work for taping down watercolor paper. Try to find a panel with a carrying slot and a metal clip attached. The panels come in various sizes and are ⅛" thick and tempered for extra strength.

- **Water containers.** Just about anything can be used to hold water, and it does not have to be deep. I use two: one for clean water and another for cleaning my brush. Do not leave your brush in the water because it will damage the brush tip, rust the ferrule (metal band), and cause the handle finish to crack and fall off.

- **Artist's bridge.** An artist's bridge is a transparent plastic shelf raised above the drawing surface. An essential tool, it allows you to add details to your painting or drawing without smearing, to rule straight lines with a brush or a pen, or to steady a shaking hand. A good size to use is 18" long. I use an architectural triangular scale held on edge.

- **Frisket film.** This transparent masking film (see figure 1.6) is compatible with almost all surfaces and just about any medium. Easy to peel, it is backed by translucent paper for ease in cutting and to allow the line drawing underneath to be seen. Be sure to purchase low-tack frisket film because it is easy to lift and reposition.

- **Masking fluid.** Art masking fluid is used for setting aside areas of work to be protected from subsequent washes of color. When dry, masking fluid creates a water-impervious film that can be removed by gently peeling or rubbing.

Tip! To make your own artist's bridge, tape stacks of coins to a sturdy see-through ruler or triangle. Raise it enough so the tip of your brush can glide on the paper, and the ferrule can rest on the edge of the ruler. Ellipse templates or French curves can also be used.

- **Salt.** Because it is absorbent, salt can help create interesting textural effects (see figure 10.22c). Dried bread crumbs, coffee grounds, or cement powder can do the same.

- **Bleach.** Spraying, spattering, or dropping bleach into marker or watercolor media results in washing out color and sometimes can bring white back to the paper. The pitfall is permanent damage to the paper that may cause it to disintegrate over time. A dampened white Mr. Clean® sponge is also effective in lifting out color.

- **Light box.** A light box is useful for tracing drawings and creating overlays to develop pattern guidelines.

- **Dry-mounting machine.** Access to one of these machines is desirable for dry mounting, in which heat and pressure are applied to layers of paper, mounting film (reversible adhesive), and board.

- **Tacking iron.** Access to a tacking iron, used for mounting and patching, is also desirable. It can be used to reheat and remove an area that has been cut to receive a correction patch.

Additional Resources

- **Papers:** www.strathmoreartist.com

- **Watercolor pigments:** www.watercolorpainting
.com/pigments.htm#staining; www.talens.com/
english/technical/default.asp?subID=1

- **Brushes:** www.princetonartandbrush.com

- **Palettes:** www.cheapjoes.com/art-supplies/
4568_watercolor-palettes.asp;
www.dickblick.com/categories/palettes

*Tip! To steady a shaky hand when holding
a brush or a marker, rest the tip of your small finger
on the paper surface.*

Assignments

1. Research. Go through this book to study the watercolor and marker colors used, making notes of colors and supplies that you need. Keep in mind that the printed colors in this book or on the manufacturers' color charts will not precisely match the actual colors. Research the colors just as you will later when purchasing colors to match your design material samples. Make a preliminary list before going to purchase supplies.

2. Get ready. Purchase the materials you need and be sure to take a sketchbook or a notebook with you. Purchase marker paper before buying the markers. Tape a few blank pieces of the marker paper in your sketchbook for testing markers at the store.

a. *At the art supply store*

- Test different marker nibs of various manufacturers.

- Make notes of the properties of each and what you like and dislike about them.

- As your budget allows, purchase what you will need to practice the exercises in this book.

b. *Setting up your studio space*

- The drawing surface should be tilted at about 15 degrees.

- A reference area works best to the right of the drawing surface (if you are right handed); switch this around if you are left handed.

- Sit in your chair, and extend and swing your arm in a large half circle to determine your reach. The arc distance is your comfortable reach; it should not be larger than the work surface area.

- Try to stage a combination of artificial light with natural light. Most artists prefer a north-facing window (for constant, unchanging light) to the left. A fluorescent light fixture with one cool white tube and one warm white tube comes close to natural light colors.

3. **Create a color matrix.** Create a matrix of your marker colors similar to the one in figure 1.2. Use the same type of paper that you plan to use for your illustrations. Apply the markers vertically and then horizontally in the same color order. Note what the colors are on one side as well as on the top or bottom. Create the same type of matrix using watercolors. Keep both at hand for reference each time you study color choices for an illustration.

4. **Experiment.** Get used to handling a marker and a brush. Write your name in cursive and architectural lettering styles with different marker nibs. Paint various marks on paper using different brushes. Try painting with ordinary objects, such as the tip of a brush handle, a palette knife, the side of a credit card, or a crayon loaded with paint. Draw with them, and scrape with them. Vary the pressure of your grip when trying all of these suggestions. Seek to understand how the tools feel in your hand and respond to your gestures.

5. **Practice.** Practice the illustrations shown in figures 1.1, 1.4, 1.5, and 1.8 before beginning the next chapter. Likewise, practice all of the step-by-step illustrations in each chapter before beginning the assignments or moving on to the following chapter.

6. **Pat yourself on the back!** Using your favorite marker or rendering tool, write a confirmation statement to yourself.

Beginnings are exciting. You will blossom regardless of your skill level. Students with energy and enthusiasm but little or no knowledge of art can develop into brilliant interior illustrators. As you start out, take advantage of all the energy and enthusiasm you are generating. Bravo!

Markers and Watercolors

Your new job title is interpreter—because the interior illustrator has to make many of the same decisions as a fine artist makes when planning a composition, beginning with the choice of media. In working with markers and watercolors, you will learn a few simple techniques drawn from fine-art studies that also apply to design illustration. One difference is that interior illustrations typically combine several media to enhance and reinforce one another.

Tord Boontje collection for Moroso and an Emma Gardner area carpet (watercolor)

2.1. This sketch combines marker, watercolor paint, gouache paint, and colored pencils.

Comparison of Media

Markers and watercolors have their own unique characteristics. In time you will prefer one to the other. With each, you can achieve great transparency as well as good color mixing and blending. Most interior illustration is a combination of media: base colors can be achieved with marker or paint, details are quick and easy when drawn with pencil.

- **Markers.** Relatively inexpensive, markers allow you to work rapidly and are excellent for drawing crisp edges.

- **Watercolor paint.** Watercolor is superior for creating large areas of color wash and achieving a limitless color range. Its fluidity and blending qualities help produce a serene effect and soften the look of hard materials.

- **Gouache paint.** With its ability to achieve both softness and hard lines, gouache is the traditional medium for interior illustration. Although time consuming to use, gouache as well as tempera have an opaque nature that allows for easy corrections.

- **Oil paint.** Oil paint is not a typical medium for illustrating interiors, but it creates more of a pure artistic expression.

- **Pastel chalk and pencil.** Pastel chalk and pencil impart a soft feeling and facilitate infinite blending capabilities. These media were often used during the mid-twentieth century, while highly detailed, texturized, and well-blended pencil illustrations gained popularity in the 1980s.

2.2. Markers with a small amount of white gouache are an excellent choice for capturing the crisp edges of this sofa grouping.

2.3. Gouache was once traditional for interior illustrations. The reduction of detail in Nadim Racy's gouache illustration here is outstanding.

2.4. This transparent watercolor illustration was enhanced with black pencil.

2.5. *Using oil paint, the artist Julian LaTrobe communicates an inviting room atmosphere through his selection of values and assertive brushwork. His brush was loaded with paint, creating thick impasto strokes.*

2.6a. *Although time consuming to use, pastel chalk and pencil allow great blending capabilities and crisp detail work, as can be seen in this illustration by José M. Reinares Méndez.*

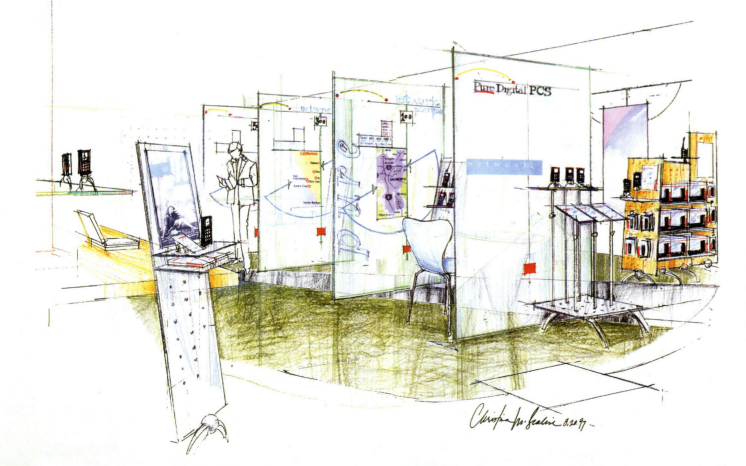

2.6b. *Colored pencil on bond paper and photocopy collage were used for this prototype retail design. Pencil was chosen because it is easier to indicate the text in the graphics with it, and it offered the ability to softly blend material colors and textures.*

Color Mixing

PAGE 22 Because markers and watercolor paint are transparent media, we rely on them to create optical color—tones that will show through a second layer of transparent color. Color dominance, often achieved by applying an undertone, unifies a rendering. Mixing or blending colors can produce the best rendition of a challenging interior color or texture. Note that each color's saturation amount does not become apparent until it is dry. The results will vary depending on the colors used and their specific layer order.

This would be a good time to review what you have learned in previous study about color theory (reference to these theories is made throughout this book). Remember this for color mixing:

- **Primary colors** are red, yellow, and blue. Any other color can be achieved by mixing these colors.

- **Secondary colors** of orange, violet, and green can be created by combining primaries.

- **Tertiary colors** are created from secondary colors. As low-chroma versions of the primary colors, these grayer tones create color harmony because they contain parts of all the primary hues.

- **A color's complement** is its opposite on the color wheel—for example, the complement of violet is yellow.

Basic color terms used in color composition are chroma, hue, saturation, tint, tone, shade, chromatic, achromatic, and value.

- **Chroma** is hue or color, including all tints, tones, and shades.

- **Hue** is a single undiluted color.

- **Saturation** is the degree of vividness. For instance, a diluted watercolor wash has less brilliance than a wash containing more pigment. Figures 2.7a and 2.8 are examples of various degrees of saturation using marker layers.

- **Tint** is a hue with the addition of white. White is not added to markers or watercolor paint because the transparent nature of these media uses the white of the paper.

- **Tone** is a hue with the addition of grays; figures 2.9 and 2.10 are examples.

- **Shade** is a hue with the addition of black.

- **Chromatic** refers to all hues, tints, tones, and shades.

- **Achromatic** refers to the range of gray from white to black. Figure 2.12 shows a value scale representing several grays between white and black. (A value scale is usually ten values in gradation, with white at the light end and black at the dark end of the scale.) How to plan a composition's value range is discussed in chapter 3.

2.7a. *Showing from one to five layers of 4525T, this example illustrates how gradation can be used with markers by letting a dark background color gradually get lighter as it comes into the foreground, or vice versa.*

Marker Layering

Value is the achromatic equivalent of the chromatics. Each hue has an equivalent value. Colors meet one another at a subject's edges; when the values are close, there is only a subtle separation. An increase in the difference in value will heighten the definition between objects. Remember this when the subjects in an an illustration blend too much with one another and read as an undesirable overall form.

Some illustrations are unsuccessful because of inappropriate color choices. Study your subject to determine which colors and techniques to use. Be sure that your marker and paint colors are in harmony with each other, and select a test paper that is the same stock as the final rendering. Do not be tempted to correct a mistake by putting the right color on top of the wrong one. This is a simple trial-and-error process; eventually you will become experienced enough to accurately predict the results.

Palette mixtures cannot be achieved with markers as they can be with paint. With markers, the illustrator is almost totally dependent on optical mixtures of color, layering one color atop another. The order of the layers is important because it will affect the result. Applying a wet layer on top of a dry layer will not produce the same blending effect as applying a wet marker on top of a wet marker.

Try this yourself with two markers, reversing the order in which each color is used. Notice in figure 2.7b that applying a wet layer to a dry layer leaves a sharper edge. You can apply as many as four or five layers before the paper reaches its saturation point and the color begins to sit on top or puddle within the paper (an undesirable effect, with a few exceptions when texture is desired). Gradation to indicate color values is also a good technique to master and one that you will use often. Figure 2.8 illustrates gradation using marker to achieve saturation and value.

a. light to dark (290T)

b. color (351T) to color (290T)

c. warm (155T) to cool (290T)

2.8. Shown is a sample marker gradation: (a) light to dark represents a marker built up in layers; (b) color to color is a gradation; and (c) warm graduates to cool.

wet (4525T) over wet and dry (263T)

wet (4525T) over wet (2707T)

wet (2707T) over wet (4525T)

wet (4525T) over dry (2707T)

wet (2707T) over dry (4525T)

2.7b. In the first box, 4525T was applied on top while a light violet (263T) was still wet; the stroke next to it is the same color applied on top when the violet was dry. The next two boxes illustrate a wet marker on top of a wet marker, but the order was reversed. The last two boxes are wet layers on top of dry layers, reversed as before. The darker color in the center of each shows a third layer of the second color applied on a dry layer.

*2.9. Tone is created with
the addition of grays to color.*

Gray Effects

Atmosphere helps sell an interior space. You can create opportunities for its use. A gray marker used in combination with other colors or gray paint produced from a mix of colors can create exciting and effervescent effects and subtleties of color. A gray marker should rarely be used alone, as it has a tendency to make a rendering look drab. If you must use gray directly from the tube, then be sure to include some white adjacent to it to keep it looking clear and crisp, as figure 2.2 illustrates.

When mixing grays, take full advantage of the fact that most materials include adjacent hues. I often use pale color tones under gray markers. My favorites are mauves and blues, such as Pantone 263T and 2706T and Cobalt Violet paint.

Practice all of the combinations presented in figures 2.9 through 2.12, and develop a few of your own. Keep them in your creation file for future reference (more details about creation files are found in chapter 3).

Cool Gray
02   04   06

4535T   473T   263T   351T   317T   182T

Warm Gray
02   04   06

2.10. These are the results of placing a layer of gray markers on top of color. Can you determine if the gray markers were applied on a wet or a dry marker layer? (They were applied after the first layer was dry; if they had been applied on a wet layer, the marker lines would not be as distinct.)

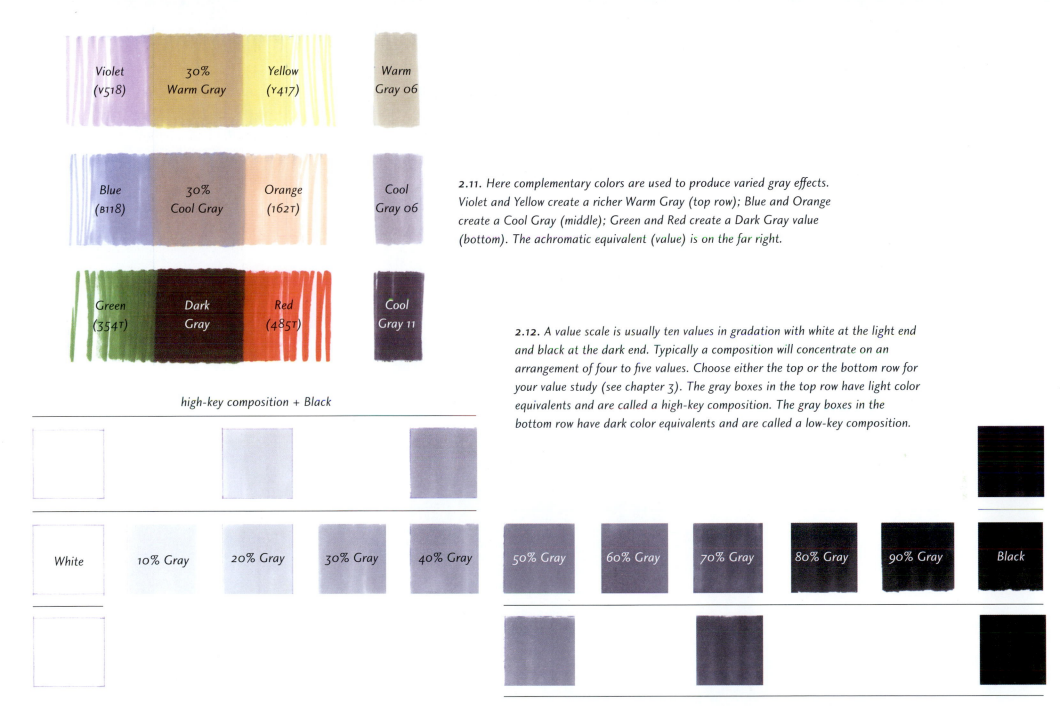

Violet
(V518)

30%
Warm Gray

Yellow
(Y417)

Warm
Gray 06

Blue
(B118)

30%
Cool Gray

Orange
(162T)

Cool
Gray 06

Green
(354T)

Dark
Gray

Red
(485T)

Cool
Gray 11

2.11. Here complementary colors are used to produce varied gray effects. Violet and Yellow create a richer Warm Gray (top row); Blue and Orange create a Cool Gray (middle); Green and Red create a Dark Gray value (bottom). The achromatic equivalent (value) is on the far right.

2.12. A value scale is usually ten values in gradation with white at the light end and black at the dark end. Typically a composition will concentrate on an arrangement of four to five values. Choose either the top or the bottom row for your value study (see chapter 3). The gray boxes in the top row have light color equivalents and are called a high-key composition. The gray boxes in the bottom row have dark color equivalents and are called a low-key composition.

high-key composition + Black

White | 10% Gray | 20% Gray | 30% Gray | 40% Gray | 50% Gray | 60% Gray | 70% Gray | 80% Gray | 90% Gray | Black

low-key composition + White

White Areas

White keeps an illustration from looking drab and maintains an energizing quality. Used next to a dark color, white helps achieve good contrast and drama. Its placement can carry the eye through an illustration and reinforce a center of interest. White can also reinforce a light source, help fade a pattern or a texture, and capture the feeling of reflections on glossy surfaces.

I have a free style of rendering that uses a fair amount of the paper's white area. This illustration technique is easy to learn and is also a great time saver for both preliminary and final interior illustrations. Plan your white areas in advance, and leave them untouched; mask them if that helps. The following eight illustrations show where to leave white paper and where to add white medium to achieve a white effect.

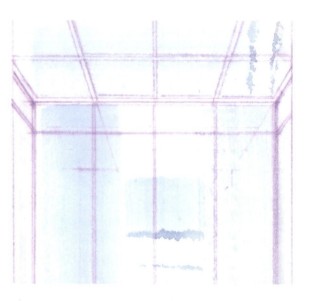

2.13c. White signifies light sources and reflections, such as in this elevator interior.

2.13a. White paper is better for a nonreflective surface such as this matte-finish aluminum table. The sketch is a gradation of color (markers 5507T and 263T) to white. Frisket film helps plan the areas to be left white.

2.13b. White provides contrast for a black glass illustration.

Tip! "White, gray, and black are quiescent places and a point of reference for color in a composition."
Frank Webb

2.13d. White adds sparkle to capture a mirror or a chrome-finish table.

2.13e. *White next to light grays communicates a soft, high-key value.*

2.13f. *White as negative space defines these window details.*

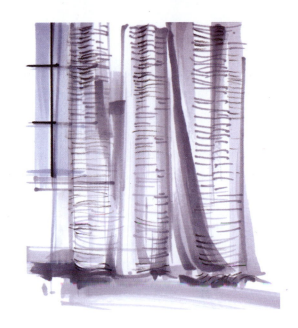

2.13g. *White denotes a fading pattern and texture or patterns within light areas.*

2.13h. *White gouache reinforces texture and reflections in dark areas, such as this terrazzo flooring.*

2.13i. *Here a white Caran d'Ache crayon is used on top of markers (9181т, 468т, 263т, and 4525т) to indicate the pattern on a linen table covering and drapery. Because some types of Caran d'Ache are water soluble, the color can be applied and then blended with a wet brush (although one was not used here).*

Techniques

As explained by Frank Webb in *Webb on Watercolor*, an illustration is a two-dimensional representation of a three-dimensional space. Numerous graphic effects may be chosen to animate these two-dimensional surfaces, using a few simple techniques drawn from fine-art studies. The following effects are the primary ways to compose an illustration:

- **Perspective.** The key method of creating and communicating a space is through the use of perspective drawings. These show the space and its objects in correct relationship to one another, resulting in an illusion of depth. This is the primary means of showing a three-dimensional space on paper, which is two dimensional.

- **Direction.** Direction comes from many elements in an illustration. Perspective creates direction leading into a drawing; high or wide elements create a dominant direction (based on proportions of width to height); and a material's texture may have a dominant direction.

- **Surface modeling** (see chapter 3). Modeling is the way to make shapes and forms read.

- **Line quality.** The quality of a line can create texture, direction, or emphasis.

- **Color.** Color is used to achieve harmony or contrast, emphasis, and balance.

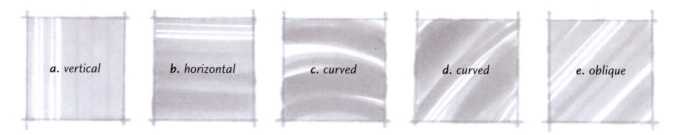

a. vertical   *b. horizontal*   *c. curved*   *d. curved*   *e. oblique*

2.14. *Basic marker direction strokes to practice include vertical, horizontal, curved, and oblique. Boxes a, b, and e use a cardboard guide, while boxes c and d are in freehand technique.*

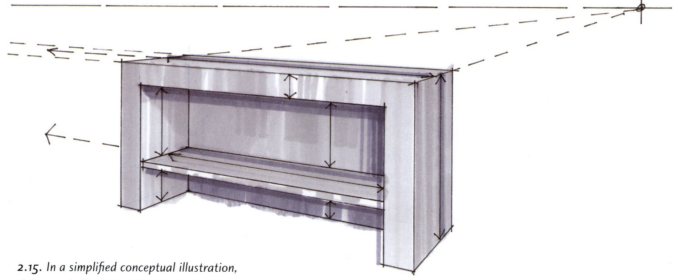

2.15. *In a simplified conceptual illustration, this console illustrates the direction of the marker strokes.*

Tip! *In capturing perspective with markers, follow the direction of the interior's perspective with your strokes. If the perspective has two points, horizontal strokes should follow the vanishing point farthest away; if one point, strokes should be parallel to the horizon line and the horizontal paper edges. Work in sections of the space in this order: floor, ceilings, walls, and then furniture. Keep strokes open and varied in width toward the foreground or near light sources. Vary the line quality: use a few straight lines and some scribbled strokes, or vary the width and the pressure.*

2.16. One-point perspective in this room includes walls rendered with vertical strokes and a floor and ceiling with horizontal strokes, parallel to the eye-level line. (VP indicates the vanishing point; EL indicates eye level.)

Just as these elements and principles are used to create an interior, they are also the techniques manipulated to create a pleasing and credible illustration. First determine your illustration's dominant direction and the room elements. Webb explains that subject matter, material, or pattern will "suggest" a direction. Do not let these control the direction. Which dominant direction will best express your concept? Is it a spatial quality or a material and a texture? Is the concept vertical or horizontal? Is it best illustrated in a vertical or horizontal format? Do you want to diminish the dominant direction or emphasize it? Determine a focus to unify the illustration, incorporate vitality, and express movement (Webb, 1994).

2.17. In two-point perspective, walls are shown with vertical strokes and the floor and ceiling with horizontal strokes, all directed to the left vanishing point.

2.18. Various marker techniques—vertical, horizontal, oblique, and subtle scribbles—illustrate basic architectural space.

Masking

Masking allows precise applications of color. Several techniques usable for both markers and watercolors follow.

- **Masking with drafting tape.** Use tape to achieve clean color edges in a rendering. When you are drawing in a horizontal direction with markers, mask the left and right edges of that area. This keeps the edges crisp (see figure 1.6). If you are applying the strokes in a vertical direction, mask the top and bottom edges. Be sure to start and finish your strokes over the tape on both sides; this prevents unwanted blobs of color and little white "holes." You can reuse the tape as long as it has enough tack. After about three or four uses, it may stretch out of shape, lose its tack, or have too much marker residue to use any longer. Atmospheric conditions affect paper and the tape's stickiness. Humidity warps the paper and decomposes the adhesive. Very dry conditions harden tape. Both conditions mar the paper's surface, so do not let tape stay on a drawing surface for an extended period of time because the tape will leave a residue on the paper and warp it.

- **Masking with frisket.** Frisket film is best to use if you have a complicated shape or want to leave something white. It is also repositionable and transparent. Once it is placed and cut, it can remain on the illustration if you are able to complete it in a few hours (see figure 1.6).

- **Watercolor masking with fluid.** Unless the illustration involves a complicated or small shape, tape is much faster than fluid for masking. However, masking fluid protects areas of watercolor work when color is applied in broad washes. Use colorless fluid to avoid any risk of staining from a pigmented material (see figure 4.5). Shake the bottle of fluid before use, then test it on the paper because it may adhere too strongly. Do not use it on wet or damp paper. Choose old brushes or dip pens to avoid damaging your brushes. Wash brushes in soapy water immediately after use. Let the fluid dry before applying the paint. You may not be able to remove it if it is left on paper for long periods of time. In addition, masking fluid may yellow coated bond paper within a few days.

Line Quality

When we sketch and illustrate, we make graphic marks on paper. These marks are representations—mere suggestions—of the quality of surfaces we wish to portray: plants, floors, reflections, textures, patterns, and the like. Then we let our audience use its imagination to synthesize and complete the images. This is great fun.

"Dot, blot, and dab" and "spatter, scrape, and scribble" are some of the illustration symbols that abound in many artists' works, imparting life and excitement. Figure 2.19 illustrates line techniques in marker, while figure 2.25 shows them in paint. It is important to learn both, because media are often combined to achieve a desired effect or level of detail. After you study and practice some of the symbols presented here, you will no doubt develop a few of your own. Get ready, relax, and have fun while you give it a try.

Tip! Use gesture! The stroke of the marker or the brush adds lovely spirit and motion to an illustration. Break the habit of merely filling in color between the lines.

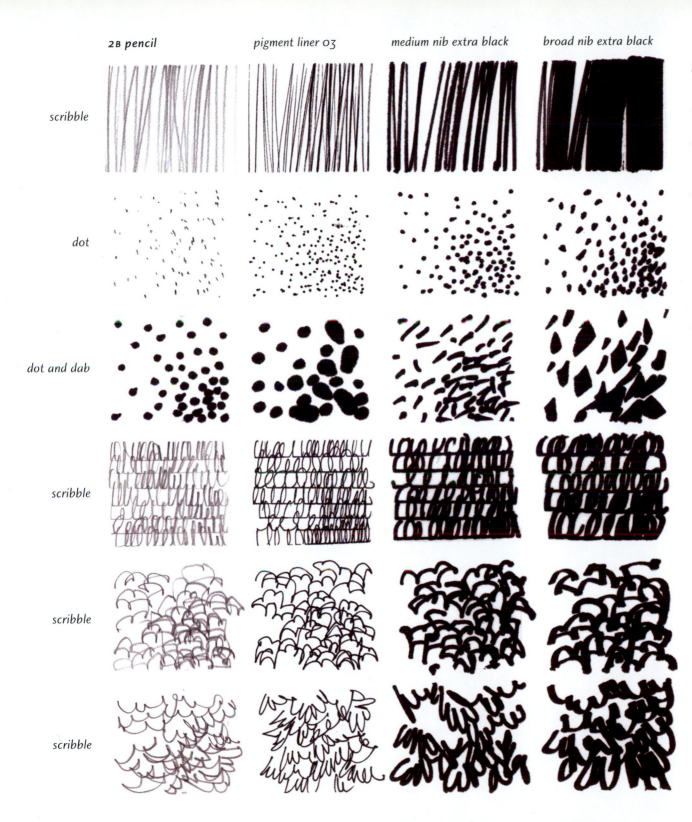

2B pencil	pigment liner 03	medium nib extra black	broad nib extra black

scribble

dot

dot and dab

scribble

scribble

scribble

Marker Symbols

Below are the key symbols used for marker line work:

- **Dot.** Textiles, carpets, and other textured and patterned surfaces translate well into dots.

- **Blot.** This mark starts out as a dot, but then the marker is left on the paper surface for a few seconds to produce a larger and softer dot. I like to use a few randomly spaced blots to show a reflection on glass, marble, or metal. Multiple layered blots can symbolize textured glass.

- **Dab.** A dab can be applied with marker or paintbrush and resembles a blot with a tail. It works well for plants, flowers, large patterns or textures, and chandelier sparkles.

- **Scribble.** Anything goes here! A controlled scribble can be used for wood-grain and marble-vein textures. Different line weights are achieved by varying pressure on the marker or the brush.

2.19. Markers and paint are interchangeable for drawing or enhancing lines.

sunset

concrete floor

glass table

wood grain

2.20. *All of the first layer is 155T, while the added scribbles are 182T, 304T, 264T, Cool Gray 04, and 2706T.*

2.21. *Can you see a beautiful scribbled sky and a warm scribbled fire in this illustration? The markers used for this scribble are 100T, 486T, 297T, 351T, and Mauve AD Marker. (For more of this pencil technique, see* Sketching with Markers, *by Thomas C. Wang.)*

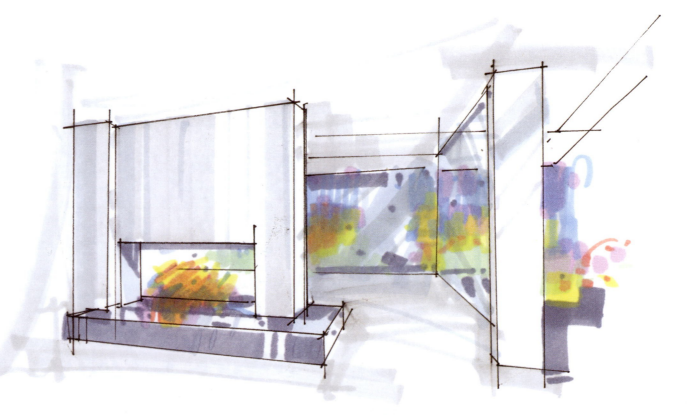

2.22. *Colorful scribbles mark the fireplace in this room as well as the exterior setting.*

2.24. *This partial room vignette employs scribbles, dots, and dabs, executed in markers and pencil.*

2.23. *Dots and dabs in markers create a vignette of a classic side chair.*

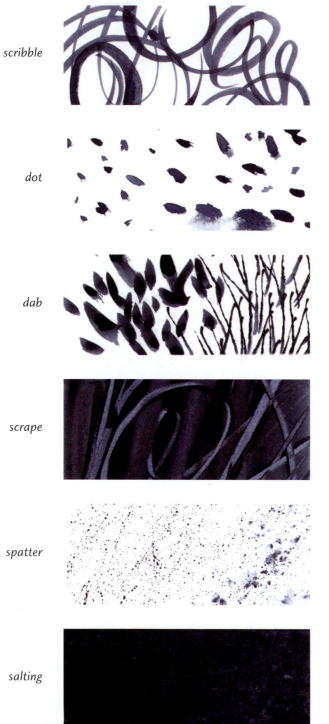

scribble

dot

dab

scrape

spatter

salting

36

Watercolor Symbols

Watercolor techniques for drawing lines are similar to those used with markers. These encompass the familiar dot, blot, and dab as well as spatter, scrape, and scribble, along with bounce, drop, and roll.

• **Dot.** This mark is quicker to achieve with a marker, but with paint it is also used for textured and patterned surfaces such as textiles and carpets.

• **Blot.** This mark is achieved using the side of a brush. Placing the brush on a wet paper area gives a larger and softer dot. Use a few randomly spaced single blots to indicate reflections, plant leaves, and flowers. Use multiple layered blots to symbolize texture; vary the color or the value.

• **Dab.** As with a marker, think of a dab as a blot with a tail. A painted dab is often used for plants, flowers, large patterns or textures, and chandelier sparkles.

• **Spatter.** Paint spatter is used frequently over marker illustration for many textures. It can be produced in different scales and works well for layering different colors in a floor surface, such as terrazzo, or simply as a finishing flair. I like to use a paint brush and either hit the wood handle on the palm of my hand or tap the handle with my fingers while holding the end of the brush. You can also use a toothbrush filled with paint and scrape it with a palette knife. Use pieces of paper to mask areas around the spatter.

2.25. Watercolor was used to create a variety of lines: scribbles, dots, dabs, scrapes, spatters, and salting.

• **Scrape.** In this procedure the pigment is scraped from the surface of the paper while the color is wet or dry. It is a good technique for plants, flowers, and some patterns or textures when you want to bring the white back to the paper. Any paper can be used. Palette knives or even credit cards will serve as good practice tools for different paper types. For the wet method, first wet the paper with water. When the paper is no longer shiny, brush in the paint color. Next place a layer of wet paint on top of a dry or wet layer. Before the top layer is dry, scrape with the end of a brush, palette knife, or credit card.

• **Scribble.** Anything goes here!

• **Bounce, drop, and roll.** Holding a brush handle at the very end, you can lightly bounce it or roll it on the paper for interesting textures and effects.

• **Salting.** Sprinkling salt on a damp watercolor wash or bleach on a dry one is another means of adding interesting texture to an illustration. The salt technique is illustrated in chapter 10 (figure 10.22c). It is more fun to spatter and more interesting to take advantage of a granulating paint color.

Tip! Try a few of these brush-handling techniques: Hold the brush on the end of the handle and paint free and loose. Twirl a flat brush by rolling the handle between your thumb and fingers. Change the pressure from firm to light while painting a line with a round brush.

2.26. The negative white space in these scribbles and scrapes achieved by scraping and can be done wet or dry.

2.27. Watercolor dabs produce a partial room vignette full of circles and swirls.

2.28. Dots and dabs in watercolor create a vignette of a classic side chair.

2.29. The spatter technique captures a granite floor in watercolor.

Watercolor Washes and Glazes

Watercolors, which are excellent for subtle color mixtures and value transitions, bear numerous similarities to markers: in their transparent qualities, in the techniques employed for watercolor glazes and washes (similar to maker layering), and in the gestures and strokes used. Once you learn how to handle a brush and paint, the process will feel relatively natural and familiar.

Interior illustrations typically use watercolor glazes and a gradation wash of more than one color. Palette mixtures of color produce results different from layers of paint on paper (a glaze). A palette mixture combines two colors that produce a third color before it is applied to the paper. A glaze creates an optical mixture on the paper, in which the first color shows through the second color.

Tip! If you want delicacy and transparency, use transparent pigments and more water. If you want a velvety, rich surface to the painting, use less water and a paint that has less transparency but lots of pigment in it.

Cobalt Violet   *Aureolin*   *Neutral Tint*

palette mix   *Cobalt Violet with Aureolin glaze*   *Cobalt Violet wash with Aureolin glaze and Neutral Tint glaze*

2.30a. Shown is a comparison of palette mixtures and layered glazes. The top row illustrates single washes, while the bottom row presents mixtures of these colors. The bottom left is mixed on the palette and then applied to the paper. The bottom middle is a wash of Cobalt Violet with a glaze of Aureolin placed on top after the Cobalt was dry. The bottom right is the same as the middle with another glaze of Neutral Tint after the previous glaze was dry.

2.30b. This painted value scale shows about five values; however, with paint many more can be achieved. Neutral Tint was applied with a flat brush.

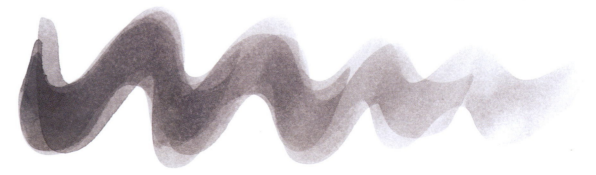

Figures 2.30a, 2.31, and figure 2.32 illustrate these watercolor techniques. Practice and try many different colors to gain more knowledge of color mixing, letting the paint dry between glazings. To begin, practice loading the brush (also called charging the brush) with paint. Wet your brush before putting it into the paint. Once you have loaded the brush, go directly to the middle of your palette and work the brush so the paint will be evenly distributed throughout the brush. It is risky to go straight to the paper even if you do not need to mix a color—a chunk of paint on the brush may not be workable on the paper. When the paint is worked in and you like the color, test it on a scrap of the same kind of paper. Remember that watercolor dries light. The most frequent error for beginners is either too much water on the brush or too little. After wetting your brush and before putting it into the paint, dab your brush on a sponge or a paper towel. Experiment and adjust the amount of water.

Rough texture and bleeds are in watercolor's nature, giving illustrations a unique character. The type of paper used has a lot to do with creating this character. A dry brush skips over most paper, creating whiter surfaces that show through the paint. If a form does not read, you can scrub over the area to take out the paint, soften the brush strokes by adding water, dampen the area with water before applying color, or do it over on a different paper. A backwash created by a puddle of water or paint in a base-color wash may be sublimated or diffused by adding the next layer or a pattern (see figure 8.44).

Because of watercolor's fluidity, free-spirited hands-on practice will help you understand exactly what it does and how to make it work for you.

2.31. *The same colors can be applied with washes and glazes to indicate a marble floor. Apply the base colors wet into wet and allow the color edges to bleed into one another (also called a variegated wash). Notice the gradation of colors and tones from light to dark as well as the vertical glazing used to indicate reflections.*

Glazes

Glazing is a process of applying paint so that the color is built up through layering—the paint version of marker layering. These glazes are a series of transparent washes applied one on top of the other, producing great depth and intensity. Each layer must be allowed to dry before the other is added; then the next layer is applied quickly and delicately to avoid picking up the previous color. The result is an optical blend of color.

A watercolor wheel developed by Zoltan Szabo shows how to work with analogous colors (adjacent to one another on the color wheel) and indicates the effects of glazing and lifting color using analogous colors. You will typically use a gradation wash of more than one color and glazes for interior illustration. Concentrate on developing your skill with these first.

2.32. The top three patches are the watercolors first mixed on the palette, while the bottom three are glazes.

Cerulean Blue
and Aureolin

Aureolin and
Ultramarine

Quinacridone Rose
and Naples Yellow

Washes

Washes, usually fairly transparent, are applied as a solid color or a gradation of one or more colors. This technique is done in either a controlled manner or a more fluid process of adding wet paint into wet paint, letting color float into another paint color or clear water. Steps in the controlled technique include the following:

- Mix color with water in a tray before applying it to the paper.

- Wet the paper with a sponge or a brush full of clear water. Then let it dry to the point that it is no longer shiny.

- Slope the paper slightly by lifting the top so the wash can move down the wet surface on its own while you are applying the paint.

- Apply the paint in overlapping horizontal bands, starting at the top and working your way down.

- Do not touch the illustration again until it is completely dry.

Light-to-dark gradation washes—ones that fade out gradually—require that the pigment be diluted slightly with more water in each horizontal stroke. Gradation washes can be created from color to color, from warm to cool, and from bright to dull.

Wet-into-wet washes leave the gradation to chance by applying the color, tilting the paper, and allowing the paint to creep on its own.

After plenty of practice, you will have a perfect wash—but keep in mind that a perfect wash is not always a desired effect when illustrating interior materials. When a color is influenced by adjacent color, different lighting, and similar conditions, it never appears as a perfect solid hue. Neither will your paint application. Gradation washes, glazing, and wet-into-wet washes have more interest and invite the viewer into the space. These same techniques create beautiful indications of texture and material.

2.33. This light-to-dark gradation wash was painted wet into wet. Notice what happened because the paper had too much water in it when the Blue and the Violet were applied as a glaze on top. This is sometimes called backwash— and something to avoid.

Assignments

1. Marker and brush control. This assignment will help develop your ability to alter the qualities of marks made on paper and show you a variety of marks that can be made by different tool handling. Focus on the tool in your hand.

a. *Precise marks.* The greatest brush control is achieved by holding a brush as you do a pencil and resting the side or tip of your small finger on the paper surface. Practice making precise marks by handling the brush or the marker as described. Now make precise marks using a guide—a cardboard guide with markers and an artist's bridge or a similar tool with a brush. You can steady the guide in your hand by resting the side or the tip of your small finger on the paper.

b. *Flowing marks.* Create more flowing marks by using your whole arm to place marker or brush strokes on the paper.

c. *Twisting marks.* Create variations of continuous strokes by twirling, rolling, or twisting a marker or a brush about 180 degrees in your hand while drawing.

2. Gradation. Trace several copies of figures A.1, A.2, and A.11 (in the appendix) with a nonphoto or nonprint pencil. Apply a single color to each drawing to achieve gradation. Create a gradual progression from light to dark colors by layering the marker or painting a wash with one color. Next indicate a gradual progression from color to color. Finally create a gradual progression from color to white.

3. Odd shapes. Changing your marker or brush position helps in coloring odd-shaped surfaces.

a. *Freehand.* Try illustrating figures A.1, A.2, and A.11 (in the appendix) without masking the edges. Use twisting, flowing, and precise marks to indicate the surfaces.

b. *Combined techniques.* Now challenge yourself to begin combining the techniques learned so far. Illustrate the drawings several more times by scribbling in the color, layering color, using washes or glazes, or floating in the color (wet into wet). Remember to use your new marker and brush control skills.

4. Gesture. Modifying the type of stroke as well as its size, spacing, and thickness can create an object with a minimum amount of gesture. Practice the techniques in figures 2.19 and 2.25 if you have not yet done so. Study the art, items on the table, and people in figure 2.1, the plants in figure 2.3, and the furniture in figures 2.5, 2.23, and 2.28; they are created with minimal gestures that are mere suggestions of the objects. This minimal style is particularly useful to illustrate small objects in an illustration where full detail is not necessary or for distant subjects within an illustration.

a. *Symbols.* Explore the different ways to create and emphasize graphic symbols by looking at varied interior objects and materials. Study textures and patterns to decide which graphic symbols you might use to indicate their properties.

b. *Gesture drawing.* Create an illustration of the chair in your room (or any other furniture object), using only three to five gestures. Seek to understand the object's elements and principles—to capture the essence of its design. Does the arm or the leg curve or sweep? Can detailed carvings be reduced to a dot, a dab, or a scribble? Whether or not the object has decorative or functional design properties, you should be able to recreate it in a few gestures.

For a real challenge, each time you recreate the subject use one fewer gesture. See if you can achieve a recognizable object with one gesture, using a continuous stroke and varying the pressure of the marker or the brush and twisting and turning as you go. Do it together with a few fellow students and set a timer as a fun group challenge. If you are timid about sharing your ideas with a group, teaming up now can help build your confidence. This will also develop your ability to do quick, conceptual sketches in a brainstorming session, during the design development phase, or with a client.

This stage is all about experimentation and discovery. Don't be shy! Just say, Let's see what happens when I do this. You will learn a lot about tools, techniques, and your own skills. Even a mistake can be a happy accident—a way to discover something new to add to your memory theater. Most of us have had the experience of looking at a drawing on white paper and feeling as if we were going to make a muddle of it. There is a great illustrator inside you. Keep practicing to give that great illustrator the opportunity to emerge.

Artistic Interpretation

Keep your eye and passion on the goal. Your aspiration is to become a better designer and design communicator. You are already a spatial thinker. What you learn in this chapter about seeing will help create a strong connection between the design process and your eye-hand skills and techniques, making you a better interpreter.

Room composition in a line drawing, featuring the Warren Platner collection (1966) for Knoll (4B drawing pencil)

Seeing with Internal Vision

The photographs of furniture, the colors, and the material samples selected during the design process explain clearly to your client what a proposed interior will look like. But you, as an accomplished illustrator and interpreter, can also create a personalized illustration that speaks to what the space will feel like. That is a great accomplishment with vast benefits in selling a space.

Surface Shapes

Light and shade affirm the volume of a shape. A line drawing creates a shape, while color and value define its form; objects display either lightness or darkness, expressed by the value of their color. Modeling or chiaroscuro is used to express the planes in an illustration. Modeling, based on what you know rather than what you can see, uses different values to make the planes distinctive. Chiaroscuro (forms rendered with a gradation of light to dark) involves replicating the values actually seen on an object. Modeling is used more often in interior illustration because it helps the objects read as planes of light and shade with clear edges.

We do not have the actual room to look at before we render a proposal, so we cannot replicate values in chiaroscuro.

The images in figures 3.1 through 3.8 show how illustrators simplify planes to three or four values: highlight, light, shade, and shadow. The use of these principles, which apply to many elements of an interior, keeps an illustration from looking like a cartoon image. The basic surface shapes in figure 3.2 can be used to capture both furniture and architectural room elements.

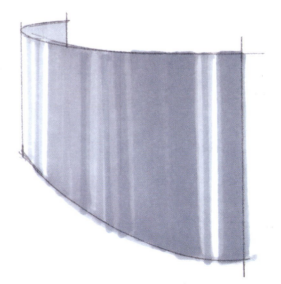

3.1. *Marker 5445T is used to render these curved wall surfaces, using value modeling to express planar forms.*

Four basic surface shapes are illustrated in marker 5445T to demonstrate values, with the light source to the front and the right of the forms. The marker can be layered to create different values.

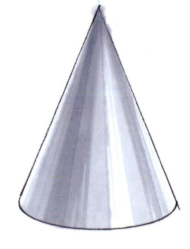

3.2a. Three values are used for this cube: light on top, dark on the front, and medium on the side.

3.2b. Four values are used for this cylinder: the highlight is white, the lightest value is on either side of the white, the medium value is in shade on the side (adjacent to the lightest value), and the darkest value, sometimes referred to as the core, is in the center of the medium value.

3.2c. Four values, applied in the same manner as on the cylinder, are used for this cone.

3.2d. For this sphere, four values are used: highlight, light, shade, and core.

Tip! In planning an illustration, do not rely on line work alone. Use color values to show an object's three-dimensional form. To help see the values of the chair or the table in your room, squint your eyes. Hold a piece of white paper at arm's length, and compare it to the values on the walls of your space.

Color and light

Assume that for a potential presentation, you have many beautiful materials to illustrate. Pin them up, look at them from a distance, squint your eyes, and observe what you can actually see. Then you can render what ought to be there.

To represent color in light, start with a shade lighter than your sample's actual hue. You can add layers of the same color (as shown in figure 3.5) or another color to achieve variation, gradation, and shade and shadow. Place your sample under both natural and artificial light, and notice the color differences. Put something in front of the light source, then study the color again in shadow. Be aware that artificial light has more intensity at the source of light, and natural light is more subtle and diffused.

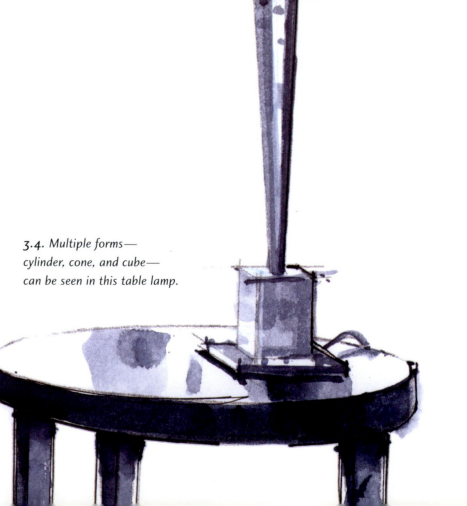

3.3. *Rotund furnishing forms express the sphere and cylinder values (table by Marcel Wanders).*

3.4. *Multiple forms— cylinder, cone, and cube— can be seen in this table lamp.*

Shadows

Illustrations need light, shade, and shadow to give clarity and form to interior objects. To achieve clarity in your illustration, here are a few key points to remember:

• When an object blocks the light, it causes a shadow.

• The shadow occurs on the opposite side of the light source.

• The surfaces of an object not receiving light are in shade.

• Light is reflected back on an object (true of both reflective and nonreflective surfaces).

• The higher the light, the shorter the shadow.

• The lower the light, the longer the shadow.

It is impractical to render every shadow in an illustration. Because an interior typically has multiple light sources, the rendering will be over-complicated if shadows from each light source are included. Instead, follow these guidelines:

• Render shadows primarily where they help the surface read.

• Emphasize an important light source or a dramatic architectural feature.

• Include enough shadow to make an illustration understandable and lively.

You can decide how best to represent shadows by developing a value study (described later in this chapter). More information about how to project precise shadows in perspective is found in Sid DelMar Leach's *Techniques of Interior Design Rendering and Presentation.*

3.5. Five values were used for this Bubble Club chair by Philippe Starck to indicate light, shade, and shadow. Light is coming from the chair's mid-right side.

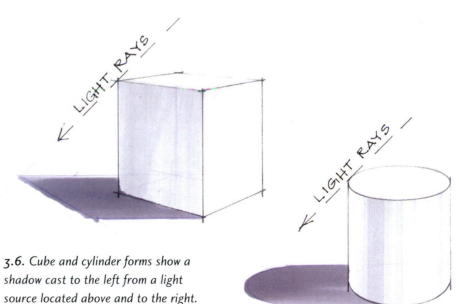

3.6. Cube and cylinder forms show a shadow cast to the left from a light source located above and to the right.

3.7. Shadows help make planes and details readable. To create them, reduce your marker palette to one, two, or three values. For close-up illustration, use three values, but for distant details use the darkest value and locate it where a shadow would occur. When rendering this type of architectural feature, detail should gradually fade out as the surfaces recede into the room (see also figure 5.53).

3.8. *The light source is offset to the front of this tall dresser. Shadow is emphasized here—it may create needed drama or be too dominant, depending on the overall composition of an illustration's room elements.*

3.9. *In this rendering of a drapery-covered window in sunlight, a minimal indication of foliage and sky outside helps the forms read. Render positive and negative space while thinking in terms of reduction: leaving a circular section white emphasizes the drapery's transparency and suggests a very sunny space—providing a cheerful emotional appeal.*

Tip! It is important to make the architecture of windows look realistic, but it is not necessary to render every detail of a window frame. Simply render a few shaded areas on the mullions and the frame so the forms will be implied.

3.10. *The waves fade and dissipate in this sculptured broadloom carpet pattern.*

Textures and Patterns

When approaching textures and patterns, ask yourself, How can I simplify them into a readable interpretation?

Again, pin up your sample, look at it from a distance, squint your eyes, and observe what you can actually see. You can then render your interpretation of what ought to be there. You are seeking a truthful interpretation, not a realistic representation. In a patterned subject you will notice the dominant shapes after squinting.

3.11. *Simplification produces a striking representation—or symbol— of a dark wood plank floor, captured in only multiple color values and lines of varying weight.*

3.12. *Ceramic tile can be symbolized by grid lines and overlapping rectangular color subtleties.*

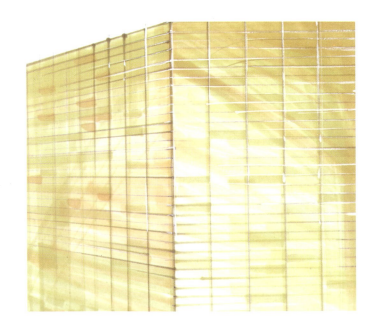

Only after this exercise can you begin your selection of marker colors, the layers required, line symbols to incorporate, and shades and shadows. Figures 3.10 through 3.13 are interpretations of interior materials. Multiple color values and lines of varying weight are symbols for a wood surface. Grid lines and overlapping rectangular color subtleties symbolize tile. A small amount of these line gestures allows our mind to complete the picture.

3.13. An economy of lines and colors produces a sophisticated rendering of glass tile.

Patterns of any type in a one-point or two-point perspective drawing require special understanding and reduced illustration methods. Patterns typically have a repeat; you must draw it in perspective with the correct repeat dimensions. The pattern in perspective diminishes in size as it recedes in space, so it is appropriate to indicate less detail as it recedes. Other methods are:

• Render foreground detail.

• Render a pattern where it is in light or shadow.

• Render the area where a surface form changes direction.

3.14. In this patterned broadloom carpet, more detail is rendered in the foreground, fading away as the material recedes from view.

3.15. Bright light dissipates the pattern and color in this patterned window covering and bedding.

3.16a and 3.16b. Stripes in shade and light change value and recede in perspective. Black Caran d'Ache was used to shade the chair frame and yellow to shade the cushion stripes.

3.17. Detail in this crochet table is emphasized at the surface edges.

3.19. For this floral chair, pattern is indicated only on the edges of the fabric folds.

3.18. The line quality used for this side chair is emphasized on one face, and then it changes at the edge and gradually fades out toward the opposite edge.

Details and Shapes

Drama is dispelled when too much pattern and too many details are placed in an illustration. Detail is naturally eliminated from vision as it recedes into the distance; so should the amount of texture you illustrate. An illustration's foreground and center of interest will have more detail than the background. This concept is illustrated well in figure 3.20.

The world is not flat, but our paper is, so we must present interior objects as readable flat shapes. You will have to develop the ability to interpret three-dimensional objects to fit a two-dimensional presentation. You can help the shapes read using value, color, and texture. Each object's shape can be simplified and varied in viewpoint to create more interest; figure 3.20 exudes this quality.

3.20. Julian LaTrobe's masterly rendering of Anne Morgan's dressing room in New York City, an Elsie de Wolfe design, exemplifies the emotional power of illustration over computer drawings. The table in the left foreground is fashioned from six simple brush strokes, while the negative space created at the base of the table is echoed in both the exquisitely detailed area carpet and the chandelier.

Synthesis and Interpretation

Throughout the process of creating a design concept and preparing a presentation, you will be interpreting the client's desires and needs. Remember that the goal of any illustration is a truthful interpretation of a concept, not a realistic representation—the latter would be a photograph. Once you simplify an idea as an understandable interpretation, the viewer's mind can complete the picture.

You are beginning to understand how to visualize and simplify details such as pattern and texture on paper and in perspective. Of great importance are an object's perspective and how to indicate it in a simplified manner in "paper space." In real space the human eye cannot possibly see all of a room's detail at once. Interior illustration thus uses symbols, synthesis, and interpretation. A key concept to keep in mind is that in illustration, as in fine art, one does not render exactly what is there—you should render what ought to be there (Webb, 1994).

This is where computer-generated renderings fall short. By indicating too much detail and modeling, they look implausible. Computer programs also may produce inferior color renditions; many examples consequently are dull and gloomy because of the amount of gray used with colors to achieve value modeling. If an illustration looks unnatural or makes the client feel uneasy, then it fails as a sales tool. So do not be misled by your desire to create everything with a computer— a rendering that looks like the interior in a computer game setting is very hard to warm up to as a living or working space. Illustrations such as figure 3.20 and those that follow are far more pleasant to look at and will engage clients on an emotional level, right where you want them.

It is fine, however, to use computer-generated perspective drawings that can be retraced and illustrated with traditional media. They will help you compose the perspective and can also help you place an overall pattern repeat in correct perspective. Try a computer-generated rendering with base colors applied, but use traditional methods to create pattern detail, shading, and shadows. Computers also excel in creating rendered floor plans.

Tip! Darken a value behind a light object. The darker value recedes in space and pushes the lighter shape forward. Try to achieve a readable form without relying on line work. The illustration will hold together and read well at a normal viewing distance.

Composition

As you look at your proposed floor plan, think broadly about how to arrange the illustration. First study the plan's placement in an abstract manner by looking at the different perspective viewpoints. Which shapes are dominant and interesting as possible focal points? Perhaps a display, a fireplace, a sofa, a window, or an important wall? Choose a feature that best expresses the concept. Develop concept perspectives on tracing paper to determine the best composition. The line work, shapes, textures, colors, and values will give form to the interior's full expression; see the example of figure 3.21, with its prominent vertical focus. Approach the rendering in a broad, simple, and abstract way. Study the four to seven largest or most dominant areas in your room; they should be the most distinguished in your rendering (Webb, 1994).

3.21. Notice the vertical format here, emphasizing the height of this duplex suite in the Wasserturm Hotel, an old water tower in Cologne, Germany, renovated by Andrée Putman in 1990. The circular stair and the shape of the curved area rug sweep your eye into the space, while the vertical white shapes bring it up and back down. The perspective lines and the light value of the left wall plane constitute another directional element.

Tip! Where a plant may be too dominant to place in the foreground of a rendering, use the power of suggestion. Placing the shadow of a tree on a wall and creating an interesting shadow on the floor, adjacent to the foreground furniture, produces a great framing device. It dances into the page and contrasts with more formal techniques in the rest of the illustration.

3.22. *In this watercolor rendering by Nadim Racy of a New York living room designed in 1972 by Ellen McCluskey Associates, the floor pattern leads into the space, while the tree and the plant in the foreground help frame it. Composition perspective techniques employed include repetition of forms and the diminutive size of various shapes.*

Outline of a Drawing

When you have completed your perspective composition study, it is time to study the drawing's outline. Remember that with perspective drawing, you are creating the illusion of a space that the viewer's mind can comprehend intuitively. But you are able to direct how the viewer visually moves through the space or persuade him or her to see it the way you choose.

Consider your illustration's perimeter. Does the rendering have a motivating shape, an opening into the illustration? In both figures 3.23 and 3.24, turned chairs pull the viewer's eye into the spaces. An aisle, as in a retail environment, would be another natural opening into an illustration. A classic technique directs movement from side to side, makes a sweep into the illustration space, and then moves forward. Keep that in mind when placing furniture, colors, and the floor plan in the initial perspective. In the accompanying illustrations, foreground chairs, tables, plants, and trees are planned gateways and foreground devices.

Let your line work create an interesting shape at some edges, using elements of the floor plan or the placement of a figure, a plant, or some other enhancement. Elements placed in a composition's foreground help keep the viewer's eye engaged with the illustration. These elements can be intensified with strong lines, bold strokes, or significant contrasts with something nearby. One more line technique to experiment with is continuous line. Using tissue overlay studies on your perspective drawing, try to find a continuous line to emphasize; it can change direction and flow from one element to another.

Tip! Critique your own work often during the development process, and view public critiques as information-gathering sessions for improvement. That way they are less devastating.

3.23. In this perspective study for a sketch are several interlocking negative spaces at the drawing's lower perimeter edges. Study and manipulate foreground elements in your perspective drawings to achieve similar results.

silver chairs

silver leaf

floor?

3.24. *Julian LaTrobe paintings typically show a truthful likeness of the room reflected in mirrors, as seen in this arched wall mirror (compare this to the unidentifiable symbols used in figure 3.25). This rendering shows Elsie de Wolfe's own entrance hall at the "Little House of Many Mirrors."*

Point of View and Center of Interest

What are the important elements or special features of your space? Is there a great selling point for the design? If so, emphasize it by making it the center of interest. Points of view and perspective angles can be diverse in look and feel. Note the placement of the fireplace and the mirror in figure 3.25: the contrast of light against dark grabs your attention, and the perspective of the long bench in the center forces the viewer's eye into the space. In contrast, the desk in figure 3.27 makes the foreground a center of interest. Truthfully show the contents of a space and its primary features. Focus on a room's special features, and try to make these the strong center of interest. These are your selling points.

3.25. *Illustrations by the interior designer Jeremiah Goodman, such as this gouache rendering of a drawing room, always have an inviting appeal.*

Value Study

Before placing color on your illustration, complete a quick value study as a reference. You cannot rely on color or texture alone to achieve clarity. Develop several studies of the space with shade and shadow. Make a copy of your line drawing or place a piece of white tracing paper over it. You can use watercolor paint (Neutral Tint), a graphite stick, gray markers, or a soft carpenter's pencil. Build up the values based on what you know to be true from your study of how to render shapes and shadows. This will help you see where you may have problems with getting a shape to read. Generally your study will save areas of white, include two middle values, and have a dark value or black, or both. Contrasts hold our interest.

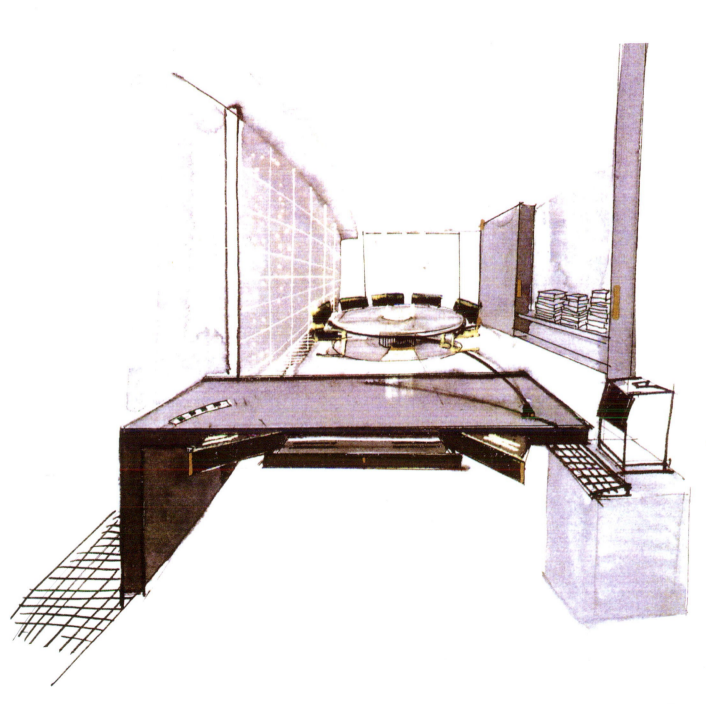

3.26. A value study using Neutral Tint paint establishes the areas in which to use contrast and the locations for the range of values. The next step is to develop a color study, as shown in figure 3.28, where the actual color values are considered. Both are created before starting a full-color final illustration, as shown in figure 4.5.

3.27. Whites placed adjacent to black areas create drama, holding the viewer's interest with the contrast between the two values. This office for a private company in Belgium was designed in 1990 by Andrée Putman.

Color Study

Each material selected for an interior illustration must be fully studied before you can begin your rendering, as shown in figure 3.28. Topics to address include which medium to use, which colors, the order of the color application if more than one color is needed to achieve a desired effect, and which colors to use for shade and shadow. This procedure takes quite a bit of time but can make or break a presentation.

Think of color unity as your goal: unity for the illustration and unity for the entire presentation if more than one illustration is to be included. Limit your color marker or paint palette for the illustration. Four hues of green or blue or any other color can be distracting when one or two could have been used instead. For example, the beige in your marble sample may not be an exact match to your beige paint sample, but they are similar enough and in accord. The best solution for synchronization in the illustration would be to use the same beige marker or marker combination for both the marble and the paint. Color synchronization was used for figure 3.29. Be as realistic as harmony allows. Change the value and intensity to add interest.

Tip! A good rule to follow is to avoid rendering every inch of the paper surface. Soften the edges by leaving a lot of white at the perimeter.

3.29. A color study representative of color synchronization is created with marker.

3.28. Watercolor is used for this color study of figure 4.5.

Sighting

Part of the artistic process is to research before we create. For discovery and exploration, we have our eyes, our instinct, our intuition, and our passion. Your own curiosity can take you on a journey to discover for yourself—for example, by visiting different spaces to actually observe subjects in an interior setting. After doing several of the step-by-step exercises, you will begin seeing materials and spaces in a new way. "The question is not what you look at," said Henry David Thoreau (*Journal*, August 5, 1851), "but how you look and whether you see."

Sighting Expeditions

You may find yourself in a restaurant or a lobby, looking at color values and textures with an eye to how they would translate into an illustration. This situation research should also take into account what you observe about light, shade, and shadow under different lighting conditions and various times of day. Observing only the color of an object reveals vast information. Instead of seeing a pool of water or a reflection on a table, you will see yellow, pink, blue, green, and the shapes of those colors. Pretending that you are a marker or a paintbrush when observing a plant can help you imagine how to reproduce the subject with gestures.

Invite a friend on a sighting expedition. A visit to a museum to study the art may introduce you to a new technique that you might want to mimic. You are bound to find a painting by one of the masters that helps you understand where to place the lightest values to their best effect. By studying color palettes, you can discern which colors achieve contrast or color harmony. A gold mine of information can be observed and assimilated from painters such as the impressionists Renoir, Monet, Cézanne, Degas, and Manet. Go out to "see" at least once a week.

You are imagining all the time, although you may not realize it. Looking at a geometric sculpture and how it relates to the space surrounding it can set the stage for imagination. Can you imagine it as a spatial enclosure or a dramatic focal wall statement? Can you imagine how it could be illustrated—which medium, which colors, which techniques? The reason that visionary artists, designers, inventors, and architects rarely had an issue with placing a mark on a blank sheet of paper is because they fully developed their imagination skills. Their creations were completely envisioned and developed in their mind before ever approaching paper. Perhaps their mental curiosity included many questions beginning with, What if? Mental images grow from questioning, and creative results blossom from those mental images.

Develop your own imagination skills and apply them to illustration. Being able to illustrate your vision quickly, skillfully, and with originality is a direct track to great rewards in your career as a designer. Use internal, mental vision when selecting your materials and seeing them before rendering. This process requires careful study of your subject matter, probing and digestion of concepts, and visual information. Now imagine being proficient enough in rendering so that you do not have to look at this book any more. You will be.

3.30. *Robert Martin's gouache rendering of a night scene in a living room, designed in 1970 by Yale R. Burge, shows a dramatic yet subtle use of dark blue and brown to depict the windows. The light reflections, placed next to the dark values throughout, are crisp and sharp.*

Great Illustrators

Lovely, enticing, wonderful—these are some of the impressions we get when looking at the work of great illustrators. That is precisely how you want your client to feel when you make a presentation. If your illustration reflects your passion, it is quite contagious!

Many great professional illustrators have my admiration and respect, among them Jeremiah Goodman, Robert Martin, and Nadim Racy, whose work all takes my breath away. Julian LaTrobe produced paintings of interiors designed by Elsie de Wolfe in the early twentieth century that were brimming with natural light and delicate impressions; his unrestrained free strokes and exquisite discernment of what to leave out made him a master of reduction and light. Significant designers who also have great skill in illustration have included the late Billy Baldwin as well as the venerable Albert Hadley.

Look for those who inspire a passion in you. I would love to illustrate as the great illustrators do, so I study them and try to emulate their techniques. Of course my illustrations do not look like theirs, because I developed my own style—one somewhere between concept and presentation rendering. Most interior designers are not professional illustrators, but their presentations ought to look skillful. You will develop your own style by practicing and studying the professionals' techniques.

I studied in workshops with the watercolorist Frank Webb. He is a master of color, making me always in awe of his beautifully placed gestures of Quinacridone Violet.

A good place to start your research is *The Illustrated Room: 20th Century Interior Design Rendering*, by Vilma Barr and Dani Antman, a wonderful book of illustrations by accomplished professionals. Jeremiah Goodman's *Jeremiah: A Romantic Vision* is a source of the illustrator's own magnificent illustrations. *Albert Hadley: Drawings and the Design Process*, by Mark Hampton, Mario Buatta, David Anthony Easton, and Mariette Himes Gomez, is a compilation of the designer's stunning illustrations and design process drawings. Also look at the Web site of the American Society of Architectural Illustrators (www.asai.org). In addition, there is much to learn from illustration books for product design, fashion design, and fine art painting. The illustration books on my own shelf are listed in this book's Resources.

3.31. Nadim Racy, a Brazilian architect who has directed restorations of many classic hotels, such as the Plaza in New York City, made this gouache rendering of a model living room for W. & J. Sloane in New York City in the early 1960s. Study its well-planned color harmony and skillful detail indications.

Tip! Great illustrators are masters of reduction. The best way to learn what to reduce or leave out is to study a subject in detail to understand its important elements. Then it will have a place in your memory theater.

3.32. Julian LaTrobe exquisitely rendered the many society interiors designed by Elsie de Wolfe in the first decades of the twentieth century. In this bedroom LaTrobe used very soft brush strokes for the large chintz pattern. White intensifies sunlight coming through the window sheers, pours onto the floor, and is repeated on the screen.

71

Creation Files

You probably have a stack of photographs, samples, furniture tear sheets, and articles that you are saving to use some day on a project. These are your creation files. The fact that you saved these items means that there is something about a photograph or a sample that stimulated you. This is a great habit of creative personalities.

Architectural and interior photography, to take one item, has so many great compositions to learn from. The light placement, foreground devices, and points of view have much to teach you. Research and study such photographs. Trace a composition on tissue. Does it give you any ideas regarding composition to try in your future masterpiece?

Keep compiling or begin collecting and organizing the items mentioned above. Drawings of people, plants, illustrations, and techniques are also helpful to have. Such a file is a good source of motivation. Add your own marker and watercolor studies for future reference. Make it an ongoing research project, because it should be kept up-to-date. Your creation file will be a great time saver when adding enhancements to your drawings.

Assignments

1. Value studies. Use figures A.1 and A.11 (in the appendix) for this exercise. Trace several copies of the drawings with a nonphoto or nonprint pencil. Illustrate the forms using the values in figures 3.1 through 3.5. Value gives the illustration its painterly quality and helps hold an illustration together, providing readability from the viewing distance of a normal presentation. Try to achieve a readable form without relying on lines for these exercises:

a. *Gray.* Create a value study with gray.

b. *Light color.* Create a value study with a light color.

c. *Dark color.* Create a value study with a dark color.

Remember that you can add layers of the same color or a complementary color to darken a color. Incorporate what you learned from the rendered forms in figures 3.1 through 3.5 (how to simplify the planes to three or four values: highlight, light, shade, and shadow).

2. Patterns. Select a patterned surface material or upholstery textile. Study it closely, noticing the dominant shapes, directions, and colors. Now close your eyes. What you recall about the item with your eyes closed is in all probability the simplified interpretation of the pattern that you should render. Illustrate a few of those impressions.

3. Refinement. Select a perspective drawing from a current or previous project that you have completed, or use figure A.17 or A.18 (in the appendix). Select a paper and a medium of your choice. The suggested size of the sketch is 11" by 17" or larger.

a. *Framing and opening.* Modify the sketch to create a more interesting outline that frames the sketch. Consider the shape of the perimeter edges. Can you add to or subtract from the sketch to create a motivating shape or a more interesting opening into the illustration?

b. *Value study.* Create a value study of the sketch developed above. If you have difficulty with this part of the assignment, it may help to first make black-and-white photocopies of other illustrations or photographs of rooms and study their value placement.

c. *Color study.* Develop a color study using colors and materials of your choice. Keep in mind that every color has a relative lightness (high key) or darkness (low key). The value expressed by the color will either create a contrast with adjacent colors or create ambiguity because the values may be identical. The more contrast in values between adjacent colors, the more they will appear separate from each other. Make a black-and-white photocopy of your color study to see your value placement more clearly. From there you can decide if you should alter the relative lightness or darkness of a color to support the spatial relationships.

4. Research. As inspiration, do some research into the work of great leading illustrators. Keep these treasures handy as you practice your skills. Complete the research suggested throughout this chapter, as it will provide valuable reference material as you progress in the study of interior illustration.

5. Creation files. Begin to add more categories to your creation files. Start by doing some situation research into light, shade, and shadow. Photograph the same room (your living room or bedroom, for example) under different lighting conditions: morning daylight, afternoon daylight, artificial light, a combination of daylight and artificial light, and any other combination that you can think of. Study the different effects of the lighting on each object. Keep these photographs as a reference for rendering.

6. Personal inspiration. Select something from your creation file, and render an illustration of it. It is your own personal inspiration.

Act as if you are already a great illustrator. You really are, but your dexterity needs some time to catch up with your passion. Use these lessons to learn courage and personal style. They are intended to be instructive, but please have fun along the way!

Room Vignettes

If the essence of a space is the color, then make the color look glorious. If it is texture, then capture it with gesture. If it is translucency, make it appear transparent and ethereal.

Parson-table console and a Mademoiselle chair (Philippe Starck), showing subtle differences in mirror, plastic, and chrome (marker)

The Design Concept

A rendering is one of a designer's most influential sales tools. Its primary purpose is to communicate the design concept to the client. Whatever we can do to help clients visualize a space makes the final design presentation and other recommendations smoother and quicker. The client's decision is made from the first glance at an illustration and is based on desire. The presentation goes well when the client makes a strong emotional connection to the visual. It is a memorable experience to see a glowing smile from a client—at that moment your job becomes easier. You helped make his or her dream and the project goal a reality.

Refer often to the vignettes. Look at how the architectural and furnishing subjects come together to create a whole. Recall what you know about the elements and design principles, and look for the echoes of those concepts in the illustrations. Remember that to sell a space, an illustration must support the design concept. Let these illustrations be a source of inspiration in setting new goals for improving your design communication abilities. Believe in yourself, your ability, and your desire to learn.

4.1. For this conference room, rendered in watercolor on two-ply Strathmore™ 500 series Bristol, a minimal palette is used. The color placement adds to the subtle transitions.

Commercial Spaces

A conference room setting, as shown in figure 4.1, is best presented in a vertical format to deemphasize the horizontal nature of a long, rectangular room that contains a table of this size. In this case, a horizontal format would be too static. The crop line at the bottom was intentional, to avoid distortion and the visual clutter of spidery chair bases. The vertical direction of the watercolor used for the walls and the floor emphasizes the reflective quality and color harmony of the room. The same direction was also applied to the ceiling elements, achieving overall unity in the illustration. A rhythm created by alternation in minimal color and contrast brings the viewer's eye into and around the space.

For additional instruction, see figures 5.36 (ceiling), 6.39 (walls), 7.20 (floor), and 8.51 (chair).

An illustration of a typical workstation (manufactured by Teknion) looks more interesting when framed with a foreground device such as the screen in figure 4.2. The panel system shown (manufactured by Herman Miller) has translucency and makes the small space in the foreground feel more expansive. Office system illustrations are a good place to show ghost people. Details, such as the computer on the desk, help keep the eye on the center of interest—the workstation system elements and the task chair to be sold by this vignette.

For additional instruction, see figures 5.4 (ceiling), 8.19 (chair), 8.31 (desk), and 8.33 (credenza).

4.2. Office panels, files, and desks are much easier to render with markers because of their ability to achieve crisp and clean edges. Here markers are used on Letraset Bleedproof marker paper.

Retail Spaces

An illustration is a must for retail and is required for most mall tenant-approval submissions. For a storefront, the illustration must show four primary elements: entrance, signage, merchandise display, and storefront materials. The shop-front design for the Lori Jewelry Boutique, seen in figure 4.3, incorporates the store's name and graphic brand identity. The opaque nature of the black glass is minimized by its reflective qualities and the pattern's floating nature. Both are illusions but realistic interpretations.

For additional instruction, see figures 5.25 (storefront material), 8.36 (lighting), and 9.44 (displays).

For the retail shop concept in figure 4.4, the translucency of the interior materials and the merchandise presentation are of primary importance. The effect of scrim panels is achieved by layers of watercolor glazes as well as the texture created by the interaction of water with the paper. The heavyweight plate-finish illustration board used is not made for the amount of water added to the paint, but it is perfect for creating the essence of these interior materials. The more color glaze applied to the paper for the concrete floor, the richer the texture produced by the paper. Color was applied lightly for the aluminum surfaces, as the metal has a smooth surface quality, and mere brush strokes were employed to signify the clothing on display. The distribution and proportion of the color red and the black-and-white placement of merchandise create a strong balance in the composition.

For additional instruction, see figures 5.44 (window), 10.8 (platform), 10.21 (scrim), and 10.34 (floor).

4.3. To help communicate the ethereal quality of this shop concept, merchandise is indicated merely with simple brush-stroke gestures. Watercolor is used on heavyweight-plate Strathmore™ 500 series illustration board.

4.4. Retail illustrations usually include people, such as shoppers with the retailer's shopping bag in hand. This rendering of the Lori Jewelry Boutique uses marker, white pen, and pencil on Letraset Bleedproof marker paper.

Hospitality Spaces

Watercolor lends itself well to an eclectic design concept and creates a mood of intimacy when soft and subtle transitions occur—some areas simply melt into mystery. The salon in figure 4.5 exemplifies this on the left of the space, around the tea table, the sofa, and the floor as well as under the side tables in the back.

For additional instruction, see figures 5.35 (ceiling), 5.45 and 5.46 (window), 8.11a (chair), 8.43 (sofa), 8.54 and 8.55 (table), and 8.67 (lamp).

The beauty of the bedroom study in figure 4.6, besides the color blending, is the combination of the free marker stroke gestures. They are dynamic and help move the viewer through the space. Without them this could have become a static representation because of the character of the geometric patterns. Many colors are blended into the floor, wall, and ceiling—a great technique for making a monochromatic scheme more vibrant and achieving interesting variation through color transition on large surface areas.

For additional instruction, see figures 5.3 (ceiling), 6.7 (walls), and 7.12 (carpet).

4.6. The free strokes used for this bedroom suite vignette study create movement, pulling the eye through the rendering. Markers are used on Letraset Bleedproof marker paper.

4.5. To render a salon in a private club, watercolor on Crescent cold-pressed watercolor board offers a soft, fluid quality. (For a value study of this room, see figure 3.26.)

Residential Spaces

The three loft illustrations here and on the next two pages were executed for a residential loft presentation. All are consistent in approach and show a tight style of illustration.

Inspired by studying a photograph, the perspective and furniture locations shown in figure 4.7 were planned to create a geometric rhythm in the living room. The red colors lead the viewer into and around the space, while the grays and the blacks help the whites read. This is a very simple vignette for beginners to try.

For additional instruction, see figures 8.1 (sofa), 8.30 (table), 8.32 (credenza), and 8.38 (lamp).

With an open plan layout, you must decide whether to have a view looking over furniture in the foreground or leave out the foreground furniture. In the dining room illustrated in figure 4.8, foreground furnishings are omitted in order to show the floor covering materials. The area carpet is a strong directional element that takes the viewer into the space; it is balanced by a bold art element on the left. The room's tight rendering style and rigid geometric shapes are softened by the view through the window; there a hazy winter scene adds some color and helps outline the table and chairs. Repetition of rectangular shapes controls eye movement through the illustration.

For additional instruction, see figures 5.17 (window), 7.17 (area carpet), and 7.19 (floor).

Changing the medium within a design presentation is not the norm. It works in figure 4.9 because the style used for the loft kitchen is similar to that of the dining room in figure 4.8. Watercolor is a perfect medium for indicating dark colors, as it is easier to soften the feeling and achieve value transitions. The room has a delicate balance between the floral wall mural and the colored crystal chandelier. Note that the same blue colors are used throughout figures 4.7 to 4.10, giving color unity to the presentation, as do the colors of the flowers and the fruit in the different spaces.

For additional instruction, see figures 5.34b (ceiling), 6.42 (wall mural), 7.24 (floor), and 8.65 (chandelier).

4.7. Geometric rhythms set apart this loft living room, rendered in markers on Letraset Bleedproof marker paper.

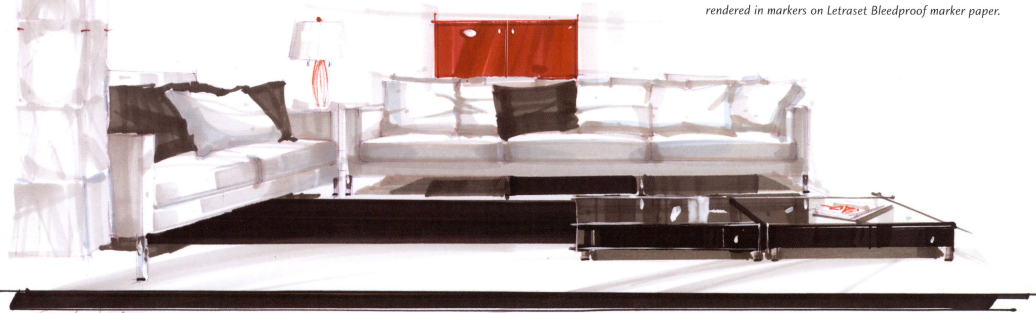

4.8. *For the loft's dining room, created with both markers and paint on Letraset Bleedproof marker paper, the view skips over the foreground to focus on the dining set in front of the prominent window.*

Choose a few room photographs to experiment with. Use them to learn what occurs with light and materials in perspective. Trace the photograph and then reinterpret what you see in a marker or watercolor illustration. The illustration in figure 4.10 is an experiment of that type to study pattern in light, shade, and perspective. Decisions have to be made regarding where to emphasize patterns and where to allow them to dissipate. Here the pattern is strong at the center of the subject, and then it fades as it recedes in the space and becomes lighter where the pattern changes direction. Notice how dark the wall value is under the counter, created with a few discernible pattern strokes. When illustrating a bath space, it is sufficient to show and highlight key design elements, such as the wall design, fixtures, and the shower enclosure.

For additional instruction, see figures 6.44 (wall), 8.63 (track lighting), and 10.4 (shower).

4.9. A simple one-point perspective places the center of interest on the Boffi system in the loft kitchen rendering, executed in watercolor on smooth surface Bristol.

4.10. To study patterns in light, shade, and perspective, this bathroom was recreated from a photograph of a hotel suite designed by Marcel Wanders in his Lute Suites near Amsterdam. Watercolor is used on smooth surface Bristol.

Imagination Illustration

Illustrations prepared to communicate a preliminary design are the most fun phase of the interior design process. Creativity flows in amazing directions when you render studies to express your design concept—giving sight to words and flight to fantasy. Said Albert Hadley of his own dots and lines on a sketch: "This was simply a drawing I did creating a big modern room . . . but the dots indicate pattern" (*Albert Hadley: Drawings and the Design Process*). Because of the free-spirited nature of good concept drawing, concept studies are often far more representative of a design concept than the final design illustration. Figure 4.11 is a concept study for a retail boutique.

4.11. The line work in this rendering of Christian Lacroix's Las Vegas boutique has a fluid and abstract quality that emphasizes its spontaneity.

Tip! "Go some distance away because the work appears smaller and more of it can be taken in at a glance, and a lack of harmony and proportion is more readily seen." Leonardo da Vinci (1452–1519)

Assignments

1. **Practice rendering.** Render figure A.16 or A.17 (in the appendix) on paper no smaller than 11" by 17". You may think that it is too soon to do this, but try it anyway. Apply the skills and the knowledge you have learned to date. The results of the study will show what you do well and lead to areas where you need more practice. Render the subject a second time to improve on the first version. Or render it using the techniques that you love.

2. **Graphic drawing.** You are next going to create an illustration of a graphic quality, rather than in a painterly style (in which each interior item is indicated and modeled with color values). Begin by studying figures 2.27, 3.13, 3.20, and 4.1; also look at figure 4.6, but turn it sideways. Take a brush (without paint or water) or a marker (with the cap on), and without touching the images, mimic the gestures for applying the background color. Do not stop the gesture until you reach the edge of the page. Use your whole arm.

a. *Coloring.* For the next part of this practice, use figure A.18. Make the drawing as large as possible, up to 24" high. Imagine your color scheme, and then choose a few colors to illustrate with. Use any medium. Think more about the medium's effect as background color—color swings the mood of an illustration—and let it express the mood of your imagined color scheme. Simply lay in color, in a vertical direction, covering most but not all of the paper. Ignore the lines of the drawing. You may leave some white areas. Let the rendering dry if you used paint or a large amount of marker layering.

b. *Calligraphy.* The final part of the practice is placing graphic lines and symbols to represent the room's subjects. Apply your skills of variation and gesture, considering which lines you want to leave out; for example, you could focus on the contours of the furniture and the architecture, or you could decide to create pattern. Your lines may be freehand or assisted by tools. Any medium may be used over the background color; this is a good exercise in which to mix media. Your line work does not have to be black. This type of line work is often called calligraphy, and your illustration is referred to as a graphic drawing because of the interesting line work, in contrast to a more painterly style.

c. *Variations.* Try some variations to represent the following:

• Color and mood.

• Contrast (light and dark, warm and cool, solid and void, and so forth).

• Pattern and line.

• Black and white.

3. **Imagination illustrations.** Try a few imagination illustrations. No pencils allowed. Use marker or paint, and render several concepts in a freewheeling way. This will help loosen up and diminish any nervousness you may have about illustrating. Be spontaneous!

4. **The masters.** After you study some illustrators whose work you love, apply their techniques to any wild and fancy ideas you have. Or apply their technique to a drawing in this book. Add it to your ideas or creation file.

5. *The Yoga of Drawing.* Read this book by Jeanne Carbonetti if you would like to explore more drawing and painting techniques on your own. Variations of those explained by Carbonetti appear as some of the assignments and warm-up exercises throughout this book.

"Do just once what others say you can't do," suggested Arthur C. Clarke, *"and you will never pay attention to their limitations again."* To help you become an exceptional visual artist, let's make that even more personal: if you do just once what you think you can't do, you will probably never again pay attention to the limitations you place on yourself!

Interior Architectural Elements

In the design of interiors, spatial voids help reveal solid forms, and in an illustration, shape, color, and texture establish the dominance of any form. Geometric shapes prevail in architecture; even the shapes of our body parts can be abstracted into basic geometric forms. Your interior concepts will use shapes in their purest geometric form or will combine and vary them—highlighted with color and texture—to achieve the proper emphasis, harmony, or balance.

Design presentation illustration for gourmet food boutiques and a restaurant (1983) (marker and gouache)

Minimal Illustration Technique

Interior design is best approached with a minimal illustration technique. Study the shapes and forms in your own compositions. Do not overrender. Do not overdetail. Rather, suggest details with gesture. Most of the time I complete an entire rendering only through step 1 (overall application of color and values), so that I do not illustrate too much detail or place it where it is not successful.

Because illustrators often mix media, it is best to prepare the paper surface accordingly. Final touches of wet media, such as paint spatter over marker, should be applied to a stiff, sturdy surface. Bond paper can be dry mounted to board, or the marker illustration can be done on heavy Bristol or illustration board. Tightly tape unmounted marker bond paper to a hard surface, and then apply paint gestures such as spatter or simple strokes for details and plants. Be careful with the paint consistency, as too much water will warp the paper.

Step back from your work and critique it between steps. Check for color or gesture errors. It is easier to make adjustments during the process than it is after a rendering is complete. Because you may lose spontaneity from constant step-by-step practice, after doing the steps, practice the exercises again with quicker gestures.

Markers

In working with markers, remember these basic guidelines:

- **Perspective.** Follow the direction of the perspective with the marker strokes. For two-point perspective, horizontal strokes must follow the left or right vanishing point. For one-point perspective, work parallel to the horizon line and the horizontal paper edges.

- **Gesture.** Keep strokes open and varied in width toward the foreground or near light sources.

- **Line work.** Vary the line quality. Use a few straight strokes and some scribbled strokes, for example, or vary the width and the pressure.

- **Masking.** Taping edges helps achieve a crisp transition between surfaces.

Ceilings

The ceiling illustrations here use a variety of techniques, including loose, tight, and scribbles. When rendering ceilings, use a minimal application of marker. Drawing all of a ceiling's detail will look too cluttered. Keep it somewhat indistinct, so the viewer remains focused on more important areas of the illustration. Following are instructions for various ceiling types and approaches, to be studied in conjunction with the illustrations indicated.

Tip! Trace the drawings in this book if you have not had previous drawing and perspective instruction. If you understand perspective, use a perspective grid and draw the subjects on your own without tracing.

5.1. Basic marker application, tight technique

For this flat ceiling, the marker strokes (aided by a cardboard guide) start at the back and gradually work toward the foreground.

5.2. Basic marker application, loose technique

The strokes (aided by a cardboard guide) start at the ceiling's back; about midway into the foreground, they gradually sweep across and are worked into the foreground without the guide.

5.3. Basic marker application, scribble technique

Up to five layers of marker can be scribbled in with a sweeping motion. Fewer color applications are placed near the window and in the foreground.

Grid ceiling

Step 1:

• Apply the base color, using a loose marker application technique. Note that a ceiling is lightest in the foreground.

• Define the grid lines for the ceiling tiles.

Step 2:

• If needed for fluorescent lights (not shown), add darker lines to define the square outlines of the recessed ceiling lights.

• Add white gouache within the lights if necessary in darker areas.

Tip! To apply very long strokes with a marker, turn your paper in a direction comfortable for you. It is easier to steady your hand for a long vertical stroke than for a long horizontal one.

5.4. Grid ceiling

Slanted ceiling

Step 1:

- Tape the edges of the slanted ceiling surface, which is painted drywall (part of a condominium project designed by Richard Meier).

- Use a cardboard guide to apply straight marker strokes to the ceiling, following the same direction as the line where the back window wall meets the ceiling. Use multiple layers of marker (427T) and varying stroke widths. Leave more white paper showing as you reach the foreground of the space.

- Remove the tape.

Step 2:

- Tape the edges of the soffit underside.

- Scribble in 427T, applying the marker in a horizontal direction.

- Remove the tape.

Step 3:

- Create a triangular tape mask to stop the marker strokes.

- Add triangular shadows to the wall surfaces.

- As an alternative, you can tape the top and the sides of the wall sections, and then apply the marker in a diagonal direction.

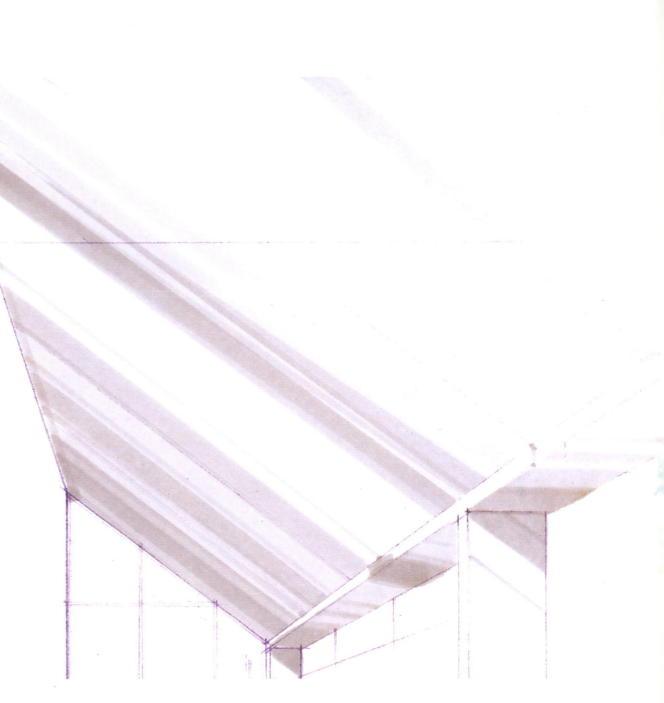

5.5. *Slanted ceiling*

Painted exposed ceiling

Step 1:

• Tape each section as you work. Establish where to place the whites and the three additional values.

• Apply the light value (Prismacolor Eggshell) first, using a combination of freehand and straight strokes made with a marker guide.

• Next apply the middle value (Eggshell).

• Finally apply the dark value (Eggshell + 155T) to the underside of the surfaces.

Step 2:

• Add a few deeper values (481T) to finish.

• Detail the water pipes and the light fixtures (dark gray and black marker, pencil, or paint).

5.6a. *Value study created before beginning the illustration*

5.6b. *Painted exposed ceiling*

Light wood exposed ceiling

Step 1:

- If the material is a light wood, use the same colors as in figure 5.6b. Other marker choices include 2706т, 155т, 134т, 168т, 263т, 473т, 492т, 4655т, 464т, 469т, and Warm Gray 03.

- Allow more white paper surface to show.

Step 2:

- Apply lines with a marker to indicate the wood grain, but do not overdetail the ceiling. Use dabs for knots in the foreground.

Floating ceiling

Step 1:

- Plan areas of white for this high-gloss painted surface to indicate the light cove source.

- Mask the ceiling's top and bottom edges with frisket film before applying the marker.

- Apply the base color (Prismacolor Blondwood), leaving white at the curve of the plane and where the cove light will be reflecting on the ceiling planes.

Step 2:

- Apply the next color (AD Marker Beige) on top, allowing some of the previous color to show.

Step 3:

- Deepen values with the final color application (Blondwood and 466т).

5.7. Light wood exposed ceiling   5.8. Floating ceiling

Curved ceiling

Step 1:

- For the two lightest shades, layer one marker (Prismacolor Blondwood).

Step 2:

- Apply a darker value (466T) for the shade areas.

Tip! If strong colors and values dominate the surrounding architecture, a curved ceiling can simply be left unrendered. This technique allows the line work or the adjacent colors or values to reveal the form as a negative shape.

Painted coffered ceiling

Step 1:

- Plan the white areas. Mask the surfaces as you work.

- Apply the light value (9181T) to all surfaces, excluding white areas.

Step 2:

- Apply the next value (468T) to the back vertical surfaces of the box and the trim at the top of the left vertical surfaces.

Step 3:

- Apply the darkest value (466T) where surfaces change direction in the corner of the box and where molding meets molding.

5.10. Painted coffered ceiling

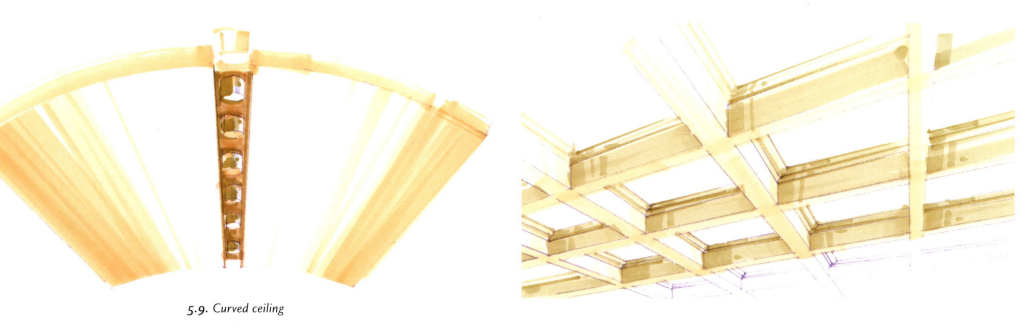

5.9. Curved ceiling

Wood coffered ceiling

Step 1:

- Plan the value locations. Mask the surfaces as you work.

- Apply the base undercolor (Prismacolor Light Peach) on the underside areas and the trim on the left in the coffer box and the front-facing section.

- Apply a darker value undercolor (4505T) to the front-facing section. Add strokes to the underside of the coffer box.

Step 2:

- Apply color (471T) to all surfaces of the box.

- Apply an additional layer of the same color (471T) to the front-facing surface.

- Apply definition (168T) between the molding, wood grain lines, and the dark value strokes where the surfaces change direction.

- Define the inside lines of the coffer box (168T) where needed.

- Note that the darker the wood, the fewer grain detail lines are needed.

Tip! When a ceiling or a room has a lot of detail (and the ceiling is a light neutral color), you may simply leave the ceiling white and render the detail in the appropriate color.

5.11. Wood coffered ceiling

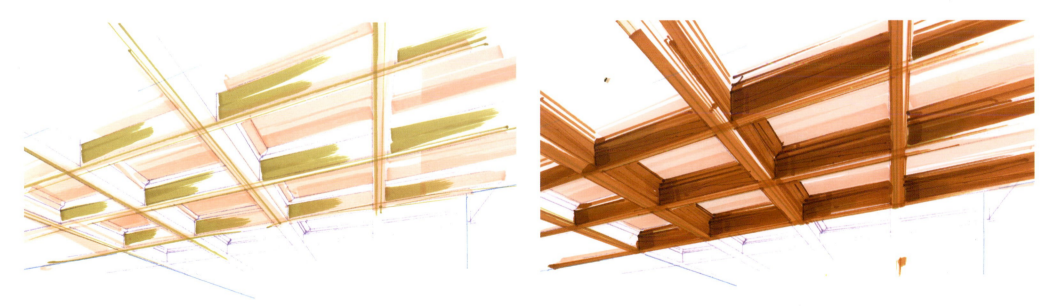

Skylight and truss system

Step 1:

- Tape the left and right edges of the skylight where it meets the wall surface.

- Apply these marker values to the structural supports: face (427T), underside (420T and 649T), and bottom piece (430T).

- Define the lines (430T) where structure meets glass.

- Use two grays (420T and 649T) for the face of the forward and back structures.

- Define the top edge (430T) of the forward structure.

Step 2:

- Mask the widest sections of the structural supports.

- Plan the whites in the skylight.

- Blend markers (2706T and 552T), working wet into wet for the rear window first.

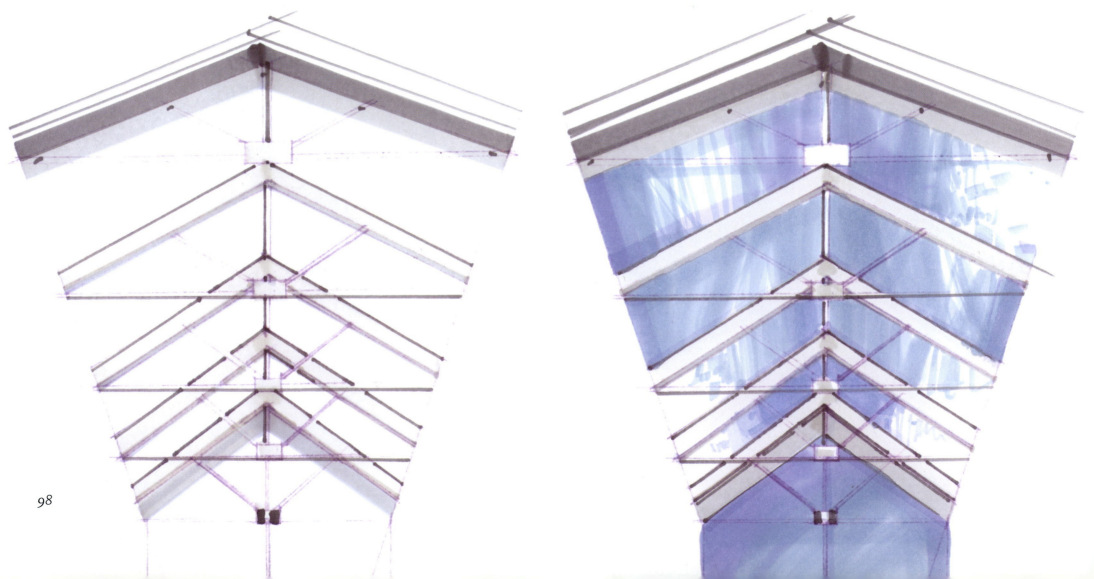

Step 3:

- Render the skylight in sections. Work quickly, and apply the markers (2706T and 552T) wet into wet, as above.

- A quick way to render the sky without taping is by following the direction of the pitch lines when applying marker colors.

- Remove all tape.

- Add definition and shadows (420T) to the walls at the sides.

- Define the vertical sides (430T, 420T, and 649T) of the rear window.

- Define the structure (430T) in the front and the rear.

- Define small elements of the middle-ground structure (white gouache).

- Add window reflections (white gouache).

5.12. Skylight and truss system

Windows

What to show outside a window is a typical dilemma. Base your decision on what will work best with both the interior and the illustration. Keep in mind the actual local setting, but romance it a bit. A vague impression is much better than a solid white or blue color to represent glass, because the latter may interrupt the visual harmony of the overall color composition. Instead combine blues and whites with a minimal suggestion of the exterior scene. Pale blue and green are color symbols for glass; reflections are added in white paint. Do not make the window the most dominant element in an illustration unless it is a focal point or a center of interest.

Glass, trim, and sill

Step 1:

- Place the detailed line drawing underneath your paper.

- Follow the lines of the drawing underneath to render the values, defining the window-frame elements without black line work; instead suggest the details with color and values (427T or light grays).

Step 2:

- Tape the edges of the window sections.

- Render the outside foliage and scenery with dabs of color (olive green).

- Indicate the sky color (pale blue) along the window's top sections.

- If you lose the whites, you can get them back with a white pen.

5.13. Glass, trim, and sill

City view from a window

Step 1:

- Mask or tape the window-frame elements.

- Apply the base color (2707T) where the sky meets the buildings.

- Apply the sky color (B128).

- Blend in hues (2706T) where the above two colors meet.

- Scribble in color (2706T) where the sky and the top frame meet.

Step 2:

- Apply the building colors (Y616, Ice Gray 07, B418, C429, and G138).

- Remove the mask or the tape.

Step 3:

- Apply color (Ice Gray 03 and Ice Gray 07) to the window-frame exterior.

- Use black for the window-frame interior.

- Add reflections and glass detail (white gouache).

*5.14. City view from a window
(basic marker technique for windows)*

Ocean view from a picture window

- Use a simple color-to-color gradation technique.

- Apply the markers wet into wet with a gentle over-lapping stroke, giving the impression of waves.

- Work from side to side at a slight angle, because waves typically break that way.

- Keep the horizon line perfectly straight; the color of the water is darkest at that point. The sky is usually lightest at the horizon line.

5.15. Ocean view from a picture window

B128

290T

535T

292T

3105T

317T

C429

Light Sand

Day and night city views from a window

Step 1:

- Scribble the base color (2707T) where the sky meets the buildings.

- Blend in the next color (2706T) where the two meet.

- Scribble in the sky with the next color (2707T).

Step 2:

- Apply the building color using grays and blues.

- Detail the window frame (Ice Gray 03 and Ice Gray 05).

Step 3:

- Add reflections and glass detail (white gouache). Let it dry.

Step 4 (for a night city view):

- Apply dark blue (541T) to the window. The values change where the colors and white paint are applied underneath.

- Add the stars and building lights (white gouache).

5.16. Day and night city views from a window

Winter view from a window

Step 1:

- Create the color behind the trees (2706T, 552T, and 2707T) with a scribble technique applied wet into wet. (You can change the colors to reflect any season or time of day.)

Step 2:

- Define the tree branches with colored pencils (Lilac and Sepia).

Step 3:

- Use a black marker for the window frame.
- Add reflections (white gouache).

5.17. Winter view from a window

Tip! Ask your clients for their favorite time of day. Render your design presentation to capture the same time of day.

Doors

Try not to render a door as an illustration's center of interest or focal point. To make the door look convincing, however, it is important to indicate door operational elements. Various door types—flush panel, raised panel, glass, French, louver, and shop fronts—are discussed here and shown in the following illustrations.

5.18. *Flush-panel painted door and wenge wood door*

Colors used for the painted door are 427T, 430T, and black, with white gouache dabs on the door lever. For the wenge wood door, the base color is Light Suntan, with Warm Gray 08, 440T, and black added, plus white gouache on the door lever.

5.19. *Painted French doors with glass*

Colors used are 649T, 420T, 134T, 155T, and 552T. Use the techniques learned in figure 5.13.

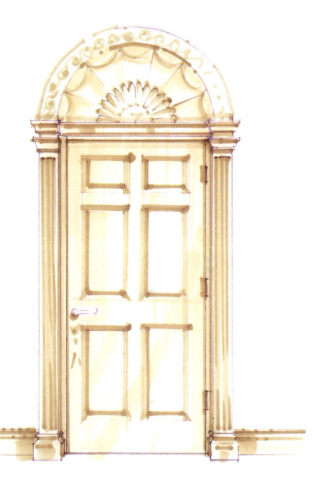

5.20. *Painted raised-panel door*

This illustration shows the use of three values (918T, 468T, and 466T) to indicate the surface detail. It can be achieved with one, the darkest value. That is the quickest approach and could be all you need.

Clear glass curved door

Step 1:

- Plan the white areas, masking them if that helps.

- Apply the colors (9181T, 468T, and 466T) for the space beyond the door, indicating them with an abstract and broken line or a shape.

- Leave areas of white to show the reflective quality of the glass.

- Apply colors (2707T and 427T) for the glass.

Step 2:

- For the metal door elements, use one light value and one dark value (427T and Cool Gray 09).

- For flat glass doors, use the same colors and techniques.

5.21. Clear glass curved door

Pocket door with engraved, sandblasted glass

Step 1:

• Plan and mask the white areas.

• Blend as you apply the glass colors (427T, 2706T, and 2707T) by overlapping the application.

• Apply the same colors for the metal frame and the wall base.

Step 2:

• Make the vertical strokes fade off into the floor to indicate a white reflective surface.

• Define the inner surface of the metal frame (Cool Gray 09) with a fine nib.

• Apply horizontal lines to the glass (gray colored pencil) to indicate the engraved design detail. Vary the pressure of the strokes.

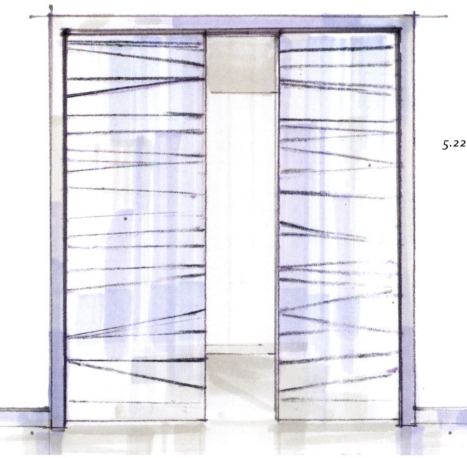

5.22. Pocket door with engraved, sandblasted glass

Tip! Soft and diffused color application is the best way to show sandblasted glass or similar materials. For a less generic glass look than the typical pale blue or green, include the colors of the room beyond a glass door.

Sliding door with acid-treated glass

Step 1:

- Apply the base colors (468T and 466T) to the walls and the ceiling.

- Apply the base color (466T) to the wall base.

- Apply the glass color (20% Cool Gray), leaving some of the white paper showing to represent the acid-treated glass. The glass can be rendered wet into wet to achieve a softer effect.

Step 2:

- Darken areas (20% Cool Gray) near the horizontal and vertical door-frame members.

- Place the darkest value (5425T) adjacent to the vertical frame members to help them read.

Step 3:

- Add gouache to the frame members.

- Render the floor with the base color (466T).

5.24. *Louvered door*

The base color is 9181T, and the values are 468T, with Raw Umber pencil and a white pen used for definition. Use this same technique for shutters, deepening the values if needed.

5.23. *Sliding door with acid-treated glass*

Opaque glass storefront

Step 1:

- To create the floating pattern and the shop name, draw the design on the wall surfaces (white pen). Let it dry.

- Tape sections as you work.

- Use a black marker to apply the color to the wall, as explained in figure 6.22.

Step 2:

- Add definition to the sign by outlining the letter shapes (white pen).

5.25. Opaque glass storefront

Stairs

A basic principle to keep in mind when rendering stairs with overhead lighting is that the lightest value is on the top of the tread (because of overhead lighting), the middle value is on the riser, and the darkest value is on the stringer area. You will thus typically need three values.

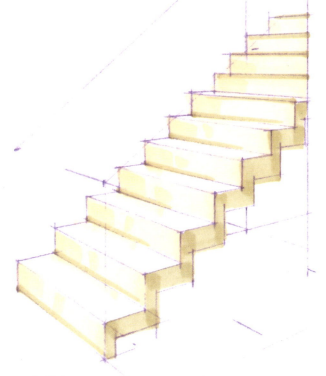

5.26. *Stairs*

Following the principle for rendering stairs, one color and three values are used. Colors used are 918T, 468T, and 466T.

Glass-and-timber stairs

Step 1:

- Apply the base colors (Y919 and Y216) on the glass treads of this antique stair assembly made of timber and thick, Coke-bottle green glass.

- Apply the base color (AD Marker Light Sand) on the timbers.

- Apply a deeper value (466T) on the timbers.

- Fade the illustration by rendering less detail at the top of stairs.

Step 2:

- Apply detail (365T) on the glass treads.

- Indicate the edge of the glass treads (365T and G136). (The thicker the glass, the greener the glass colors.)

- Apply the darkest value (O527) on the timber.

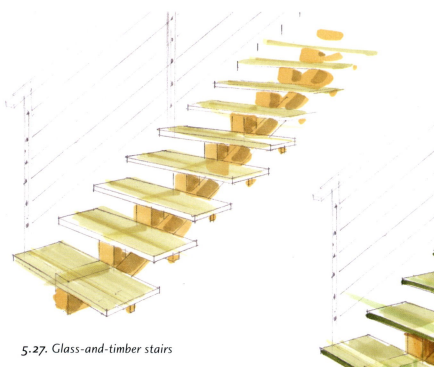

5.27. *Glass-and-timber stairs*

Aluminum stairs

Step 1:

- Apply yellow (Y417) for light reflections. Work wet into wet for softer value transitions.

- Apply the base color (Ice Gray 02).

Step 2:

- Apply the middle values (Ice Gray 04 and Ice Gray 05).

- Use a darker gray value for shadows and reflections.

- Apply highlights (white gouache and white pen).

5.28. Aluminum stairs

Columns, Molding, and Ornament

On column capitals with a lot of detail, it is best to have a minimal amount of line work. Try to suggest the detail, such as marble veins or wood grain, with a limited but readable gesture, and place it in areas with the lightest value. Do the same for any highly decorative subject matter, such as molding and other architectural ornament. The amount of detail shown for the cove ceiling molding in figure 5.33a would not be typical, but exceptions are made for elements in the foreground or close-up vignettes.

5.30. *Greek and Roman Ionic columns*

Place values as illustrated here, and define the detail with value by using simple strokes. Ice Gray 08, Ice Gray 05, and 431T are used here.

5.29. *Tuscan column*

Whatever the material, place values as illustrated here and on the cylinder in figure 3.2b. Details such as marble veins or wood grain can be placed in areas with the lightest value. Ice Gray 08, Ice Gray 05, and 431T are shown here.

5.31. Base and window trim

Always indicate a horizontal value for form definition where a profile changes shape and near the window glass. Deepen the values for shadow areas on the trim adjacent to any window covering. Colors used are Ice Gray and 468T.

5.32. Ceiling and base trim

One light and one dark value are sufficient to indicate trim. Apply the darkest value under a change in the trim profile. Colors 9181T, 468T, and 466T are shown here.

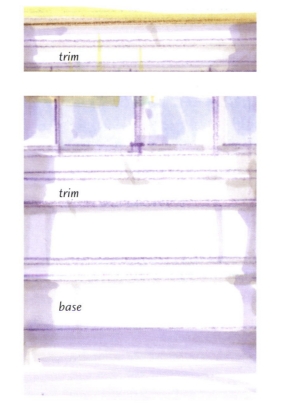

trim

trim

base

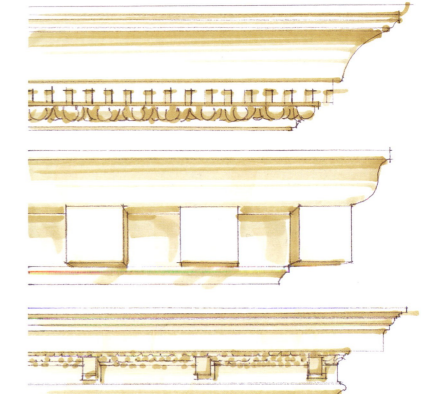

5.33a. Trim, moldings, and frieze detail

This example shows where to place values and how to indicate detail. In most illustrations of room settings, this much detail is not drawn. Exceptions are any elements in the foreground or close-up detail vignettes. Marker colors used on these examples are 9181T, 468T, and 466T.

5.33b. Painted ceiling medallion

Light to dark values used are 9181T, 468T, and 466T. Use an ellipse guide to help maintain the oval shapes and profiles.

Watercolor

Watercolor can be intimidating for beginners, but it is worth learning because it creates countless atmospheric qualities in a rendering. The value of watercolor over marker for the many subjects you have to illustrate will become apparent when you use and practice both. The secret to mastering watercolor has much to do with knowing what is possible. Warm-up exercises such as the following are designed to help you discover this potential.

Leonardo da Vinci and Albert Einstein imagined being the subjects they were studying and the problems they were solving. You too can do the same thing. Close your eyes and pretend that you are a ripple and can float and flow from dry to wet. It may sound a bit outlandish, but do it anyway to see the results. Use a large, flat brush, and sweep some water onto the surface of your paper; there will be some dry areas and some wet areas. Load your brush with paint, and begin your brush stroke on a dry spot and stop it halfway into a wet area. Let the color float and flow into the wet areas on its own. When dry, the results produce interesting edges and soft transitions from color to white paper surface—the exciting passages in an illustration.

Ceilings

The basic techniques for applying color washes to ceilings are illustrated in figures 5.34a and 5.34b. Remember to be restrained in applying paint for ceilings. By using a big brush, you will not be tempted to put in too much detail and you will have a wider brush stroke. Think sweeping gestures.

Flat ceiling with track lighting

Step 1:

• Apply the base color wash (Neutral Tint + Cobalt Violet + Raw Sienna), using a large, flat brush. Begin the horizontal strokes at the back and work toward the foreground, creating broad, sweeping brush strokes. Apply a stroke in the foreground at a slight angle or a broad curve. Let it dry.

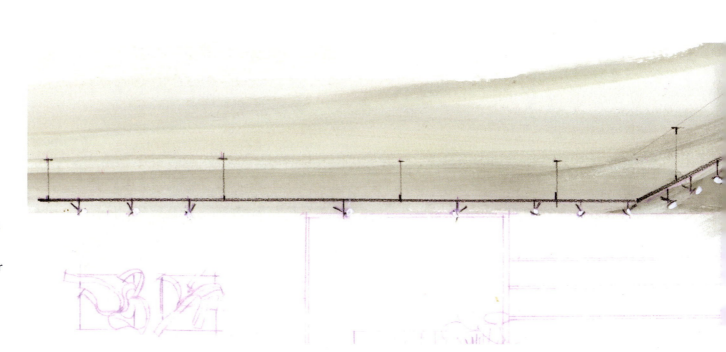

5.34a. Flat ceiling with track lighting

Step 2:

- Tape the ceiling lines at the walls. Add a darker stroke (Neutral Tint + Cobalt Violet + Raw Sienna) where the ceiling meets the wall. Let it dry.

- Detail the track lighting (Neutral Tint) with a rigger brush and an artist's bridge (or marker or colored pencil, if that is easier). Let it dry.

- Add dabs of paint (white gouache) for the lights.

Flat ceiling

Step 1:

- Tape the ceiling lines at the walls.

Step 2:

- Apply the base color (Neutral Tint) to dry paper, using a large, flat brush and a horizontal application.

- Add a base color wash, using broad, sweeping brush strokes.

5.34b. Flat ceiling

Recessed ceiling, horizontal application

Step 1:

• Use the same techniques as described in figure 5.34a, adjusting the base color paint. Use any light-value color (such as Cobalt Violet + Cobalt Blue + Neutral Tint).

• Apply the base color to the ceiling and the soffit, using a combination of tight and loose applications. Let it dry.

Step 2:

• Tape the edges of the soffit. Add a deeper value to the soffit underside. Let it dry.

• Remove the tape. For the face of the soffit that is not receiving light, add a dark value with more Neutral Tint in the paint mixture.

• Detail the trim with dabs of a darker-value paint.

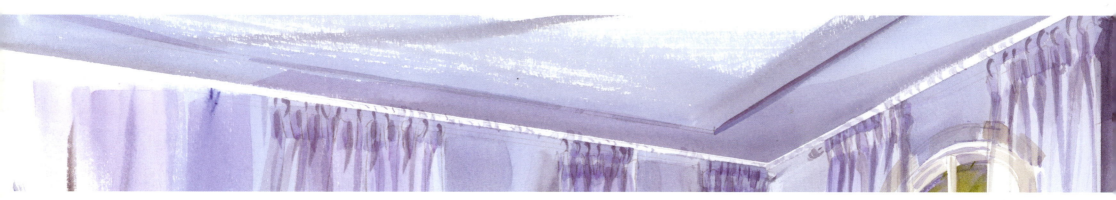

5.35. *Recessed ceiling, horizontal application*

Recessed ceiling, vertical application

Step 1:

- Plan the white areas, and mask the left and right soffit edges.

- Mix a flat color wash for the base color (Raw Sienna + Cobalt Violet + Neutral Tint), and apply it vertically with a large, flat brush. You may also apply the colors as individual glazes.

- Layer the color glazes on top of one another to achieve variations on the base color, using large and medium flat brushes. Allow each layer to dry before applying the next color.

- Apply all base color washes in a vertical direction to achieve a unified presentation.

Step 2:

- Mask or tape sections as you continue to work.

- Apply a darker glaze (Cobalt Violet + Neutral Tint) in a horizontal direction to the underside of the soffit, using a flat brush. Let it dry.

Step 3:

- Remove all tape or masks.

- Define the soffit surface at the rear with pencil or a fine-tip marker.

- Apply dabs of paint (white gouache) for the recessed lights and vertical lines for the rear lighting.

5.36. *Recessed ceiling, vertical application*

Slanted ceiling

Step 1:

• Tape the edges to help achieve a crisp transition for the surfaces of this angled ceiling, the vertical soffit edge, and the soffit underside before applying brush strokes for the individual surface planes.

• Leave more white paper as you reach the space's foreground.

Step 2:

• Apply multiple washes (Neutral Tint + Cobalt Violet), using a large, flat brush. Apply the strokes to the ceiling in varying widths, following the direction of the line where the back window wall meets the ceiling. Let the paint dry between washes.

5.37. *Slanted painted drywall ceiling*

Painted exposed ceiling

Step 1:

- Establish where to place the whites and the three additional values.

- Tape the edges while working on each step. Let them dry between washes.

- Apply a light value wash (Raw Sienna), using a large, flat brush.

Step 2:

- Apply the middle value (Raw Sienna + Neutral Tint).

Step 3:

- Apply the darkest value (Raw Sienna + Neutral Tint) to the underside of the surfaces.

- Add a few deeper values to finish.

- Detail the water pipes and the light fixtures (dark gray and black paint), using a small, round brush.

5.38. Painted exposed ceiling

Dark painted exposed ceiling

- Follow the instructions described for figure 5.38, except in step 2 do not use the middle value for the beams. Dark elements are more indistinct.

- Make the circular ductwork and the water pipes the darkest elements (Neutral Tint).

5.39. Dark painted exposed ceiling

Curved ceiling

Step 1:

• Plan the white areas.

• Apply a light wash (Neutral Tint + Cobalt Violet), using a large, flat brush. Make broad strokes, first to the vanishing point and then following the front and back curves. Let it dry.

Step 2:

• Add another glaze of the same colors, defining the edges with it. Use a large, flat brush. Let it dry.

Step 3:

• Detail the ceiling recess (at the cylinder light fixtures) with a darker glaze.

• Detail the lighting fixtures (Neutral Tint, white gouache, and dark gray fine-point marker).

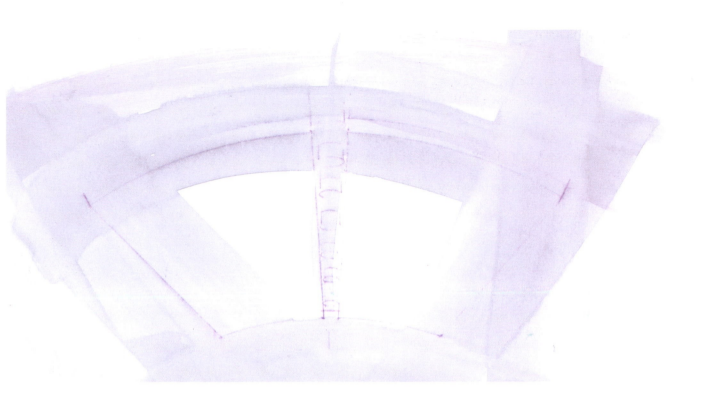

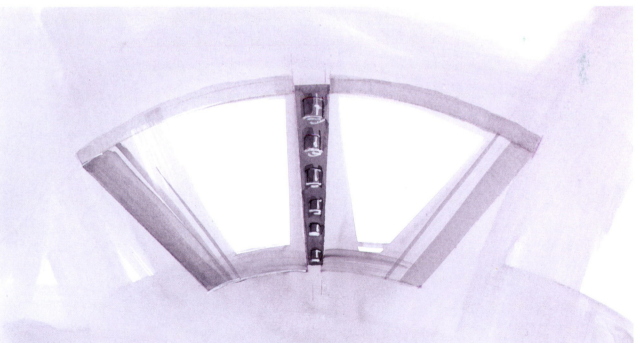

5.40. Curved ceiling

Curved aluminum ceiling

Step 1:

- Apply a light wash of the base color (Cerulean Blue), leaving some white areas. Use a medium, flat brush. Let it dry.

- Apply a wash layer (Cerulean Blue + Cobalt Violet) on the top, slightly offset to the first wash layer. Let it dry.

Step 2:

- Apply a wash (Neutral Tint) of darker values. Let it dry.

Step 3:

- Add details and definition (Neutral Tint), using a small, round brush.

5.41. Curved aluminum ceiling

Painted coffered ceiling

Step 1:

• Plan the white areas. Tape the edges as you work in each section.

• Apply a light value wash (Raw Sienna + Neutral Tint) to all surfaces, excluding white areas. Use a large, flat brush. Let it dry.

Step 2:

• Apply the medium value of the same colors to the back surfaces of each coffer box and the trim at the left of each box. Use a medium, flat brush. Let it dry.

5.42. *Painted coffered ceiling*

Step 3:

• Apply the darkest value (Raw Sienna + Neutral Tint) where surfaces change direction in the corner of the box and where molding meets molding. Use a medium, flat brush.

Step 4:

• Detail the molding with fine line work, using small, round brushes and an artist's bridge.

Skylight and truss system

Step 1:

- Tape the structural members and the edges of the skylight and the window.

- Plan the white areas in the sky. Using a flat brush, develop the sky with washes (Cobalt Blue and Cobalt Violet). Let it dry between washes.

- Develop the window with washes (Cobalt Blue and Cobalt Violet). Let it dry between washes.

Step 2:

- Remove the tape.

- Develop values (Neutral Tint) for the structural supports. The face is the lightest value, the underside is a middle value, and the bottom is a dark value.

Step 3:

- Add definition and values (Neutral Tint) to the walls on each side.

- Define the structure at the front and the rear.

Step 4:

- Add window reflections (white gouache or a white pen).

5.43. *Skylight and truss system*

Windows

When rendering windows in watercolor, washes are typically applied in a vertical, oblique direction to indicate a glass surface. Crisp white areas are created by tape or frisket film or by leaving space unpainted. Let each wash dry before applying another so your colors stay clear and the edges sharp.

5.44. *Basic glass window*

Basic glass window

Step 1:

- Plan the white areas, masking them if necessary.

- Apply a light wash (Cobalt Blue), using a large, flat brush. Paint straight through the window frames in a vertical direction. Let it dry.

- Apply a light wash (Cobalt Blue). Let it dry.

- Add values (Cobalt Violet and/or Neutral Tint).

Step 2:

- Detail the window frame last (Neutral Tint or black), using a small, round brush or a black marker.

- If needed, add white highlights (white gouache or a white pen).

French windows with drapery

Step 1:

- Tape the window-frame elements and the drapery rod.

- Plan the white areas on the outside wall and the drapery. Draw light guidelines on the drapery folds to continue the shape of the window frame.

- Apply a light wash (Cobalt Blue + Cobalt Violet) to the outside wall, inside wall, and drapery folds, using a flat brush.

- Apply a light wash of olive green to the tree shapes. Dab in a darker green value before the first green wash dries, using a round brush.

- Let all washes dry.

Step 2:

- Apply darker blue values (base color + Neutral Tint) to the walls. Let it dry.

- Apply darker values to the drapery, using a round brush. Let it dry.

- Remove the tape.

5.45. French windows with drapery

Step 3:

- Detail the drapery rod, using a small, round brush.

- Add a few shaded areas to define the mullions and the window frame, using a small, round brush. Indicate the outdoor foliage and the sky to help the window read.

5.46. French windows with drapery

Window with a city view

Step 1:

- Tape the window-frame elements.

- Apply a light wash (Cobalt Blue) to the sky, using an angled flat brush. Let it dry.

- Apply a light wash (Cobalt Violet) where the sky meets the horizon. Let it dry.

- Apply a light wash (Neutral Tint) to the buildings.

- Add diagonal washes (Cobalt Violet) to the window.

Step 2:

- Add deeper values (Cobalt Blue and Neutral Tint) to the buildings, defining the windows in the foreground.

- Remove the tape and develop the values (Neutral Tint) on the window frame. Let it dry.

Step 3:

- Add open metal blinds with a white pen. Render both the interior and the exterior window elements first. Add horizontal lines to indicate the blind (gouache or colored pencil in the blind color). To indicate the cords and the wands, add vertical lines (white pen, colored pencil, or black ink).

5.47. Window with a city view

Doors

In this section some new techniques are introduced and previously learned ones are reinforced—for example, how you can achieve an interesting surface by having two paint colors on the brush. Other illustrations indicate where to place the values for ornate trim details and raised-panel designs or moldings to achieve the same effect. It is a time saver to use a fan or a hand-held blow dryer to dry layers of paint between washes.

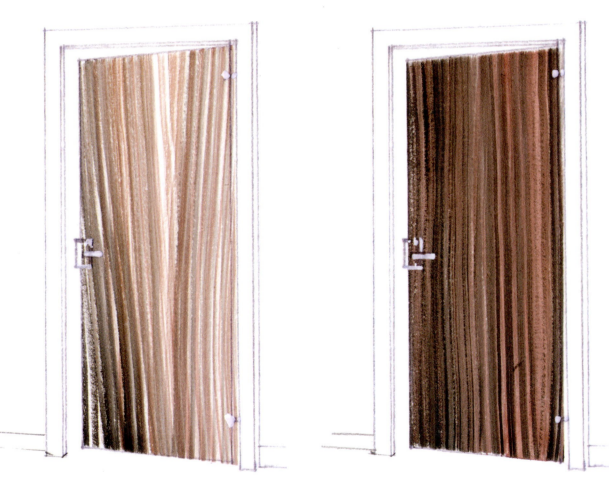

5.48a. Flush-panel door in wenge wood

5.48b. Flush-panel door in wenge wood

Flush-panel door in wenge wood

Step 1:

- Use two paint colors on a flat brush or an angular brush. Load the left side of the brush with a chocolate brown mixture (Burnt Sienna + Quinacridone Magenta + Ultramarine Blue) and the right side with Peach Black.

- Apply the paint in vertical strokes, working from left to right. Let it dry.

Step 2:

- Detail the door hardware (black paint and white pen).

Alternative:

- As an alternative to step 1 (see figure 5.48b), paint the base color (chocolate brown mixture above). Let it dry.

- Apply vertical strokes of the second color (Peach Black), using an angular brush and splitting the brush hairs. For greater control, use a flat brush or a round brush.

Painted raised-panel door

Step 1:

- Paint the door freehand with a flat brush, using a triangular scale as an artist's bridge to achieve straight lines; if you are not comfortable with a guide, use tape, but it is more time consuming.

- Work from light to dark values. Allow the paint glazes to dry in between each layer.

- Apply the light and middle values (Raw Siena) to help the primary shapes read.

- Apply dark values (Raw Sienna + Neutral Tint) and details where needed, using a small, flat brush. Keep it clean and simple.

Step 2:

- For the arch, steady your hand and start the color application from the bottom of the arc to the other side using a small, round brush or splitting the hairs of a flat brush. Stop the application at the point where you think that you may lose the curve.

- Repeat, starting from the opposite side.

- Turning the paper 45 or 90 degrees can also help in painting the arch, or make a circular artist's bridge to use as a guide.

5.49. *Painted raised-panel door*

Clear glass door

Step 1:

- Plan the white areas.

- Apply glazes (Raw Sienna) to the architecture surrounding the door, using a flat brush. Work from light to dark. Let the paint dry between each glaze. You may use an artist's bridge to help maintain a straight brush stroke.

- Apply glazes (the same color and Neutral Tint) to the architecture seen through the door. Let it dry.

Step 2:

- Apply blue (Cerulean Blue) to the glass on the door.

Step 3:

- Detail the metal hardware (Neutral Tint), using a small, round brush.

- Apply white highlights to the metal hardware (white pen or gouache).

5.50. Clear glass door

Tip! When you plan your white areas as well as what you see through a glass door, an illustration can be quick and easy.

Pocket door with engraved, sandblasted glass

Step 1:

• Plan the white areas. If it helps, tape the top and the bottom of the door elements.

• Apply a light base color glaze (Neutral Tint) to the door, frame, and architectural elements, using a flat brush. Let it dry.

Step 2:

• Use the brush as you would a marker by turning it at an angle to create the metal door frame's diagonal values, which are built up with glazes (Cerulean Blue + Cobalt Violet).

• Apply vertical strokes of paint (Cerulean Blue) to the glass with a flat brush. Let it dry.

• Apply a glaze (Cerulean Blue + Cobalt Violet) on the glass, allowing some previously applied blue to remain untouched.

Step 3:

• Detail the horizontal design with a gray pencil (Prismacolor 968).

5.51. Pocket door with engraved, sandblasted glass

Molding and Ornament

Foreground elements and close-up vignettes are exceptions to the general rule that not much detail is drawn in illustrations of room settings. For architectural trim, moldings, friezes, and other ornament, reduce the palette to one, two, or three values. Use three for close-up illustration; for distant details, use the darkest value, as shown on the examples here. Start with the wash colors for the base color application. Finish the detail work after the entire room illustration is complete. It is easier to discern how much detail is needed to emphasize ornament at the later stage.

Painted molding and light cove

Step 1:

- Mask the light cove area to retain the white surface.

- Apply the base color wash (Peach Black + Payne's Gray) to all surfaces, using a large, flat brush. Let it dry.

- Mask molding details with dabs of masking fluid. Let it dry.

5.52. Decorative molding

The paint colors used on these examples are Raw Sienna for the base color and a mix of Cerulean Blue, Neutral Tint, and Raw Sienna for the values. Start with the base color and then go from light to dark values. Detail should gradually fade out as the surfaces recede in perspective.

Step 2:

- Apply a deeper value of the same paint color to moldings and the right wall surface, using a large, flat brush.

- Pull out some of the paint along the molding lines, using a damp flat brush. Let it dry.

Step 3:

- Remove all masks and masking fluid.

- Add a warm yellow (Cadmium Yellow + Raw Sienna) to the edge of the light cove to indicate the light source, using a flat brush.

- Apply definition (Peach Black + Payne's Gray) to the molding details, using a round brush.

5.53. Painted molding and light cove

Assignments

1. Ceilings. Practice basic ceiling illustrations using marker and watercolor. Trace three different ceiling configurations from a magazine or your creation files. Apply any color using the techniques in this chapter. Be sure to try this with both media.

2. Natural drawing positions. From the exercise above, choose the ceiling that was the most difficult for you. Render it again, but turn your drawing upside down or sideways when applying color. This exercise will stimulate your inner drawing ability, but the practical result will be to find your natural drawing positions for individual subjects. Natural drawing positions are more comfortable for you.

3. Time of day. Trace the drawing of the windows in figure 5.16 or 5.17. Illustrate the view with three different times of day: morning sunlight, late afternoon daylight, and late evening with a dark sky and stars. A good reference for an evening sky is figure 3.30; study it closely, because the view through the window is very subtle.

4. Glass doors. From a manufacturer's catalog, select three of your favorite glass door designs—they are a major design trend for both passage doors and spatial divisions. Trace the doors, and then illustrate the glass and the hardware. Apply the techniques explained in this chapter.

5. Door systems. Suggest a door and its detail with color application and values; do the same for the door frame, jambs, and hardware. Place a detailed line drawing underneath your paper, and then apply color and value, using the lines underneath as a guide. Remember that doors are typically not the center of interest in an illustration; when they appear, they should be understated. Use minimal line work or none at all.

"Creativity is good rehearsal, visualizing the outcome of a project or a feeling or design soon enough and clearly enough to improve the plan before action."

Peter Glen

No one expects your illustrations to look exactly like the ones presented throughout this book. What matters is that your work resemble the material you want to portray and that you learn how to use the appropriate tools to embody your design. After much paper and practice, you will develop your own style and technique—likely ones much better than the illustrations in this book!

Walls

Atmospheric and emotional qualities surround us in interior spaces. Just as we intuitively respond to these qualities in a room, the client intuitively responds to them in an illustration. Make it a favorable response by rendering a space so that the colors and application techniques match the design concept. Color, technique, and the medium's response to the paper have everything to do with how you attain such effects as texture, transparency, or opaqueness—choices that allow you to achieve an atmospheric quality.

Color technique study for a lobby or gallery space (watercolor)

Markers

Before you practice the illustrations in this chapter, try to mimic the steps by first imagining yourself performing them. Act as if you are illustrating each image by lightly touching the surface and following the marker strokes with a closed marker. Following are some techniques to help you gain insight and engage you in the process of putting down media to achieve various effects for wall surfaces.

Painted Walls

You are familiar with the application techniques used in figure 6.1 from lessons in the previous chapters. The techniques shown in figures 6.2 through 6.6 are new. They will help you master various wall textures, directional materials, and surface patterns, perfecting your judgment as to where and when to fade color or to leave it out. Get plenty of paper ready, because it is important to practice each example in perspective and with different color hues and values. These techniques can also be tried on floor surfaces when you reach chapter 7.

Smooth painted wall

Step 1:

- Tape the lines where the wall surfaces meet the ceiling and the floor.

Step 2:

- Use straight and scribbled strokes in any color, vary the spacing, and apply more layers to areas for value changes.

- See figure 2.18 for another example.

6.1. Smooth painted wall

Textured and directional surfaces: horizontal direction

- Use this technique as a base to indicate stone, brick, wood, grass cloth, and other materials and textures with a horizontal direction.

- First practice with any light color marker and then try again with a darker color.

- Try to prevent the marker strokes from overlapping. If the placement is controlled, however, the overlap can work for you, especially as a shadow or a grout line.

- Keep the horizontal strokes going in the direction of the vanishing point. This takes much practice, gradually adjusting the marker guide as you apply the strokes.

6.2. Horizontal textured surface

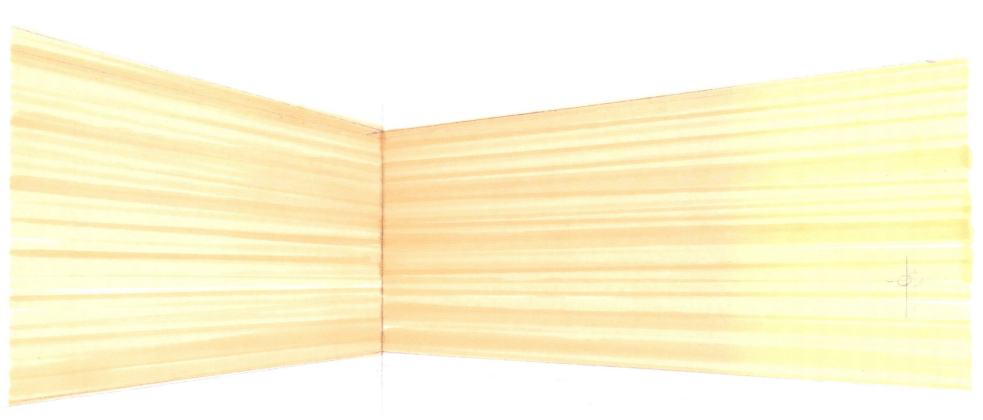

Textured and directional surfaces: "patch into patch"

- Use this technique, taught by Frank Webb in his watercolor workshop, as a good base for numerous paint textures and wall-covering patterns. It translates well into marker or watercolor.

- Use one marker color (920T) and repeatedly overlap square and rectangular shapes.

- Add line-work detail for any material that may have depth or more texture, using a fine-point marker or a colored pencil.

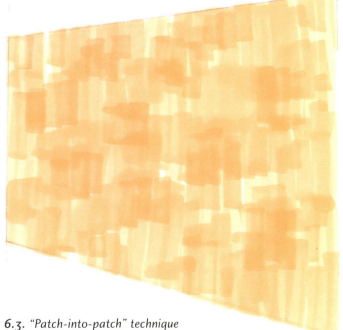

6.3. "Patch-into-patch" technique

Textured and directional surfaces: irregular course patterns

- Use this technique for irregular masonry units such as flagstone, as well as some special paints and wall coverings that have a ground pattern with an irregular rhythm.

- Apply horizontal strokes (20% Cool Gray), using a cardboard guide to help keep the perspective correct.

- Place freehand horizontal strokes next, in a rhythm that varies the size, the location, and the color.

- Add grout lines or pattern overprint details.

6.4. Irregular masonry course pattern

Textured and directional surfaces: curves and undulating patterns

- Hold the marker at an angle while it is placed flat on the paper surface, and then draw a curving line. The broad nib creates a wavy-looking line if you do not turn the marker or remove it from the surface. Simply move your arm up and down while dragging the nib across the paper.

- Gently and firmly repeat the process, overlapping some lines and placing the next curved line at an offset to the previous line. If you are holding the marker properly, the nib creates thin-to-thick strokes as you draw the line (see figure 6.5). This is much like a calligraphy line stroke.

- For a vertical example, follow the steps described above. Use the narrow side of a broad nib to achieve a regular line thickness. For the solid-looking sections, continuously overlap the line application (see figure 6.6).

Tip! If you find figures 6.5 and 6.6 difficult with a marker, try them with a flat brush to get into the flow of the technique.

6.6. *Vertical undulating pattern*

Faux finishes

Step 1:

- For a suede-finish painted wall, apply multiple layers of the appropriate color, working the layers wet into wet.

Step 2:

- Use fewer marker strokes in the lighter area to create a difference between the lightest value and the darker surface. The darkest wall area has as many as four to five marker layers, creating a rich-looking painted wall surface.

- This technique also works for suede, velvet, chenille, velour, and similar fabrics.

6.7. *Suede-finish wall*

Tip! Flooding the marker color on the paper and working multiple layers wet into wet achieves a velvety surface.

Painted raised paneling

Step 1:

- Tape sections as you work.

- Apply marker colors in layers from light to dark.

- Apply the base color (9181T) to the panels, using a vertical scribble technique.

- Apply the base color to the trim and the molding, using a horizontal direction.

Step 2:

- Allow shade and shadow to reveal the changing surfaces. As the wall recedes, draw and render less detail.

- Define the panels with the middle value (468T), deepening the values at the edges.

- Detail the moldings and the trim with the dark value (466T).

6.8. Painted raised paneling

Wood

Very detailed indication of wood can make an illustration look too busy. Study your overall composition to decide where you will place the emphasis for this material. Too much grain can produce a shape that does not read as a whole or that looks like too many pieces of color. A simple rendering technique for a wood wall finish is to add wood grain lines (with a colored pencil, fine-point color marker, or black pigment liner) to a base wall color, such as those in figure 6.1. For instance, to show a simple light wood you can use a base color of Eggshell, apply some medium and dark values with 4535T or 4525T, and indicate some grain with a Nougat watercolor pencil (Faber-Castell Albrecht Dürer 8200-178) or a Sepia colored pencil (Prismacolor 948). Remember to save your dry markers, because they are useful for indicating a convincing wood grain.

Wood color and grain

Step 1:

- Using a scribble technique, apply the markers following the direction of the wood grain. The overlap of the scribble strokes simulates the grain.

- Apply the lightest color first, gradually adding each additional color from light to dark.

- To soften a darker color, apply another layer of the lightest color or use a marker blender.

Step 2:

- Add pencil lines to indicate grain detail.

- See chapter 10 for additional wood colors.

6.9a. Wood color and grain

Colors used here are 527T, 168T, 469T, 535T, and 440T.

6.9b. Wood color and grain

Colors used here are 168T, 535T, 168T, Warm Gray 11, and 440T.

6.9c. Wood color and grain

Colors used here are 2706T, 155T, 473T, Warm Gray 03, and Terra Cotta and Nougat watercolor pencils.

Mahogany raised paneling

Step 1:

- Tape the sections as you work.

- Apply the base color (168T) to the panels, using a vertical scribble technique.

- Apply color to the trim and the molding in a horizontal direction.

Step 2:

- Define the panels with a darker value (469T).

- Deepen the values (469T) at the panel edges.

- Detail the moldings and the trim (469T).

Step 3:

- Add the highlights (white gouache).

6.10. Mahogany raised paneling

Diagonal patterns

Step 1:

- Work in sections, individually taping each section.

- Apply the base color (Y119), stroking the marker in a diagonal direction.

Step 2:

- Apply lines of varied spacing (Y216 and Y217), using a brush-tip marker.

- Apply the final color (Y717) with the fine tip.

6.11a. *Diagonal diamond-match veneer*

Figured Korina veneer

Alternative 1:

- Tape the left or the right section to create a hard line where the chevron pattern meets (see figure 6.11b).

- Apply color (Y216) in the oblique directions.

- Remove the tape.

- Indicate the grain colors (Y119, Y116, and Y117) by applying the marker in a vertical direction.

- Blend with a marker blender, applying a few strokes in the direction of the chevron.

Alternative 2:

- Apply the base color (Y119) in a vertical direction (see figure 6.11c).

- Individually tape each section to create a hard line where the chevron pattern meets.

- Apply chevron lines with a white pen. Let it dry.

- Remove the tape.

- Apply a vertical grain (Y216 and Y717).

- Blend with a marker blender, applying a few strokes in the direction of the chevron.

6.11b. *Figured Korina veneer, alternative 1*

Bamboo pattern

Step 1:

- Tape the top and the bottom of the wall edge.

- Apply the base color (Y119).

Step 2:

- Apply the bamboo color (Y217) with a brush tip, leaving a space between each line of color.

- Follow with the same strokes. This time use a start-and-stop motion to create blobs of color (Y216) with the brush tip.

Step 3:

- Place a few dabs (Y216) directly above each blob, using a fine tip.

- For a warmer look, apply a few strokes of 155T.

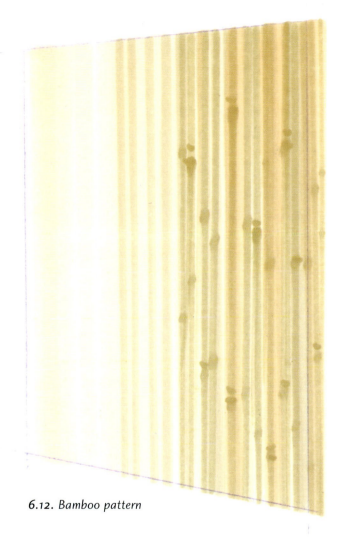

6.12. Bamboo pattern

6.11c. Figured Korina veneer, alternative 2

Tile

By its nature, tile is a very hard material that comes in numerous geometric shapes and sizes. To help achieve the character of individual tiles, subtle marker strokes are placed atop an overall base color for the wall. Although line is important in depicting the relative size of tiles, please do not overdo the line work. Incorporate just enough marks, or symbols, to help the viewer complete the picture. For tiles with an ornate decorative pattern, it is easier to detail the design with paint after application of the marker base colors and values. Again, do not overdo the indication. If you practice your skills in applying the two basic base color techniques here, you will be able to resist the tendency to place choppy color or too many lines.

To research tile in actual room settings, see the videos presented on the Bisazza Web site (www.bisazza.com). The videos feature prominent designers and artists discussing their tile projects. The settings are fun and irresistible.

Ceramic tile

Step 1:

- Tape as needed at the top and the bottom of the wall surfaces.

- Apply the base color (Prismacolor Eggshell).

- Apply a darker value (4535T) at the ceiling and the sides.

Step 2:

- Deepen the color value (4525T) at the top of the wall.

Step 3:

- Detail tiles with a randomly spaced color application (Y727, Y616, and Eggshell).

- Detail the grout with a fine tip (Y727 and Y616).

- Add white gouache to feature several grout lines.

6.13. Ceramic tile

Glass mosaic tile

Step 1:

- Scribble in the base colors (2706T, 155T, 134T, 552T, and 182T), wet on wet. The goal is to use multiple marker layers and offset lines to help convey the tile's transparency.

Step 2:

- Apply vertical strokes (486T, 479T, 535T, and 466T) on top of the base color, leaving it lighter at the center. The markers' irregular placement produces a multicolor effect.

- Add vertical and horizontal grid lines to indicate the grout, using a nonprint blue pencil.

- Dab the small squares (486T, 479T, 535T, and 466T) in a concentrated area, spacing them farther apart into the center.

Step 3:

- Add grout lines with a Caran d'Ache watercolor crayon (white), slightly offset from the previously drawn blue lines.

- Dab and spatter reflections (white gouache) to finish the iridescent effect.

6.14. *Glass mosaic tile*

Stone

The illustration techniques for stone are the same whether this surface material is used for interior walls or for floors. You may find that you have an easier time illustrating one and not the other, perhaps because of your own natural drawing positions. Turning your paper to adjust to your hand coordination will solve the problem. To achieve the many textures and compositions of stone materials, paint is almost always used on top of marker base colors. Using paint spatter instead of marker dots is much quicker and produces a more realistic-looking illustration. (See chapters 7 and 10 for additional examples of stone.)

White marble

Step 1:

• Tape the edges as you work on the sections to keep a clean edge where surfaces change.

• Apply the base color (427T) for the receding surfaces.

• Add large veins (427T) by twisting and twirling the marker. Vary the pressure.

• Add dabs (427T).

• My preference in illustrating marble is to stop at step 1 (see figure 6.15a). If you prefer more detail, complete step 2.

Step 2:

• Detail the veins in shadow (427T and gray pencil).

• Detail veins as needed on other surfaces (427T and pencil).

• Define the edges (430T).

• Add reflections (427T) with vertical and diagonal strokes (see figure 6.15b)

6.15a. *White marble (minimal style)*

6.15b. *White marble (detailed)*

Pattern-matched onice ivory (onyx)

Step 1:

- Tape sections as you work. Make your pencil guidelines lighter than those shown in the illustration for light-colored onyx.

- Use broad marker strokes for the base colors (Y417, Y919, Y217, and Y717).

- Follow the vein direction. Blend well and apply wet into wet.

- Allow the base colors to dry.

Step 2:

- Use the same colors as in step 1 to detail the veining.

- Use a brush tip and apply as in step 1.

Step 3:

- Define the panels (colored pencil).

- Define the veins (subtle colored pencil and white pen).

- Define the match lines (white pen) with very fine lines.

- Define the veining for added translucency (white gouache and white pen).

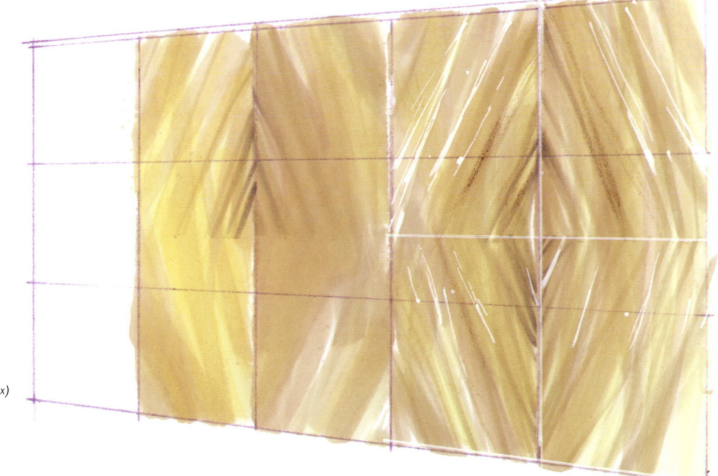

6.16. *Pattern-matched onice ivory (onyx)*

Black granite

Step 1:

- Tape the top and the bottom.

- Apply straight vertical strokes (Warm Gray 11), leaving a section of white paper untouched.

- Create a tape line on the wall surface, suggesting reflections from the ceiling.

- Apply straight vertical strokes (black).

Step 2:

- Remove the tape.

- Apply black strokes.

Step 3:

- Spatter with black paint and then with white paint.

- Detail the slab lines (white pen).

- Add reflections (white gouache).

Giallo granite

Step 1:

- Use a scribble technique for the base color (2706T, 155T, 134T, 552T, and 182T).

Step 2:

- Scribble another layer (466T) to warm and deepen the base color.

Step 3:

- Add tile grid lines (black).

- Add black diamond inserts (black).

- Spatter with paint (Burnt Umber and Neutral Tint).

- Add white gouache, spattering it lightly.

- For the reflections, apply a few brush strokes and dabs of paint (white gouache).

6.18. Giallo granite

6.17. Black granite

Tip! If you leave enough paper untouched, white gouache is not needed for highly reflective surfaces.

150

Flexible Wall Coverings

Given the huge selection of wallpaper and wall textiles available to a designer compared to the limited space in this book, here are only a few basic selections. (See chapter 10 for textures and chapter 11 for patterns.)

Relief wallpaper

Step 1:

- Flood in marker color (482T) with scribble strokes. Vary the pressure, and work wet to capture the texture of this suedelike wallpaper by Anya Larkin.

- Define the relief pattern lines (2706T), using a guide and a pointed nib.

Step 2:

- Define some of the pattern lines with a water-color pencil (Prismacolor Mulberry 2995).

- Go over some of the gridlines on top of the pencil with a pointed nib (482T).

- Finish with white pencil lines.

6.19. *Relief wallpaper*

Mural on silver leaf

Step 1:

- Indicate the silver leaf (see also figure 10.9 as well as figures 10.12 and 10.13).

Step 2:

- Apply the base mural design colors (5445T, 2706T, and 420T) on the silver-leaf background.

- Apply the ground cover base color (.003 Caran d'Ache).

- Apply the trees and the reeds (.245 Caran d'Ache).

- Apply leaves around the flowers (.45 Caran d'Ache).

Step 3:

- Finish the pattern design (.005, .045, .249, and .049 Caran d'Ache).

- Add yellow or orange to the flowers.

- Add brown to the birds and the vase.

6.20. *Mural on silver leaf*

Fabric panel

Step 1:

- Concentrate color in the foreground on the left and the underside of each panel section.

- Apply the base color (9181T).

Step 2:

- Apply more values (9181T) to shape the form. Concentrate color in the foreground on the left and the underside of each panel.

- Apply a darker value (9220T).

6.21. Fabric panel

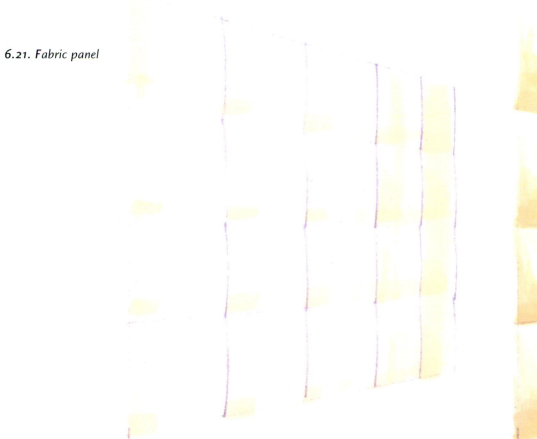
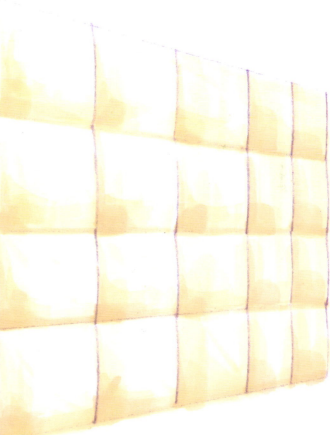

Special Finishes

Keep in mind that techniques used for other surfaces in this book can also be applied to wall surfaces, and vice versa. Materials such as stone and wood are used on various interior surfaces.

Tip! To keep vertical marker strokes consistent and correct, align your guide parallel to a vertical line in the drawing or a vertical line on the subject.

Black glass wall

Step 1:

• Tape the raised hearth, flames, rock reflections, and top and bottom of the glass to maintain the white areas.

• Apply straight vertical strokes (Warm Gray 11). Leave a section of white paper untouched.

• Tape the reflection of the hearth on the glass surface.

• Apply straight vertical strokes in black.

Step 2:

• Remove the tape.

• Dab in the stone color (Warm Gray 01).

• Dab in the stone reflections (Warm Gray 04).

• Render the hearth (Warm Gray 04).

• Add shading to the hearth (Warm Gray 08).

Step 3:

• Apply black strokes to the glass.

• Detail the stones (Warm Gray 04 and Warm Gray 08).

• Detail the flames (white gouache and 290T marker). (See figure 9.32 for an alternative flame coloration.)

• Spatter the hearth with black paint.

• Add white gouache for the reflections if needed.

6.22. Black glass wall

154

Stainless steel and white Plexiglas

Step 1:

- Apply a few strokes of blue (290T) to indicate the luminous ceiling of this elevator cab.

- Apply blue reflections (290T) on the walls.

- Apply the floor color (Ice Gray 10).

- Apply the base color (Ice Gray 10) to the walls and the door frame.

- Add the middle values (Ice Gray 08) to the frame.

Step 2:

- Apply a deeper value (Ice Gray 08) to the lower wall sections.

- Deepen the values (Ice Gray 04) on the lower wall section and the frame.

- Define the lines (Ice Gray 04) on the walls and the ceiling.

Step 3:

- Define the front surface of the frame (Ice Gray 01).

- Define the floor at the frame (Ice Gray 01).

- Add highlights (white gouache) to complete the metallic look.

Sculptural wall

Step 1:

- Cut a template guide from a sheet of acetate by following the basic curves of the relief design here.

Step 2:

- Use this guide to apply the marker strokes, either in the controlled marker strokes illustrated or in freehand (see figure 6.5). Place the guide so it overlaps and offsets the previously applied marker.

- Apply one color (9181T) for the entire wall.

- Place small sections of a darker value (9220T), using the guide.

6.23. *Stainless steel and white Plexiglas*

6.24. *Sculptural wall*

Window Coverings

Drapes do not wiggle from top to bottom; they fall in a soft straight line. Render the folds so that they look straight. Of course some treatments may slightly flare out or puddle a bit at the bottom. It is useful to line up the edge of a triangle at the bottom of a pleat to achieve a straight line where a pleat meets the fold, as in figure 6.25. Do this as you draw and render a pleat.

Drapery pleats and folds

Pleats:

- Use a darker value of the appropriate color between the pleats.

- Rely on soft line work to define the pleat. Do not overdetail these elements of the drape.

Folds:

- Apply the base color in a vertical direction along the folds, trying to keep it lighter at the front face.

- Use a darker value on the inside of the folds.

- Finish by detailing the hem and the top hardware.

6.26. Drapery folds

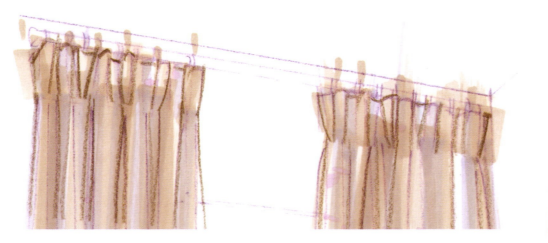

6.25. Drapery pleats

Sheer drapery

Step 1:

- Tape the wall at the top where the drape ends. Tape the floor where the drape ends at the bottom.

- Indicate the outside shadows (2707T).

- Indicate the window frame (649T).

Step 2:

- Detail the drapery folds (2707T).

Tip! Rendering techniques for drapery folds can be used to indicate ruffles on chairs and sofa skirts.

Step 3:

- Remove the tape.

- Add horizontal curved strokes (2707T) for the hem.

- Detail the pleats and the tucks at the top (649T)

- Apply a pale gray marker to the outside foliage shapes on the back of the paper (Borden & Riley 100S Smooth Comp) if they do not read well enough.

6.27. *Sheer drapery*

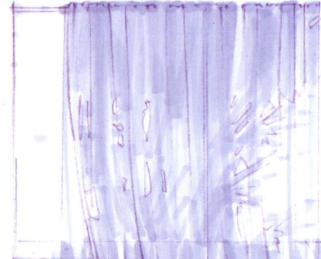

Sheer drapery with a pattern

Step 1:

• Follow the previous instructions, using four markers (Cool Gray 30 and Cool Gray 50, B118, and black).

Step 2:

• Add the details with watercolor pencils (black and white).

6.28. *Sheer drapery with a pattern*

Drapery or room divider

Step 1:

• Apply the background (B118 and Ice Gray 06).

• Concentrate the marker color in the small folds that are in shadow. Use the cylinder value principle, gradually bringing the color into the large soft folds and fading to white.

Step 2:

• Capture a drape effect at the top by concentrating the same colors where the drape attaches to the rod. Pull down the color and let it fade into white.

• Add the hardware and hem details (Ice Gray 06).

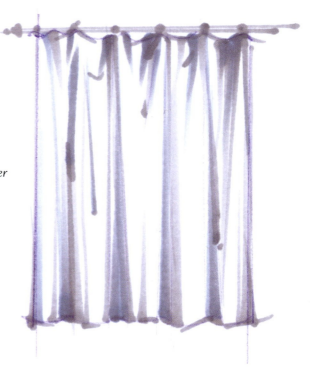

6.29. *Drapery or room divider*

Swags

Step 1:

- Follow the techniques used in figures 6.26 and 6.29.
- Use a base color (20% Gray).
- Add the values (30% Gray and 60% Gray).

Step 2:

- Fill in the details and the dark values (80% Gray).

6.30. *Swags*

Tip! The basic differences between sheer and opaque drapery folds are that (1) a sheer is lightest on the inside of the folds, and the hems are visible; and (2) an opaque drapery is darkest on the inside folds.

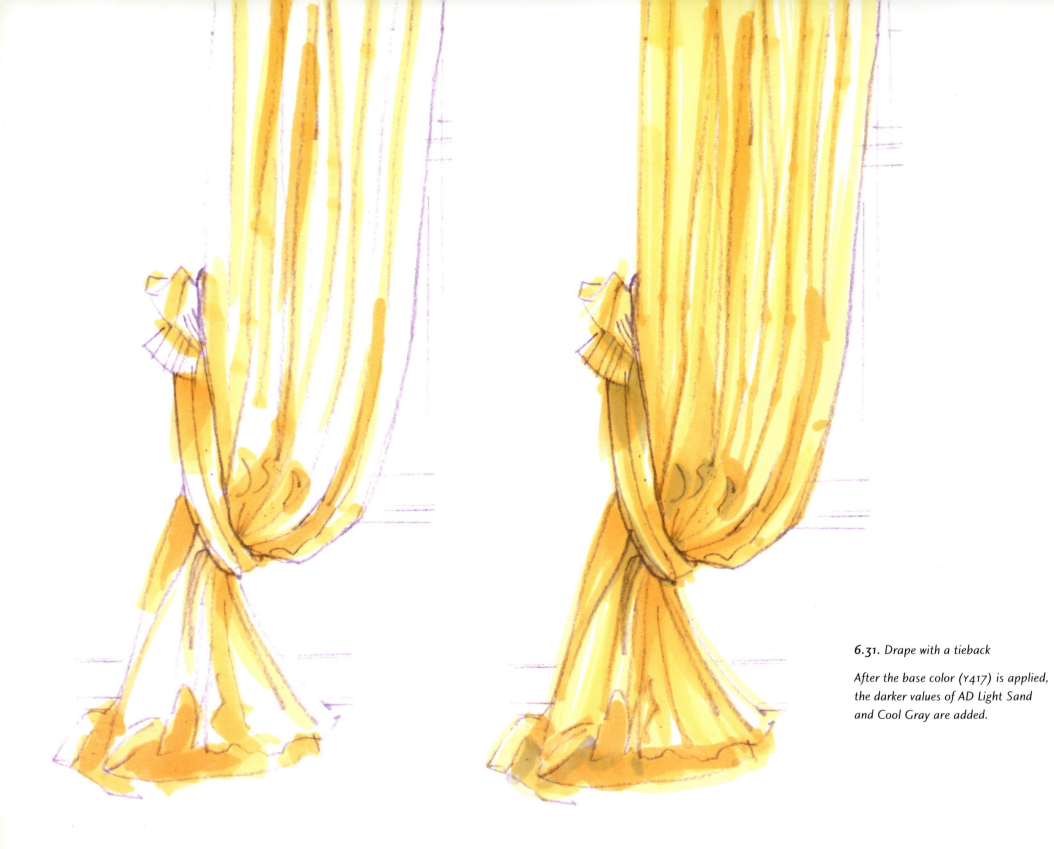

6.31. Drape with a tieback

After the base color (Y417) is applied, the darker values of AD Light Sand and Cool Gray are added.

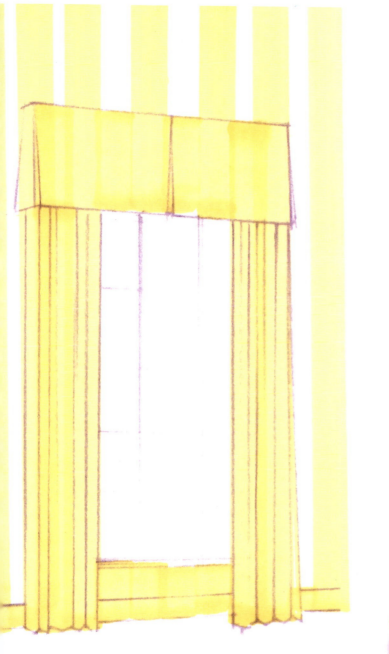

6.32. *Pleated box valance*

A base color (120T) is applied, and then the values are defined with layers of marker (263T).

Miniblinds with a sheer drape

Step 1:

- Apply the base color (Prismacolor Blondwood) to the drapery folds. Leave some white on the inside folds.

- Apply the horizontal lines (Blondwood) to indicate the window blinds.

Step 2:

- Apply the same color (Blondwood) to indicate the hem.

- Apply a darker value (649T) to the lower section of the blinds.

Step 3:

- Apply a darker value (466T) to the drape's outside folds.

- Detail the blind straps in black.

6.33. *Miniblinds with a sheer drape*

Sheer pleated shade

Step 1:

- Working from light to dark values, apply the base color (9181T) to capture the outside light. Let it dry.

- On top of the first layer, apply color (9181T) to the window frame adjacent to and behind the shade. Let it dry.

Step 2:

- Apply color (9181T) to the underside of each pleat. Let it dry.

Step 3:

- Apply color (9220T) to the underside of the pleat where the window frame shows through the shade.

- Illustrate the window details behind the shade with a darker value. (A sheer pleated shade transmits plenty of outside light, making these details visible.) Apply the lightest value first, working to the darkest value.

6.34. *Sheer pleated shade*

6.35. *Wide-slat metal blinds*

Using 4525T as the lightest value and 4535T as the dark value, the blind slats are rendered lighter where more light comes in; the blind strap is added in 440T. The same technique can be used for shutters, replacing the black with a narrow vertical line in white gouache to indicate the tilt bar.

Drapes and a shade

Step 1:

- Scribble in the pattern with a fine-point marker (Y417).

- Define the values on the shade and the drape panel folds (AD Marker Light Sand).

Step 2:

- Define the drapery rod.

- Delineate the window detail and the wall surface (Pale Blue and Cool Gray).

Shades

Step 1:

- Apply the base color (9181T), using a directional stroke following the curves of the fabric folds.

Step 2:

- Apply deeper tones (9220T) to the top hem, soft folds, and stacked folds.

Step 3:

- Add definitions in the same areas (Prismacolor Brick Beige or 155T).

- Add shadows (535T) in the folds.

- Define the edges of the folds, cords, and hems with watercolor pencil (Nougat).

- Lightly detail the window frame (427T).

6.36. Drapes and a shade

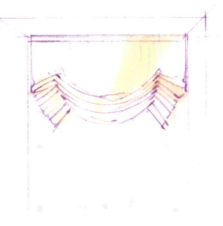

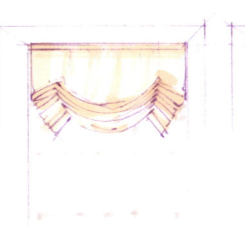

6.37a. *Shades*

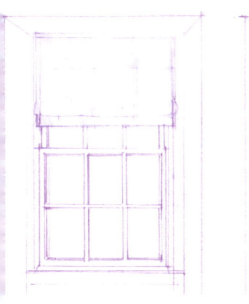

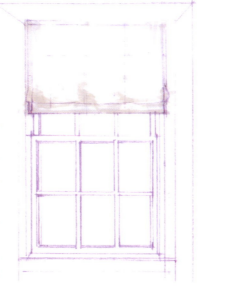

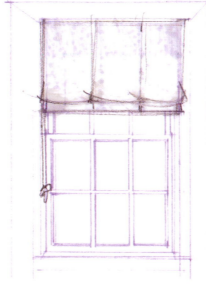

6.37b. *Sheer-pattern Roman shades*

Sheer-pattern Roman shades

Step 1:

- Indicate the shadows (649T) of the window frame, placing the strokes at a slight offset to indicate a deep window.

- Define the top, bottom, and side hems (649T).

- Apply a few strokes (649T) at the shade's top to indicate puckers.

Step 2:

- Apply definition (427T) for the hems.

- Sketch in fullness for the bottom of the fold (427T).

Step 3:

- Stipple dots (2706T) to indicate the pattern.

- Sketch in a few lines (2706T) to add softness to the fabric.

- Define the stitch lines, cords, and fabric edges (black pencil).

Watercolor

Watercolor is a quick medium for applying a simple toned base color to walls, but do not stop there. Building up washes and glazes creates beautiful color variation on a broad wall surface and lets you develop shade and shadows. This requires skill in knowing what happens when paint is applied to wet, damp, or dry paper.

Here is a warm-up exercise for determining how much water and paint to use and where you could use more fluidity in an illustration. Making a mess is allowed, so prepare your work area accordingly (old beach towels placed on your work surface are perfect). Have plenty of paper handy, and use different large brushes.

Secure your paper to a board, load your brush with lots of color, and let it drip down the paper as you apply the brush strokes. You can also apply color on top of wet paper, apply color on top of wet color, apply color on top of dry color, and do any combination of the same. Tilt the board up, down, sideways, or at an angle to coax the paint in a different direction. Remember what happens to the paint as it moves on its own through the water or previously applied color and what occurs with the different moisture content of each paper as you applied paint or as it dried.

After finishing the warm-up, you will see that if you apply the paint wet into wet, it is very fluid, and you do not have total control over the results. If you let the first wash dry and apply another one, the result is a hard edge. If you let the first wash dry slightly and then apply the second color, the two colors will blend and have soft edges.

Painted Walls

Watercolor is versatile for applying basic paint to walls and floors. Variations in the brush stroke width and direction are not as limited as with markers. Light and shadows are suggested by sweeping brush strokes, creating a dynamic wall surface.

6.38. Smooth painted wall

Smooth painted wall

Step 1:

• Mix the watercolor wash on your palette.

Step 2:

• Apply the paint in three stages, beginning with the light value first, then the middle value. Use a large, flat brush.

• Use wide, sweeping brush strokes, from left to right and from top to bottom.

• Build up the layers of paint.

Textured wall

Step 1:

- Mix a flat base color wash (Raw Sienna + Cobalt Violet + Neutral Tint) on the palette.

- Use a very large flat brush to create a simplified rendition of this back wall.

Step 2:

- Complete the art and credenza accessories.

- Add the darker wall values (Cobalt Violet + Neutral Tint).

- Spatter paint (Raw Sienna, Cobalt Violet, and Neutral Tint) as the final touch.

- This technique can be used equally well for a fine texture, such as a faux sand finish or evenly pitted travertine surfaces.

6.39. *Textured wall*

Handpainted wallpaper

Step 1:

- Apply the base color palette mixture (Raw Sienna + Neutral Tint).

- Use a flat brush for a light, dry brush technique, applying it in vertical and horizontal overlapping strokes.

Step 2:

- Repeat step 1 with a slightly darker value for the color.

Step 3:

- Place strips of tape lining up with the pattern direction to create hard line edges.

- Using a split, dry brush, apply brush strokes (Cobalt Blue + Cobalt Violet) in vertical and horizontal directions. Assert more pressure where the lines begin.

6.40. *Handpainted wallpaper*

Trompe l'oeil wall mural

Step 1:

• Try a painterly approach to this wall mural illustration, imagining that you are Julian LaTrobe, working with watercolors instead of oil paint.

• Apply a light wash of the base color (Raw Umber + Aureolin) for the wall surface.

Step 2:

• Define the crown molding.

• Add a shadow under the crown molding (Burnt Umber + Cobalt Violet).

• Define the background colors of the wall design, using a loose technique to give only a general impression of the subject.

Step 3:

• Detail the patterns, using a darker value of the colors depicting the wall background. Complete the darkest details (Olive Green). Render more detail in the foreground and less as the wall recedes in perspective.

6.41. Trompe l'oeil wall mural

Floral mural

Step 1:

- Dampen the paper with a damp sponge or a brush filled with clear water.

- Paint the base colors of yellow and red, working wet paint into wet paper. The yellow will float into the red, creating areas of orange.

Step 2:

- While the first wash is still wet, float in the middle values. The paper will begin to dry when the middle values are floated in, so expect some soft blending and hard color transition lines. (That is the beauty of this watercolor technique—there is always a nice surprise.)

- Let it dry.

Step 3:

- Define the petal shapes with light glazes of color.

Tip! Too much rendered detail will dominate a room illustration, creating overall disharmony and weakening the center of interest. Think in terms of reduction.

6.42. Floral mural

Tile

Scraping paint from the paper is a great way to achieve tile grout patterns. This would be a good time to refresh what you learned in chapter 2 regarding watercolor line techniques as well as watercolor washes and glazing.

Ceramic tile

Step 1:

- Work quickly after first reading through all the steps.

- Wet the paper.

- Apply a very light wash as the base color.

Step 2:

- Add more color gradation from dark to light, using a very wide, flat brush. You may introduce subtle color variation in this step.

Step 3:

- Do not let the washes dry. Quickly begin the next step.

- Using the slanted end of the brush handle, scrape out the grout lines. Where the paint is still too wet to scrape, it will leave a dark line. Where the paint is too dry, it will leave a faint blue line. Where the paint is at the perfect moisture content for scraping, it will leave a white line. (If you add another layer of paint after scraping, the lines appear darker and you can scrape it out again to get white lines.)

- Alternatively, grout lines can be detailed with a white pen after the color washes dry.

- Results vary based on the paper used; the illustration here was made on smooth Bristol. The dark, medium, and white lines work well and suggest shade and highlights.

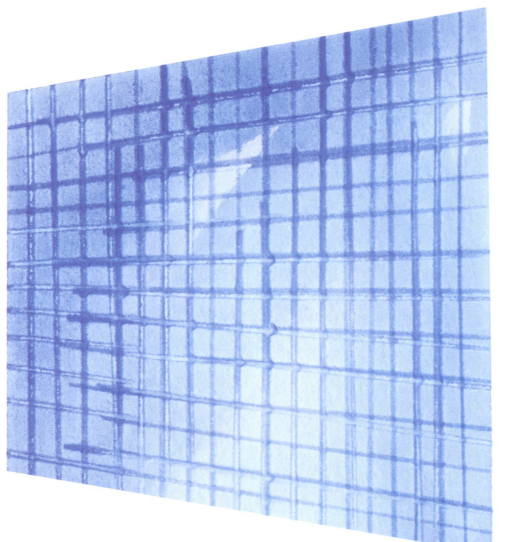

6.43. *Ceramic tile*

Ceramic mosaic

Step 1:

- Apply the base wall colors, which in this case are values of gray (Neutral Tint). Use a flat brush. Let it dry.

Step 2:

- Apply the pattern, using a round brush and varying the pressure to go from thick to thin lines. Here the pattern is darker at the area nearest the sink and the counter, the subject's center. It fades as it recedes in the space and becomes much lighter where the wall and the pattern change direction.

- Sweep in a glaze (Cerulean Blue + Cobalt Violet) on the far right side.

- Apply the darkest wall value under the counter, using only a few pattern strokes.

Step 3:

- Apply a minimal number of grout lines (white pen or gouache) for the tile at the top, on the light wall.

6.44. Ceramic mosaic

Stone

The stone surface techniques illustrated here can also be applied to floors, shower and bath enclosures, countertop surfaces, fireplace surrounds, and furniture. As a basic guideline, determine which characteristics of the material you want to emphasize. Does the pattern design take precedence over the texture and tile size, or vice versa? For example, if you wish to characterize an aged or a rustic appearance, the texture will be most important. Watercolor is well suited for capturing the variegated layers and jewel-like quality of onyx.

White marble

Step 1:

- Apply clear water to the paper on the area to be painted.

- Develop one surface plane at a time, beginning with the values (Payne's Gray). Use a large and medium flat brush.

- Pull out some paint with a damp medium, flat brush.

- Add vein detail by scraping with the end of the brush handle. Let it dry.

- When developing a full room rendering, complete the marble detail through step 1 only. When the rendering is near completion, then finish with step 2 only where it is needed.

Step 2:

- Define more vein detail as necessary (Payne's Gray and white gouache), using a rigger brush.

- Define the edges (dark gray pencil).

6.45. White marble

Diamond-patterned granite

Step 1:

- Apply a wash of base color (Cerulean Blue + Cobalt Violet + Neutral Tint), using a wide flat brush. Vary the color mix to achieve different values to indicate variation, rather than a flat-looking color. Let it dry.

Step 2:

- Tape each section of the diamond pattern as you work.

- Apply the same color combinations on top of the previous wash, following the direction of the diagonal pattern with the brush strokes. Begin and end each stroke on top of the tape.

- Spatter the composition with the same color. Let it dry.

Step 3:

- Squeeze some water out of your brush, separating the base of the bristles.

- Apply the color mix on the left side of your brush and Neutral Tint on the right side.

- Apply the color as in step 2, this time using a small wavy motion. Let it dry.

Step 4:

- Add white highlights (white gouache and a white pen).

- Spatter the composition (Indigo Blue).

6.46. Diamond-patterned granite

Flexible Wall Coverings

Here's hoping that you do not overdo it with the wall coverings! When illustrating a room, the walls are the background; therefore, wall coverings are rendered in a loose, minimal technique. Even the most ornate and detailed patterns are reduced to basic overall color and value, with only mere suggestions of texture or pattern.

6.47. *Mural on silver leaf*

Mural on silver leaf

Step 1:

- Brush in the base colors (Burnt Umber and Cobalt Violet), using a ½" to ¾" flat brush.

- Leave white spaces to create the effect of soft reflections.

Step 2:

- Add a glaze of the same colors on top to deepen the value where the wall may be in shadow or to achieve variation in the background color. Use a ½" to ¾" flat brush.

- Brush in the base color for the trees and the foliage, using a round brush.

Step 3:

- Brush in more design detail with a darker value of the color, again using a round brush.

Step 4:

- Finish the details (black, Sepia, and stronger Olive or Sap Green hues), using a round brush.

Fabric panels

Step 1:

- Apply the base color wash (Raw Sienna + Neutral Tint), using a wide, flat brush. Let it dry.

- Apply another wash in the shaded areas. Use a wide, flat brush and sweeping strokes. Let it dry.

6.48. Fabric panels

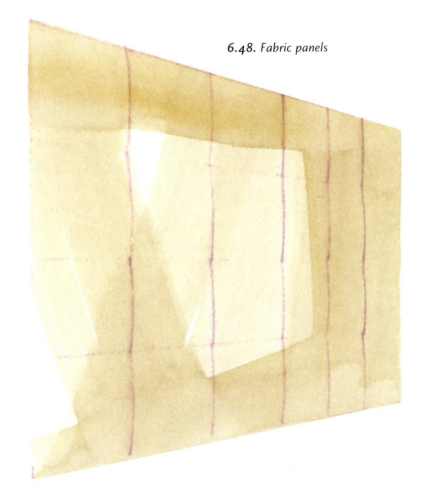

Step 2:

- Apply values (Raw Sienna + Neutral Tint) to each panel with slightly curving strokes, using a narrower brush. Let it dry.

- Repeat the above step.

- Develop shadows with a small, round brush.

Special Finishes

Exciting new materials now available through technological advancements can be a challenge to illustrate. Look for special characteristics that prevail: if they are reflective, then highlights of white can be added; if there is a combination of elements, such as reeds or a leaf pattern floating in clear plastic, the color and pattern can be emphasized. See if you can apply a technique from another material that you have rendered. Of course, you just may find that you have to create a totally new technique or two.

An artist uses a palette knife for diverse techniques, and one is watercolor painting with a knife. Load up the knife with paint and scribble lightly with the tip on some practice paper. Did you develop something that might be used for one of those new materials? Put it in your creation file.

Stainless steel and white Plexiglas

Step 1:

- Apply a few strokes (Neutral Tint + Cobalt Blue + Cobalt Violet) to the ceiling of this elevator cab, using a flat brush.

- Apply blue reflections on the walls with a flat brush.

- Apply the middle values to the walls.

- Add the light values to the walls on the sides.

Step 2:

- Apply a deeper value to the lower wall sections.

- Define the lines on the walls and the ceiling (black pencil).

Step 3:

- Define the front surface of the frame (fine-nib black marker).

- Apply the floor.

- Add highlights (white gouache).

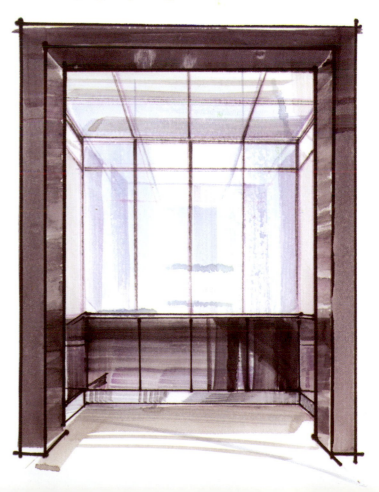

6.49. Stainless steel and white Plexiglas

Sculptural wall

Step 1:

- Cut a template guide from a sheet of cardboard or stiff acetate by following the basic curves of the relief design. Raise the guide by taping stacked coins to the back.

- Use this guide to apply the brush strokes, either in freehand or in a controlled brush application (this illustration uses both). Place the guide so it overlaps and offsets the previously applied paint.

- Apply the base color wash (Neutral Tint) for the lower wall surface, using a #24 flat brush. Let it dry.

Step 2:

- Apply a wash of sweeping strokes (Neutral Tint) at the top of the wall surface to indicate lighting, using a large, flat brush. Let it dry.

Step 2:

- Apply curved brush strokes (Neutral Tint) to the wall surface, using the guide described above and a flat brush. Let it dry.

Step 3:

- Apply slightly darker curved brush stokes (Neutral Tint), using the guide and a medium, flat brush. Overlap and slightly offset the guide when applying this step.

6.50. Sculptural wall

Window Coverings

Whether a window treatment appears in the background or the foreground of an illustration will determine how much emphasis to place on it.

For distant subjects, often very clean, quick brush strokes are enough; they can be defined a little more with additional line work.

6.51. Drapery folds

Drapery folds

Step 1:

- Mask the top and bottom edges of the drapes.

- Use various pallette mixtures (Raw Sienna and Neutral Tint).

Step 2:

- Apply the base color with vertical brush strokes, using a flat brush. Let it dry.

- Apply values to the inside folds with vertical brush strokes, using a flat brush. Let it dry.

Step 3:

- Define the drapery rod, using a small, round brush.

- For the stripes, see figure 11.13.

- For the leaf pattern, apply paint with a small, round brush. Dissipate and lighten the leaf pattern as it turns into the folds. Try to use one dab of the brush for each leaf.

Sheer drapery

Step 1:

• Tape the top and the bottom of the drapery.

• Indicate the outside shadows (Cobalt Blue + Neutral Tint).

• Indicate the window frame (Cobalt Blue + Neutral Tint).

Step 2:

• Detail the drapery folds (Cobalt Blue).

Step 3:

• Remove the tape.

• Add horizontal curved strokes for the hem (Cobalt Blue).

• Detail the pleats and the tucks (Cobalt Blue) at the top.

6.52. *Sheer drapery*

Drapery with a tieback

Step 1:

• Apply the base color (Neutral Tint). Let it dry.

Step 2:

• Apply the values (Neutral Tint) to the inside folds. Let it dry.

Step 3:

• Add the pattern detail (Neutral Tint and Sap Green).

• Define the drapery rod (Neutral Tint).

• Paint the Bubble Club chair (Raw Sienna), the sky (Cobalt Blue), and the landscape (Sap Green).

6.53. Drapery with a tieback

Pleated box valance

Step 1:

- Apply the base color (Raw Sienna). Let it dry.

Step 2:

- Define the values and the drapery folds (Cobalt Violet).

- Detail the pleats and the folds with a colored pencil (Goldenrod).

- See chapter 11 for more drapery examples.

6.54. *Pleated box valance*

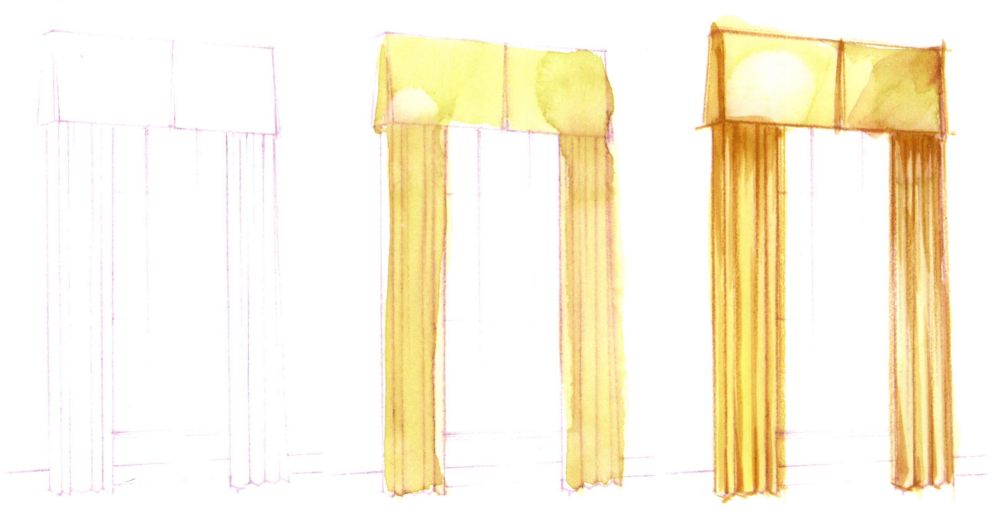

Wide-slat blinds

Step 1:

- Plan the white areas for the shade and the window trim.

- Apply the base color wash (Pale Sepia) to the wall surface, the top of the blind, and middle values on the window trim. Let it dry.

- Develop shade and shadows (Pale Sepia and Neutral Tint) on the wall surface and the top of the blind. Let it dry.

Step 2:

- Add the fabric strap detail (black or dark gray paint).

- Detail the shadows on the window frame.

- Indicate wood shutters using a similar technique. Leave out the black strap, substituting a narrow vertical line for the tilt bar (a color value or white gouache).

6.55. *Wide-slat blinds*

Shades

Step 1:

- Apply the base color wash (Pale Sepia) to the wall and the window frame.

- Apply shadow strokes to the interior of the window frame (Neutral Tint).

Step 2:

- Apply the base color wash (Pale Sepia) to the fabric. Use a directional brush stroke following the curves of the fabric.

- Apply deeper tones to the top hem, soft folds, and stacked folds.

Step 3:

- Add shadows in the folds (Pale Sepia + Neutral Tint).

- Detail the window frame (Neutral Tint).

6.56. *Shades*

Assignments

1. Scale. Illustrate several walls with marker, as shown in figure 6.1. Try these application techniques at smaller and larger scales to refine your skills in marker handling.

2. Try it again. What was the most difficult lesson in this chapter for you? Try it again now. What was the most fun? Try it again now.

3. Color schemes. Illustrate as many white walls of any material as you have colors for in marker or watercolor. This will help you learn which markers to choose for the hundreds of whites available to designers as finishes. Make notes of the colors used. Refer to these for future illustrations when you need to create color harmonies. You can place your design samples (such as paint, laminate, or tile) adjacent to each hue to determine which will work best in the illustration to capture your materials and to produce color harmony.

Do the same for a beige-to-brown color scheme, a yellow color scheme, a cool color scheme, or a color scheme that you loved in a magazine photograph.

4. Color harmony. For one of your current or past design projects, develop color harmonies for a color and material scheme. Take a minimalist approach when choosing the colors to ensure a unified color palette for the illustration. Determine which hues could be left out or used for several different materials. Fully develop the color palette for the medium, and make notations of the colors used.

5. Color and technique. Select a subject matter from this chapter. Illustrate it in a different color. Next illustrate it in a different style and technique.

6. Atmosphere and emotion. Select a subject matter and a material, then develop your rendering approach to create an atmospheric or emotional quality. Study the material's properties. Look at the manufacturer's photographs of the material; these may include a room setting. How can your choice of color and technique capture the material's texture, opaqueness, or translucency? Is its texture rough, fine, smooth, glossy, matte, shiny, or uneven? Is its color warm, cool, light, dark, or radiant? After considering these qualities, illustrate the material as a wall surface that exhibits atmosphere and emotion.

7. Render an idea. Instead of using words to explain a design idea for a wall, a feature, or a new material, quickly render it. Sit down with a fellow classmate or a friend and illustrate your idea. Allow the other person to comment while you are illustrating. Develop the concept later in your studio.

Hey, let's have some fun here! It is difficult to remember all the technical aspects you have practiced, especially color blending. This time, anything goes. Gather up a few markers and see what happens when you scribble the colors in layers. Who knows, one or more could be great. And you will have the color experiment as a reference for your creation files. Scribble away.

Floors

Imagine that you are Leonardo da Vinci, Frank Lloyd Wright, or any great designer you admire. Then imagine looking at your favorite interior or object. Think about what you like about it and how it can be translated to paper. Imagine later being able to easily assimilate it into one of your designs because it resides in your imagination. What does this have to do with rendering floors? Everything. Do the same for any interior subject, and when you need it the most, it will be right there to be recalled and synthesized.

Pattern and composition study, including a Hill House chair (1903, Charles Rennie Mackintosh) (marker and colored pencil)

Markers

Use color to broaden your perception of how to illustrate the infinite number of material choices for floor coverings. Color "voices" lurking in the shadows and the light can even be yellow, pink, blue, and purple. Apply the scribble experiments practiced at the end of chapter 6; adopt that painterly technique as the base color application for some of the floor materials in this chapter (see figures 7.8, 7.10, 7.12, and 7.13).

7.1. Basic marker application for floors

Basic marker application for floors

Step 1:

- Mask the left and the right edges of the drawing.

- Apply broad marker strokes starting at the back, placing fewer strokes as you gradually work to the front.

- Follow the perspective direction; in this case, horizontal strokes must go to the left vanishing point, not parallel to the paper edges.

Step 2:

- Using the same technique, apply another layer of color from the back to the middle ground. Add a few additional strokes in the foreground.

Wood

Keep strokes open and varied in width to indicate grain and direction, using a few straight strokes and some scribbled strokes (see figures 7.2, 7.3, and 7.4). Rendering a bit of color on the back of a drawing gives added depth of color to wood; this can be done only on more transparent papers that do not have a coating on the back (see figure 7.4). Note that parquet patterns require a considerable amount of time for masking (see figures 11.26 and 11.28).

Light wood plank floor

Step 1:

• Mask the left and the right edges of the drawing.

• Tone the back of the paper with a few strokes (2706T) to provide softer wood color transitions.

• Turn over the paper to the front. Progressing from light to dark, scribble the lightest color (155T) in the direction of the wood grain.

Step 2:

• Scribble as above (473T).

• Scribble as above (Warm Gray 03).

Step 3:

• Add strokes (473T) with a guide.

• Detail the lines with watercolor pencils (Faber-Castell Albrecht Dürer 8200-178 Nougat and 186 Terra Cotta).

• Define the grain and the planks with pencil (Terra Cotta).

7.2. Light wood plank floor

Dark wood plank floor

Step 1:

• Follow the same techniques described in figure 7.2, using the markers below.

• 4655T for the base color.

• 479T.

Step 2:

• 4505T.

• 168T.

Step 3:

• 469T.

• Black or dark brown pencil to define the grain and the planks

Tip! To help keep the marker strokes in proper perspective, place the same perspective grid used for the room line drawing under the illustration surface if you are using bond or marker paper.

7.3. Dark wood plank floor

Basket-weave plank floor

Step 1:

- On the back of the paper, mask the drawing's left and right edges.

- Using a few straight strokes and some scribbled strokes, apply color (263T) on the back of the drawing.

- Remove the tape, and turn over the drawing to the front. Mask the left and right edges of the drawing on the front. Cut frisket film and apply it to a few of the shorter planks.

- Lightly scribble in color (134T).

Step 2:

- Apply a few broad strokes of color (473T).

- Lightly scribble in color (4655T). Keep the strokes open and varied in width to indicate grain and direction. Remove the frisket and the tape.

Step 3:

- Mask the front and back edges of the short planks. Work in steps from the front to the back of the drawing.

- On the short dark planks (left in the illustration), scribble in color (464T). On the short light planks (right), scribble in color (473T). Remove the tape.

- Add a few grain strokes in the foreground with a pencil (Prismacolor 943 Burnt Ochre). Define the planks in the foreground and the middle ground with a pencil (Burnt Ochre).

- Lightly define the drawing lines (2B pencil or a fine-point black pigment liner).

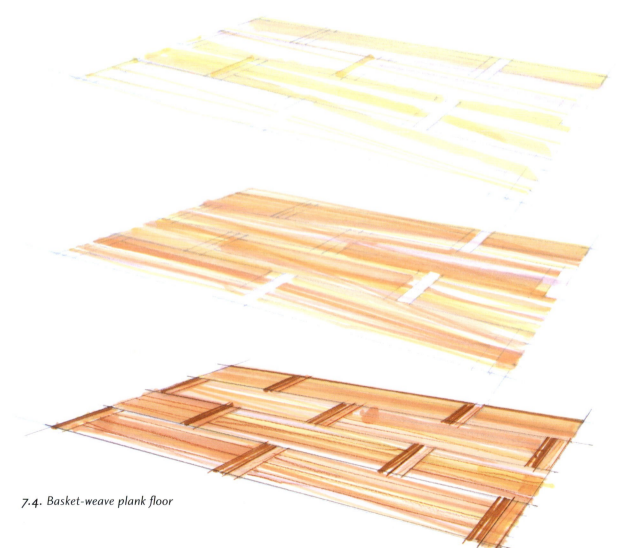

7.4. Basket-weave plank floor

Stone

If you master the few techniques that follow, you will be able to illustrate almost any stone by simply adjusting the colors. Do not apply indications of detail on top of base colors in a direction that causes confusion; look at the direction of the overall color application. Seek ways to balance line and color. Make it simple so it can read. Repeat some of the material's character marks somewhere else in the illustration to keep the texture from being too dominant in one place. Do not overdo it.

Marble or quartzite floor

Step 1:

• Plan the white areas. Mask the drawing's edges.

• Using horizontal, wavy, scribbled strokes, sparingly apply the marker (5425T).

• Gradually enlarging the same type of stroke, add several strokes (2707T) on top of the previous strokes and throughout the drawing. Leave a lot of white. (Allowing additional white would be more representative of quartzite.)

Step 2:

• Apply color (5445T) with vertical, open, and free-style marker strokes.

• Repeating the same technique, go over it again (2707T), overlapping a few strokes to get a color variation in the marble.

• Using horizontal wavy, scribbled strokes, sparingly apply 5425T, while leaving whites throughout.

7.5. Marble or quartzite floor

Step 3:

- Indicate more color variation by scribbling and dragging a watercolor pencil (Prismacolor 2901 Indigo Blue). Vary the pressure when drawing these lines.

- Indicate additional variation (Prismacolor 1903 Art Stix).

- Blend these lines with 2706T.

- Define the grout lines (5425T). Note that lines and texture fade as they recede in a complete rendering.

- Spatter a dark blue paint for more texture.

- Indicate reflections (white gouache).

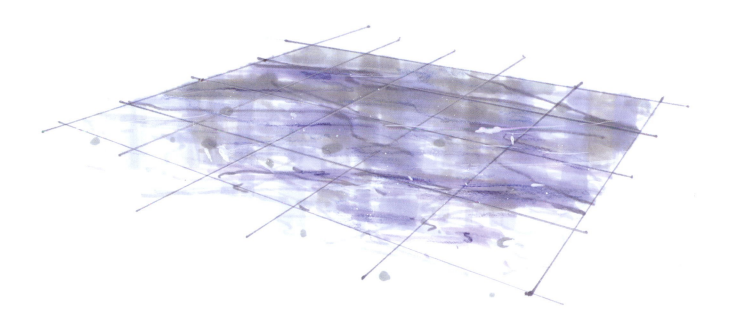

Striated marble floor

Step 1:

- Mask the drawing's left and right edges on the back of the paper.

- Using a few straight strokes and some scribbled strokes on the borders, apply a marker (134T) on the back of the drawing to make the yellow marble softer and the taupe marble less drab. Add several strokes of the same color in the center square. Follow the perspective direction; horizontal strokes must go to the left vanishing point, not parallel to the paper edges.

- Add a few strokes (2706T) to the back.

- Remove the tape, and turn over the drawing to the front. Mask the drawing's left and right edges on the front with the same drafting tape, and then mask the border edges.

- Using the wet-marker technique of flooding, apply color (Warm Gray 04) on the borders, leaving a little yellow showing through.

- Remove the tape from the inside border edges.

Step 2:

- Mask the drawing to allow work in the center squares.

- With open and free-style marker strokes, apply color (Warm Gray 01) to the center squares. To keep the floor looking level and in correct perspective, be sure to go over the tape on both sides when you start and finish the strokes.

- Go over it again (Warm Gray 01), overlapping a few strokes to get color variation to represent the marble striation.

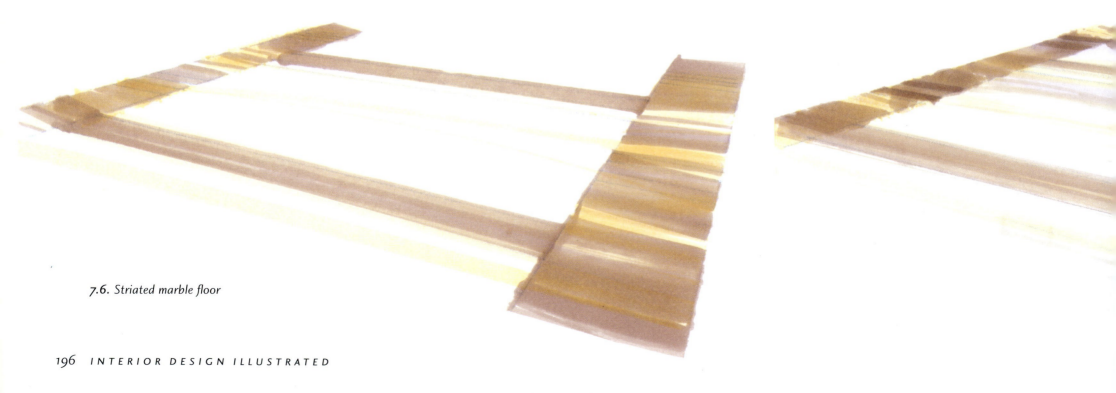

7.6. *Striated marble floor*

- Remove the tape from the center. Tape the border edges on the left and right sides.

- To indicate the dark marble inserts, apply Warm Gray 06 to the small rectangles.

- Completely remove the tape or reposition it for the next steps.

Step 3:

- Indicate vertical reflections with Warm Gray 02, Warm Gray 01, and 2706т. Note that the reflections fade as they descend.

- Add a few dabs of Warm Gray 04.

- Indicate more striation with Warm Gray 03. Drag the marker with irregular, start-and-stop line strokes, varying the pressure when applying the strokes.

- Indicate additional striation with a watercolor pencil (Nougat).

- Define the lines (Warm Gray 04 and Nougat pencil).

- Spatter a neutral gray for more texture, and indicate reflections (white gouache).

Tip! Uplift gray or drab colors with an undercolor of minimal strokes of pale yellow.

Black granite floor

Step 1:

• Tape the edges as needed.

• To determine the base color, use the color key of surrounding colors (in this case 365T).

• Apply the base color strokes (365T) in the direction of the vanishing point, using a guide.

• Repeat the above (5497T), allowing some of the base color (365T) to show.

Step 2:

• Apply color (Cool Gray 11) in the direction of the vanishing points.

• Place a few scribbles or sweeping curved strokes (Cool Gray 11).

Step 3:

• Multiply the layers in varying directions (Extra Black).

• Place reflections depending on the surrounding architectural elements, furniture, and light sources (in this illustration, black for dark reflections; or use white for light reflections). Apply vertical strokes to indicate reflections, horizontal to indicate depth of perspective.

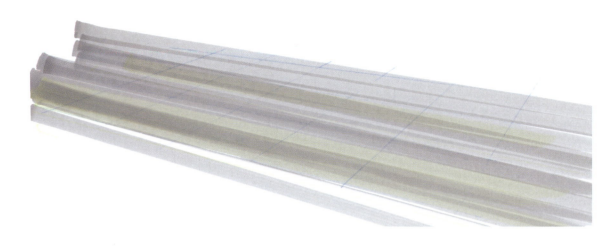

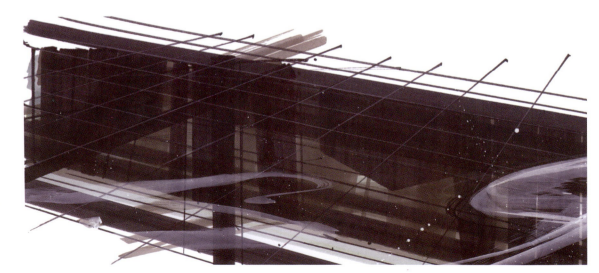

7.7. Black granite floor

Giallo granite floor

Step 1:

- For the base color, use 2706T, 155T, 134T, 552T, and 182T in the same scribble technique as described for glass wall tile (see figure 6.14).

Step 2:

- Warm and deepen the base color (466T).

Step 3:

- Add the tile grid lines with a fine-point pigment liner (black).

- Add the black granite diamond inserts with a broad nib (black). Turn the nib at an angle on the paper.

- Spatter with paint (Burnt Umber and then Neutral Tint).

- Add a light spatter and reflections (white gouache).

Tip! If you dry mount bond paper, you can spatter color for more texture and indicate reflections with white gouache. You can also spatter without dry mounting, but the paper may wrinkle and ripple; therefore, firmly tape it at the four corners.

7.8. Giallo granite floor

White terrazzo floor

Step 1:

- Apply the base color (468T), using straight and sweeping strokes.

- While still wet, work in color variation (2706T).

Step 2:

- Firmly tape the paper at the four corners if it is not dry mounted.

- Spatter three colors (Neutral Tint and Burnt Umber paint, plus white gouache). Concentrate the spatter in the foreground. Add more spatters in areas with shade and shadow (the triangular section in the middle ground on the right in the illustration).

Step 3:

- Add reflections (white gouache).

- For imperial white granite, use the same technique. Simply add more grout lines and more reflections with white gouache.

7.9. White terrazzo floor

Tile

Line is important in depicting materials to indicate their relative size and whether they have a smooth or an uneven surface. Line also illustrates texture and pattern. Figure 7.10 shows quarry tile, which usually has an uneven surface because it is either handmade or manufactured to look handmade. Although the lines used to indicate the tile edges are straight, there is no question that the tiles have an uneven surface, given the lines' locations and varying thickness. These marks, or symbols, help the viewer complete the picture.

Quarry tile floor

Step 1:

- Use 9181T, 155T, 468T, 435T, 155T, 182T, 535T, and 134T as the base color. Scribble them in, working wet into wet. Let it dry.

Step 2:

- Add grout lines (466T).

- Apply additional grout lines (466T) on top to represent the tile's uneven surface. Use heavy pressure at the corners of the tiles.

Step 3:

- Add multiple layers (466T) to darken a few tiles.

- Spatter lightly with paint (Burnt Umber).

7.10. Quarry tile floor

Glass balcony

Step 1:

- Apply the base colors (365T and 429T) to capture the glass's transparency and reflections. Consider what is below the glass, the reflections of objects above the glass, and the structural elements holding the glass.

- Apply vertical strokes (Y119 and Y216).

Step 2:

- Detail and darken surfaces and reflections.

- Apply vertical strokes (Y216, 420T, 292T, Ice Gray 01, and Ice Gray 07).

- Apply horizontal strokes (B418, B128, and 356T).

Step 3:

- Render the floor frame surrounding the glass (Ice Gray 03).

- Add reflections (white gouache).

- If the illustration feels unsettling, add more white reflections over the entire surface (as in the foreground). There is a psychological barrier regarding walking on a glass floor, so expect the possibility that it may be a controversial topic in a design presentation.

7.11. Glass balcony

Carpet

Markers are well suited to geometric patterns in floor coverings, depending on the color (although paint is the better medium for curvilinear or naturalistic patterns found in many area carpet designs). Woven cut-pile carpet will show areas of light because the yarns lie in various directions. As seen in figure 7.12, using a scribble technique to apply color is a nice way to achieve interesting variations; the many colors blended into the floor covering are the same as those on the walls and in the textiles, making the final product a rich taupe.

Broadloom carpet is by nature a soft material. Whether it is a printed, cut-loop, or sculptured pattern, it must look soft in an illustration. Try not to use hard lines to define the features. Blend colors well. Concentrate pattern indication in the foreground, fading the pattern as it recedes. When placing darker values over base colors, work wet into wet so they blend softly, as described in figure 7.15b.

Plush carpet

Step 1:

• Apply the base color (1205T), using scribbled strokes to make the monochromatic scheme extra vibrant.

Step 2:

• Blend and scribble in colors (263T, 2706T, and Prismacolor Blondwood) to achieve interesting variations in color transitions on large surface areas.

• Allow the base color to show in areas flooded with light.

Step 3:

• Add shadow lines (Cool Gray) under the drape and the bed skirt.

• Practice this technique to help a one-point perspective of a small area look dynamic and energetic.

7.12. Plush carpet

Natural-fiber carpet

Step 1:

- Scribble in various colors (9181T, 155T, 468T, 435T, 155T, 182T, 535T, and 134T) to create the base color, working wet into wet. Let it dry.

Step 2:

- Add horizontal lines (AD Marker Light Sand) to indicate the weave direction.

- Add horizontal lines (Cool Gray 03 or 2706T) to depict the weave in shade or shadow.

Step 3:

- Add dots (Light Sand and Cool Gray 05) to indicate the nubs and irregularities of natural fibers.

7.13. Natural-fiber carpet

Patterned cut-loop broadloom carpet

Step 1:

- Apply the base color (Cool Gray 02).
- Apply a deeper value (Cool Gray 03).

Step 2:

- Add very light lines (Cool Gray 02) to define rectangular areas of the pattern.
- Define the pattern's horizontal direction (Ice Gray 03).
- Define the pattern's vertical direction (Ice Gray 09).

Step 3:

- Define a simplified, horizontal direction for the pattern at receding areas (Cool Gray 02).
- Go over a few horizontal pattern lines in the foreground (Cool Gray 02). Too much sharp definition will give the appearance of a hard-surface floor covering.

7.14. Patterned cut-loop broadloom carpet

Sculptured cut-pile broadloom carpet

Step 1:

• Apply the base color (Cool Gray 10 and Cool Gray 02), working in a diagonal direction.

7.15a. Sculptured cut-pile broadloom carpet

Step 2:

• Apply a deeper base color value (Cool Gray 04) with a diagonal direction in the background.

Step 3:

• For the wave pattern (Cool Gray 05), use the marker handling technique explained in figure 6.5.

• Apply a darker shadow (Cool Gray 07), adding a thin line at the front edges on the right side, following the wave pattern.

Step 2

Step 3

Step 1

Alternative:

• Follow the same instructions, except use
  Cool Gray 01, 02, 04, 05, and 07 for the base
  color to create a softer appearance.

7.15b. Sculptured cut-pile broadloom carpet

Woven-pattern cut-pile broadloom carpet

Step 1:

- Apply the base color (Warm Gray or French Gray).

- Scribble in the medium and dark values.

- Study and lay out the pattern repeat on a tissue overlay. Use this drawing as a guide, placing it underneath your carpet illustration.

Step 2:

- Define the pattern colors (Cool Gray or Ice Gray), using less detail as the pattern recedes. Do not use too much detail for the pattern, as it may overpower the illustration.

7.16. Woven-pattern cut-pile broadloom carpet

Area carpet

Step 1:

- Mask the white areas to keep them pristine while developing the dark sections.

- Use a middle value (Cool Gray) as the base color on the right side, applying straight strokes. Let it dry.

Step 2:

- Using a dark value (Cool Gray), apply a layer on top of the right section. Allow the base gray to show in the foreground. (Marker works better than paint for this area carpet because this one is a dense, cut pile that establishes its own contrasting white shape; in addition, spatter is not necessary here to delineate texture, because it appears on the adjacent terrazzo floor.)

- At the front edge of the carpet, apply a darker line (middle value of Warm Gray) that is close to the color of the adjacent hard surface floor to help the thickness read.

7.17. Area carpet

Watercolor

If you have mastered good brush-handling techniques, floors can be effortless to paint. Your brush strokes can help the viewer feel the surfaces in an illustration and will stimulate a response, such as peace and calm or excitement and energy. Mastering watercolor with the direction, intensity, and quality of your brush strokes is a form of storytelling.

Jackson Pollack, Franz Kline, and Robert Motherwell used grand, exaggerated gestures to turn out abstract expressionist paintings daring in their experimentation. To illustrate floors with your own broad brush strokes, rich with movement and flair, get your whole body at ease with exaggerated movement. For this warm-up, select your largest flat brush and secure it to your longest ruler. Take out a very large sheet of paper (such as kraft paper or large scraps of illustration board), and place it on the floor or an easel, or lean it on or tack it to the wall. Paint! Paint long strokes, spatter, sweep your arm across the surface, and use your whole body to create gesture. If you are worried about creating a mess, just use water (artists often do this to loosen up before painting). You will feel more energized, get emotionally involved with the medium, and find it easier to work on exercises such as figures 7.18, 7.20, 7.21, 7.23, and 7.24.

Wood

Use exaggerated, sweeping gestures when you work on placing brush strokes and spatter for the floor-covering subjects that follow. To indicate wood grain, vary the moisture and paint content in your brush or drag a dry bush with paint over a dry base color wash.

7.18. Light wood plank floor

Light wood plank floor

Step 1:

- Apply a wash (Cobalt Violet) for the undercoat, using a flat brush.

- Quickly apply a light wash (Raw Sienna) to provide color variation. Let it dry.

- Apply strokes (Raw Sienna) with a flat brush, producing a darker, hard-edge color variation.

Step 2:

- Apply a light glaze (Cerulean Blue), using one stroke each, in the background and the foreground.

- Dry brush paint (Raw Umber) over portions to indicate the grain.

Step 3:

- Define with a wash (Raw Sienna) over the planks.

- Spatter paint (Neutral Tint).

- Define the plank lines and the grain with watercolor pencil (Nougat).

Dark wood plank floor with steps and a platform

Step 1:

- Tape the paper to your work surface.

- Wet the paper with a wide, flat brush. Let it dry a few seconds, until the paper is no longer shiny.

- Apply the base color wash (Burnt Umber + Quinacridone Violet). Use a wide, flat brush. Let it dry.

Step 2:

- Apply darker values (Burnt Umber and Quinacridone Violet + Payne's Gray). Use a medium-width, flat brush. Let it dry.

Step 3 (right side of floor only):

- Add darker strokes (Burnt Umber and Quinacridone Violet + Payne's Gray) to indicate the planks, varying the locations. Use a flat brush, held at an angle. If you have difficulty in handling the brush, tape the edges.

- Apply the same dark values to the risers on the steps.

7.19. Dark wood plank floor with steps and a platform

Tip! Place push pins in the location of the left and right vanishing points, and rest your cardboard guide or a long artist's bridge against them to help keep marker or brush-stroke lines in the proper perspective.

Stone

A minimal color palette with subtle transitions creates the color harmony needed for illustrations of stone. Cobalt Violet is often used, because it has grainy sediment properties and leaves a nice texture on the paper. Using a very wide brush is a quick way to render a floor. A vertical application of watercolor brush strokes emphasizes reflective qualities.

Travertine floor, vertical application

Step 1:

- Apply the colors (Raw Sienna + Cobalt Violet + Neutral Tint) with a series of glazes, starting with the lightest. Layer two or three glazes on top of one another, allowing the previously applied color to show in some areas. Use a large, flat brush. Let each glaze dry before applying the next color.

- Add a few darker values (Cobalt Violet + Neutral Tint).

Step 2:

- Spatter the same base colors (Raw Sienna + Cobalt Violet + Neutral Tint) on the floor. Spatter again (Neutral Tint).

- Define the grout lines (white pen).

- Add dabs for the reflections (white gouache).

7.20. Travertine floor, vertical application

Striated marble floor with borders

Step 1:

- Apply a pale wash (Aureolin) all over Lenox 100 paper, using a flat brush. Let it dry.

- Mask the yellow tiles.

- Apply a light glaze (Cobalt Violet + Raw Umber + Sap Green). Let it dry.

Step 2:

- Mask the edges of the dark tile borders.

- Leave the mask on the yellow areas.

- Apply another glaze (Cobalt Violet + Raw Umber + Sap Green). Let it dry.

- Add another layer of glaze (Cobalt Violet + Raw Umber + Sap Green) at the back. Add vertical reflection strokes (Cobalt Violet + Raw Umber + Sap Green). Let it dry.

7.21. Striated marble floor with borders

Step 3:

- Add a darker layer (Cobalt Violet + Raw Umber + Sap Green) on the decorative strips. Let it dry.

- Remove all masking.

- Use a dry-brush technique (Cobalt Violet + Raw Umber + Sap Green) on a rigger brush. Drag it across the illustration to detail the texture. Vary the pressure on the brush to achieve a thick-to-thin line quality.

- Add a few brush strokes (Aureolin + Cobalt Violet) to the yellow tiles and on top of the textures.

Step 4:

- Detail the tiles with watercolor pencil (Nougat).

- Spatter paint (Cobalt Violet + Raw Umber + Sap Green).

- Add light reflections (white gouache).

Senia limestone floor

Step 1:

- Plan the white areas. The goal is to achieve soft light reflections that may be coming from a window or an open door.

- Apply very light individual washes (Cobalt Violet, Aureolin, and Cobalt Violet) in vertical and horizontal directions, using a flat brush. Let it dry.

Step 2:

- Apply washes to each tile, varying the colors (first a darker mix of Aureolin + Cobalt, then Neutral Tint + Cobalt). Use a flat brush with an angled tip.

Step 3:

- Sparingly apply spatter (Raw Sienna).

- Detail the grout with pencil (Faber-Castell 50 Gold).

- For a less vibrant effect, apply a light glaze (Raw Sienna + Cobalt Violet).

7.22. Senia limestone floor

Slate floor

Step 1:

- Use the same technique as in figure 7.22. Because this is a darker floor, first apply a multicolor base (Raw Sienna + Sap Green + Red).

Step 2:

- Detail the tiles (Burnt Sienna, Indigo, Cobalt Violet, and Neutral Tint).

Step 3:

- Define the grout lines (black pencil and white pen).
- Spatter paint (Neutral Tint or Indigo Blue).

7.23. Slate floor

Tile

Watercolor creates interesting shadows and plays up any reflections on tile with a reflective surface. Take advantage of the drama that light can create on a reflective tile finish. Boldly indicate those reflections with white gouache brush strokes. Look for opportunities to place a dark shadow right next to the reflection for contrast. Contrast gets our attention.

White ceramic or porcelain tile floor

Step 1:

- Mask the walls, cabinets, and furniture.

- Apply a light wash of blue (one that works well with your overall color scheme), using a large, flat brush. Leave some white paper showing. Let it dry.

Step 2:

- Apply a light wash (Neutral Tint), using a large, flat brush. Keep the floor the lightest where the white cabinet reflects onto the floor or closest to the center of interest. Let it dry.

- Apply deeper values (Neutral Tint) at the rear, sides, and where dark furniture or casework may reflect onto the floor or cast shadows on it. Let it dry.

Step 3:

- Define the grout lines (gray pencil).

- Spatter lightly (Neutral Tint).

7.24. *White ceramic or porcelain tile floor*

Carpet

Good brush-stroke technique gives you the ability to interpret the numerous carpet surfaces available. Plush and smooth pile requires a soft wash of color. Loop and textured carpet lacks an even surface, so brush strokes can be a little more irregular.

Try the technique in figure 7.25 for commercial loop carpet with multiple colors and varying loop heights. Some areas will blend where the paper is wet, and others will have distinct edges where the paper dries quickly. This enhances the carpet's textural qualities. Change the colors to match the yarn colors, always starting from light to dark.

Figure 7.24 (without reflections or the pattern indication steps) shows a basic way to apply paint for a solid-color, cut-pile broadloom carpet. Include a little spatter in the foreground to imply the cut pile. Remember to fade the pattern and show less detail as the pattern recedes in perspective; you can also fade the pattern into the white paper in the foreground.

Tip! Use a gradation wash to make large areas of color, such as a solid-color broadloom carpet, more appealing.

Textured loop broadloom carpet

Step 1:

• Tape the paper to your work surface.

• Apply a light base color wash (Cadmium Yellow), using a wide, flat brush.

Step 2:

• While the base coat is still wet, brush in sweeping horizontal strokes (Raw Sienna). Use a fan brush, or split the hairs of a flat, damp brush.

Step 3:

• Brush in a light layer of the next color (Neutral Tint).

• Although lightweight, smooth Bristol paper helps achieve the desired carpet texture, it may become rippled because it cannot handle this much water. Flatten it with a dry-mounting machine or a stack of heavy books, or stretch it before rendering to diminish some of the rippling.

7.25. Textured loop broadloom carpet

Geometric-patterned, cut-loop broadloom carpet

Step 1:

- Wet paper with clear water.

- Apply a light color wash (Cobalt Blue for the front, Payne's Gray for the back), using a flat brush.

- Immediately draw horizontal lines with the end of the brush handle to indicate stripe widths. Allow it to dry until damp.

Step 2:

- Apply stripes in light and middle values (Payne's Gray), using an angular brush. Begin with the lightest value and work to the darkest.

Step 3:

- Spatter the lightest stripe (Payne's Gray).

- Detail the horizontal weave direction (Payne's Gray), using a fan brush or a split-brush technique to bring out the loop construction areas. More brush "wiggles" indicate a deeper pile, while fewer represent a shorter pile and a tighter weave.

7.26. *Geometric-patterned, cut-loop broadloom carpet*

Sisal area carpet

Step 1:

- Mask the edges of the canvas border.

- Apply the base color wash (Raw Sienna), using a large, flat brush. Let it dry.

- Apply a deeper value (Raw Sienna + Cobalt Violet) at the middle and the back of the carpet. Let it dry.

Step 2:

- Apply lines (Raw Sienna + Cobalt Violet) in a horizontal direction to indicate woven fibers, using a split-brush technique. Let it dry.

- Spatter texture (Raw Sienna + Cobalt Violet). Let it dry.

Step 3:

- Remove the tape.

- Paint the border edge (Neutral Tint values), using a small, flat brush.

7.27. *Sisal area carpet*

Shag area carpet

Step 1:

- Apply the base color wash (Payne's Gray), using a large, flat brush.

- While the paper is still wet, float in a few darker values (Payne's Gray) at the back of the rug. With a damp fan brush, quickly pull out some color at the edges and in the darkest areas. Let it dry.

Step 2:

- Use a fan brush to develop the shag texture (Payne's Gray).

- Apply deeper values (Payne's Gray) by dabbing the paint into some areas, using a fan brush to develop the shag texture. Let it dry.

- Add a small amount of large spatter (Payne's Gray).

- You can use this same technique with any color. Try it now.

Animal hides

Steps for a and b:

- Using a wet-into-wet technique to create a soft, natural-looking pattern, wash the area carpet with clear water.

- Lightly drop in the color, using a round brush.

- When the paper is dry, add shadows to the carpet's perimeter edges.

Steps for c and d:

- Using a combination of wet into wet and wet into dry, apply the base colors wet into wet.

- Indicate the patterns when the paper is dry.

Step for e and f:

- Apply the base colors and the patterns to dry paper.

7.28. Shag area carpet

a

b

c

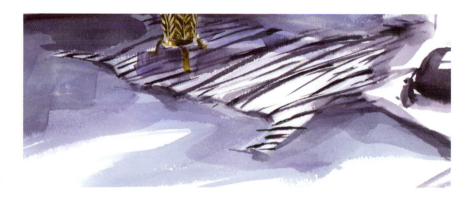

d

e

f

7.29*a–f.* Animal hides

Assignments

1. Imagine. Go to a showroom and respond to what you like. Ask yourself why you like this material, and imagine it put to use in a specific surrounding or design project. Obtain a sample or product literature to take with you; later, looking at the material, think more about the space you created in your imagination. Now put away the literature or sample. Be confident and enthusiastic, and then illustrate it. The more you do an exercise like this, the better a creative and skillful designer you will become.

2. What if? Choose three illustrations from this chapter that you would like to master for a future project. As a rehearsal for the final project illustration, consider how you could modify each one. For example, look at the black granite in figure 7.7. You may want to make a color change, add a border design, alter the direction or the size of the material, or change the placement or the color of the reflection. Consider adding a large ficus tree or a branch as a framing device; think about where the light source will be and consider the placement of the reflections; or place a piece of furniture and determine the reflection and color to use for it.

Draw the floor material and the modifying elements, incorporating all the techniques you have learned up to now. The appendix has a few floor drawings to work with for correct perspective, along with plant drawings. You could also trace other items from anywhere in the book.

3. Surfaces. From this chapter, select three floor-covering examples with pattern or texture in order to gain proficiency with surface indication. Create new drawings of them, choosing new colors to see how texture changes in appearance when different colors are used. Experiment with a variety of tools and media, including fan brush, sponge, hard-bristle brush, watercolor crayon, and pencil stick.

4. If it doesn't feel right, it isn't. Your intuition is speaking to you. It may be time for a critique. Critique in the form of feedback is a vital part of the design process. Embrace it, because it will make you a better designer. Select one of your slip-ups, then comprehensively evaluate it by making notations and possible resolutions on the same paper; use the checklist in the appendix (The Critique). Now ask a fellow student, instructor, or mock client the same questions you asked yourself.

5. A puddle of mud. Surely you have one on a drawing, hidden under a pile of paper waiting to be discarded. It happens quite frequently from too many marker layers, the wrong color, and accidental spills. Oops! Attempts at heroic saves, by covering it up with black or pulling out the color, do not always work. A puddle of mud is a dull puddle of mud forever. Do not take such an illustration to a presentation. Even if you think it is a successful cover-up, you will still see it, and this will have an effect on your confidence during the presentation. Try these patching techniques on several of your mistakes:

a. *Bond paper patching*

- The goal is to create a patch that is perfectly flush with the paper surface. Look for good transition places. Black line drawings conceal better when the patch is cut along the lines. A patch can also look almost invisible if it is a complete shape—for example, an entire tabletop or seat cushion.

- Reprint or redraw the section to be patched on a new piece of bond paper. Place it under the drawing, and then line it up exactly with the area to be patched.

- Cut through both paper surfaces at the same time with a sharp X-Acto knife. Carefully remove the area with the mistake while trying to leave the new patch in the drawing's cutout. Adjust the patch to fit, and place a piece of removable tape on it.

- Turn the drawing over. Secure the patch firmly on the back with transparent tape. Then turn the drawing to the right side, and place a piece of drafting tissue over the patched area. Rub it lightly to smooth the patch's edges.

- If the drawing is dry mounted, place the new drawing on top of the area to receive the patch. Cut both at the same time. Use a tacking iron to reheat the area to be removed, then remove it without pulling up the adhesive underneath. Put the new patch into the area. Place a piece of tissue on top, and reseal the patch with the tacking iron.

b. *Watercolor paint lifting*

- Place frisket film or masking tape around the area to be lifted out. Wet the area with a sea sponge, fine water sprayer, or brush. Let the water absorb into the paper for a minute or so.

- Using a clean, damp sponge, lift out the paint by applying pressure and blotting. Rinse the sponge, and repeat until the color will no longer lift out. Remove the mask, and let it dry completely.

- Staining pigment is difficult to remove. The paper must be gently scrubbed with a nylon stocking before removing the mask. Gentle rubbing removes the top of the paper surface. Do not expect perfect results. Do not use white paint to cover a mistake; when you paint on top of it, the color pigment looks milky.

"Mistakes are almost always of a sacred nature. Never try to correct them. On the contrary: rationalize them, understand them thoroughly. After that, it will be possible for you to sublimate them."

Salvador Dali (1904–89)

Allow yourself to make mistakes. Analyzing them will leave you with the confidence to keep experimenting. Self-analysis or analytical questions and feedback from others—underlying principles of a critique session—can generate new ideas and bring you to new conclusions. Remember that among many mistakes, there may also be a few lovely spots worth duplicating again.

Furniture

Furniture helps tell a story in a rendering. As interior designers, we are fortunate to have so many designs to choose from (and exceedingly lucky that time-consuming nineteenth-century illustration techniques, which allowed little room for error, are no longer expected). The usual technique is to paint around a room's furniture, detailing that last. When your clients see the sofa in your rendering, they will imagine sitting on it. Do your best to make it look persuasive, no matter the style or materials.

Vignette study of a Bombay chest and a high-gloss black plank floor (watercolor)

Markers

Are you a three-dimensional object, or do you merely have an outline? After your inspection, of course you can confirm that you are a three-dimensional object with form, shape, and volume. So is a chair! Illustrating furnishings, such as a sofa or a table, requires that you consider the whole subject, not only its outline or its edges. Recall what you learned in chapter 3 about rendering basic forms.

For a warm-up, focus on an object as a whole; do not render any lines. First look around you and chose three objects to illustrate—maybe a chair, lamp, vase, table, or sofa. Reduce each object to its dominant forms: cylinder, square, rectangle, and cone. Squint your eyes to see the highlights, shades, and shadows. Now, using one marker, illustrate each object as a combination of three-dimensional forms, taking just three minutes. Because there are no lines, you will not have to worry about any marks going out of bounds. Ah, but if you lose the shape or the form, your drawing will not resemble the subject at all. Remember the forms as you work through the following exercises.

Seating

Now that you can illustrate a space's architectural components and materials, you can learn how to make your furniture selections great selling points. A designer manipulates many forms within an interior. The mass of each furniture piece must be studied carefully to determine its impact on the whole. You have heard comments such as, "The sofa is too heavy for the room," or "This has a nice, light feeling." These remarks describe the visual weight of objects, which will vary depending on the surrounding colors, space, texture, and other elements.

While practicing the following subjects, keep in mind that color values are built up in layers. The placement of these values helps an achromatic or a color sofa read well.

White leather sofa

Step 1:

• Plan the white areas to capture the bright light source in front of and above the sofa, as well as from a table lamp to the left. Use a freehand stroke.

• Apply gray values (light cool gray) to the front-facing surfaces and shadows in the pillow areas.

Step 2:

• Apply blue marker strokes (pale blue) to soften the gray value placements.

• To accent the pillow, apply the base color and values (dark gray or a color of your choice), using a layered technique.

Step 3:

• Apply lines (pale blue) to the metal legs.

• Add dabs of color (dark gray) to indicate shadow or reflections.

• Add a line (black) to the bottom of the legs.

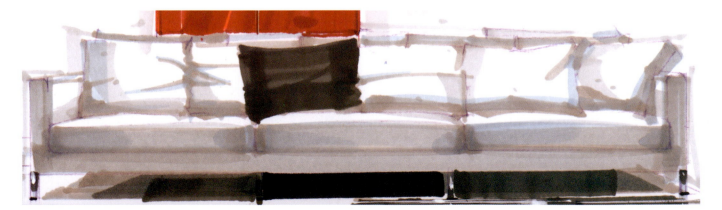

8.1. White leather sofa

Solid-color sofa

Step 1:

- Apply the base color (1205T) on all surfaces, excluding the pillows. Use a cardboard guide and a straight, horizontal stroke.

Step 2:

- Apply the middle value (1205T) on all surfaces, excluding the pillows and the top of the seat.

- Apply the dark value (4535T).

- Apply the darker value (4525T).

Step 3:

- Detail the pillows: the roll in black, the round pillow in the middle value (1205T) and the dark value (4535T), and the square pillow in two layers of the dark value (4535T) and black.

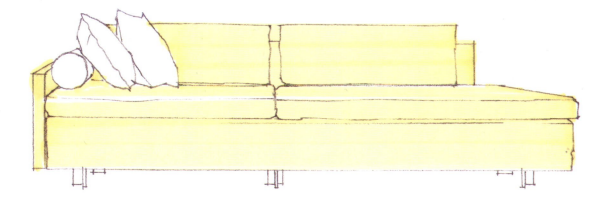

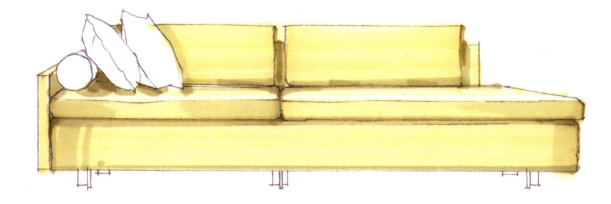

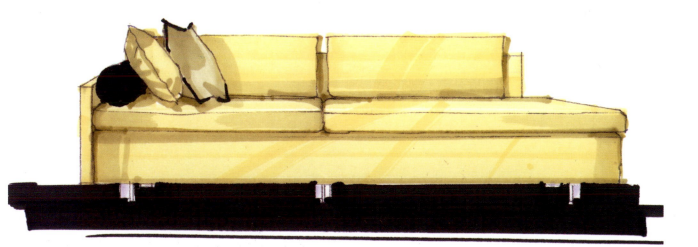

8.2. Sofa with solid-color upholstery

Gray velvet sofa

Step 1:

- Apply the base color (Ice Gray 10) for the upholstery.

- Add values to the sofa back (Ice Gray 10).

Step 2:

- Apply the middle values (Ice Gray 08).

Step 3:

- Apply the darkest values (Ice Gray 04).

- Define the fabric wrinkles (Ice Gray 08).

- Add soft scribble strokes (Ice Gray 08).

- Fill in the legs (440T and black).

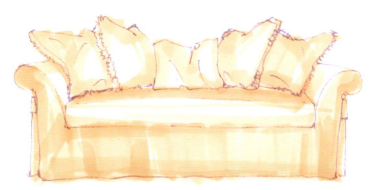

8.3. *Sofa with gray velvet upholstery*

8.4. *Sofa with polished-cotton upholstery*

Polished-cotton sofa

Step 1:

• Scribble in the base color (729T) for the upholstery.

• Leave white at the seat cushion's top front edge.

• Apply the dark values (729T).

Step 2:

• Apply the shadows (518T).

Step 3:

• Detail the pillow trim (R228 and Fuchsia pencil).

Sofa with button upholstery

Step 1:

• Apply the base color (454T) for the upholstery.

• Apply the middle values (454T). This layering technique uses the same color to achieve the value range.

Step 2:

• Apply the shadows (454T).

• Define the legs (Ice Gray 09 and Ice Gray 05).

• Detail the piping and the buttons to match the sofa, using a fine-point marker nib or a colored pencil.

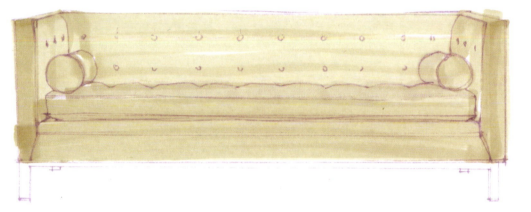

8.5. Sofa with button upholstery

Pale blue satin chair

Step 1:

- Apply the base color (c919) for the upholstery.

- Leave the white areas.

Step 2:

- Add the middle values (c919).

- Add the dark values (b418).

- Add value to the pillows (c919).

Step 3:

- Define the legs (Ice Gray 09, Ice Gray 01, and black).

- Detail the pillow pattern (Ice Gray 01 and black).

Skirted stool

Step 1:

- Apply the base color (2706t).

- Apply the middle value (2706t).

- Apply the dark value (Cool Gray 09).

Step 2:

- Apply the stripe pattern with a pointed nib (black).

- Soften and fill in the stripes (black Caran d'Ache).

- Develop the folds by sweeping in marker strokes (2706t).

- Detail the cording and the cord knots with a fine-point nib (black).

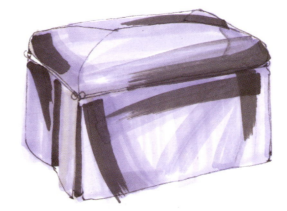

8.7. Skirted stool with horizontal-stripe upholstery

8.6. Chair with pale blue satin upholstery

Elgin chair in painted wood

Step 1:

• Apply the base color (649T), rendering in a free and loose style as if drawing with the marker.

• Leave the chair's front seat white.

• Add thin lines (1205T) for the gold-leaf finish, using a fine-point nib.

Step 2:

• Add the shadows (5445T) to the wood and the fabric.

• Add the shadows (468T) to the gold leaf.

• Define the shapes in shadow (263T).

Step 3:

• Sketch in the loose lines and dots (2B pencil or a black fine-tip marker), using a light touch to add spirit and delicacy to the chair.

8.8. *Elgin chair in painted wood*

Zigzag chair (Gerrit Rietveld)

Step 1:

- Tape the edges, section by section.

- Apply a few strokes (162T) to the areas where darker values occur, using a scribble technique and following the direction of the wood grain.

- Apply the base color (155T), using a solid scribble technique to blend the previous color.

Step 2:

- Apply light strokes (263T) to develop the wood grain.

- Continue to develop the wood grain with light strokes (468T).

- Define the edges on the left (468T).

Step 3:

- Develop the darker values and the edges (482T).

- Scribble lines (482T) in varying directions for the light wood grain on the chair seat and back.

8.9. *Zigzag chair in wood (Rietveld)*

Solid-color chair

Step 1:

- Apply the base color (134T) for the upholstery.

- Apply the base color (469T) for the wood legs and frame.

Step 2:

- Apply the middle value (134T) for the upholstery.

- Apply the dark value (141T) for the upholstery.

- Detail the wood frame (440T).

8.10. Chair with solid-color upholstery

Marie Antoinette boudoir chair

Step 1:

• Plan the white areas.

• Apply the light values (10% Cool Gray).

• Apply the middle values (20% Cool Gray).

Step 2:

• Apply the dark values (40% Cool Gray).

Step 3:

• Define the pattern's dark areas (30% Cool Gray).

• Detail the pattern (white gouache), using a very small, round brush.

8.11a. Marie Antoinette boudoir chair in painted wood and upholstery

Chair with linen upholstery

Step 1:

- Apply the fabric's base color (Y119).

- Leave a white area at the front edge of the seat cushion top.

- Apply the wood frame's base color (O727).

- Scribble in a colored watercolor pencil (Faber-Castell Albrecht Dürer 8200-178 Nougat) to develop some texture in the shadow areas.

- Blend the texture with a marker (Y119) or a marker blender.

Step 2:

- Add the darker values (464T and black pencil) to the wood frame.

- Define the upholstery piping with watercolor pencil (Nougat).

8.11b. *Chair with linen upholstery*

Louis Ghost chair (Philippe Starck)

Step 1:

• Mask the white areas.

• Apply the base color (290T) for the transparent polycarbonate material, working wet into wet for steps 1 and 2.

Step 2:

• Apply the darker values (2707T).

Step 3:

• Define a few edges (292T).

8.12. Louis Ghost chair in transparent, colored polycarbonate (Starck)

8.13. Mademoiselle chair in a clear Plexiglas frame (Starck)

***Tip!** If the Plexiglas you are illustrating is very thick, there will be a noticeable offset in what is seen through the material.*

Mademoiselle chair (Philippe Starck)

Alternate 1:

- Render what is seen through the clear Plexiglas frame, revealing white on the side of the frame facing the light source.

- Indicate grays and blue on the back of the frame.

- Render the elements beyond the frame on the frame itself, leaving white to indicate reflections.

Alternate 2:

- Render what is seen through the Plexiglas frame, without leaving any white spaces.

- Outline the frame (white pen) on the surfaces facing a light source.

Plia chair (Gian Carlo Piretti)

Step 1:

- Plan the white areas to represent the polished chrome.

- Apply the base color (649T) to the chrome frame.

- Apply the red base color (485T) for the ABS plastic back and the seat.

Step 2:

- Apply values (649T and Cool Gray 08) to the chrome.

- Add color reflections (485T) to the chrome.

- Apply the circular and half-circle shape definitions (485T) on the seat and the back.

- Highlight the edges of the circular and half-circle shapes with a watercolor pencil (Prismacolor 2938 White).

8.14. Plia chair in red ABS plastic and polished chrome (Piretti)

Series Seven chair (Arne Jacobsen)

Step 1:

- Plan the light and dark transition lines.

- Apply the base color (M555 and 2706T, with Warm Gray 03 blended in) for the lacquered paint.

- Apply multiple layers of the same colors to darken the back and part of the seat.

- Apply thin lines (cool gray) to the chrome-finish legs.

- Add dabs (gray) to indicate the reflections. Finish the leg caps (dark gray or black).

Step 2:

- Define the edges with a colored pencil (Rouge).

- Add highlights with a pencil (white) to give the chair its glossy lacquered appearance.

- Highlight the legs (white gouache).

8.15. Series Seven chair in lacquered paint (Jacobsen)

LC1 chair (Le Corbusier)

Step 1:

- Shade the surfaces (9181T) of the seat and the back.

- Apply the base color (40% Cool Gray) for the metal frame.

- Define the frame values (60% Cool Gray).

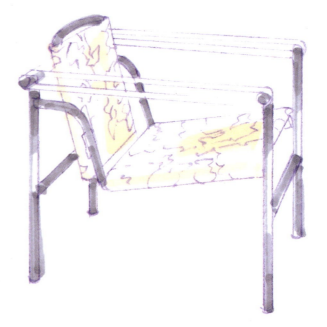

8.16. LC1 chair in polished metal with animal hide (Le Corbusier)

Step 2:

- Block in the hide pattern with a light brown (O527).

- Detail the arm straps (440T).

Step 3:

- Mask the arms and the frame. (Alternatively, render through the frame and go back over it with white gouache after the rendering is complete.)

- Define the back and the hide seat, blending in darker browns (O535 and 440T).

- Blend the animal hide pattern with a marker blender if needed. Remove the mask.

- Detail the frame (80% Cool Gray or black).

Alternative:

- To detail the hide pattern with paint instead of marker, securely tape the four corners of the paper to your work surface.

- Be sure that the seat and the back are wet when you begin; if the paper is wet enough, you can let the paint float into the surface.

- Paint in the pattern on the seat and the back.

- Spatter brown and black paint into the seat and the back.

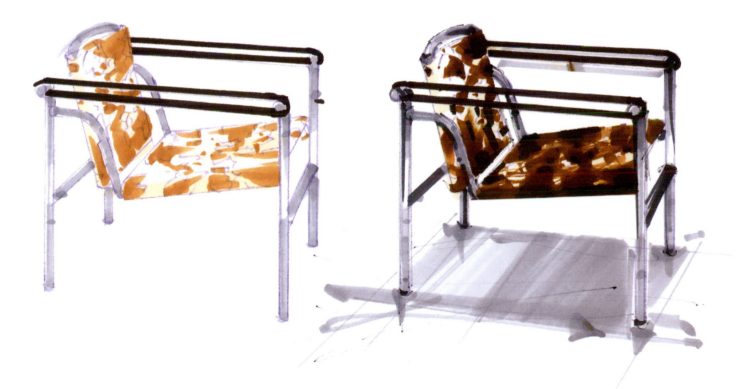

Polished metal stool

Step 1:

- Apply the base colors (cool gray and pale blue).

Step 2:

- Add the medium and dark values (cool gray and touches of lilac).
- Dab in the reflections (white gouache).
- Define the shadows (black fine-point marker).
- Add reflections (white gouache).

Management chair

Step 1:

- Apply the base color (c919) for the chair upholstery.
- Leave a white area on the seat.
- Apply a second layer of the base color (c919) to the back of the seat.
- Apply a third layer (c919) to the side of the seat and the back.
- Apply the base color (Ice Gray 01) for the metal frame components.

8.17. Stool in polished metal

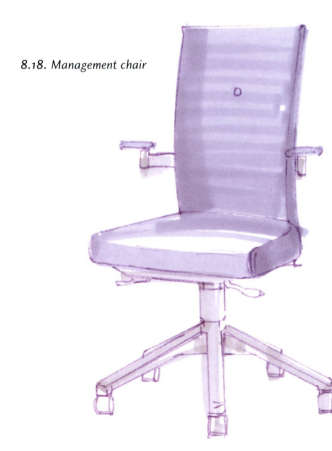

8.18. Management chair

Task chair

Step 2:

- Blend the upholstery color, and deepen the values on the back of the seat and the lower back.

- Apply the middle value (Ice Gray 06) to the metal base frame components.

- Apply a darker gray value to the metal base frame components.

- Define the casters and the areas in shadow on the frame (black).

Step 1:

- Apply the base color (649T) on the chair back and seat.

- Apply the middle values (649T or light gray) to the back of the chair.

- Apply the base color (gray) to the chair base.

Step 2:

- Define the shadows in the base components (black).

- Add a fine white line to the top edge and the side edge of the chair back and seat.

- Add dabs of paint (white gouache) to highlight the chair base.

Tip! Keep the manufacturer's photographs in view while illustrating a furniture selection. They may help if you are having difficulties with a value placement or a pattern direction.

8.19. Task chair

Tables

For tables use the techniques learned for other materials such as wood and marble. Your decision will be direction: wood grain, marble veins, and so forth. Highly reflective surfaces finished in mirror, glass, or chrome are rendered in colors that vary slightly, depending on the surrounding room elements but using the same techniques.

Antique gold-leaf table

Step 1:

• Apply the base color (AD Marker Light Sand).

• Define the values (4525T).

Step 2:

• Deepen the values (4525T, 466T, and 1205T).

Step 3:

• Add detail (4655T) to the frame, and apply the glass color (552T).

• Add the reflections (white gouache).

8.20. Antique gold-leaf table with glass

Gold-leaf table

Step 1:

• Apply the base colors (1205T and 4525T).

Step 2:

• Define the frame with values (4655T and 4505T).

Step 3:

• Detail the frame (2706T), and define the glass color (552T).

Wood-top table

Step 1:

• Mask the edges of the wood tabletop.

• Apply the base color (AD Marker Light Sand), using two layers.

• Add detail (Warm Gray 08) in the direction of the wood grain.

• Apply color (Warm Gray 11) to the base frame.

Step 2:

• Deepen the color (Warm Gray 11) of the tabletop's grain direction.

Step 3:

• Apply dark grain detail (440T) in the direction of the tabletop's wood grain.

• Detail (440T) the base frame.

8.21. Gold-leaf table with glass

Step 1   Step 2   Step 3

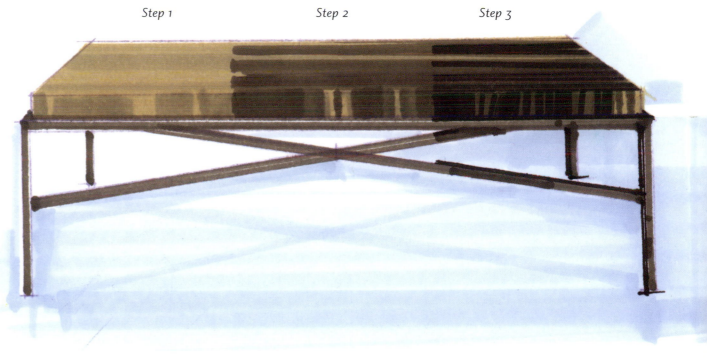

8.22. Table with a wood top and a metal base

Marble-top table

Step 1:

• Mask the edges of the marble tabletop.

• Apply blue (B118) to the top.

• Apply color (Ice Gray 03) to the base frame.

Step 2:

• Add gray veining (Ice Gray 07) to the tabletop.

Step 3:

• Detail the marble (black pencil and white pen).

• Detail the base frame (Ice Gray 03 and black).

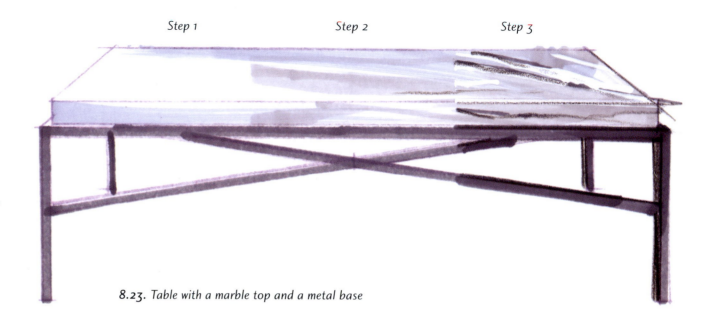

Step 1   Step 2   Step 3

8.23. Table with a marble top and a metal base

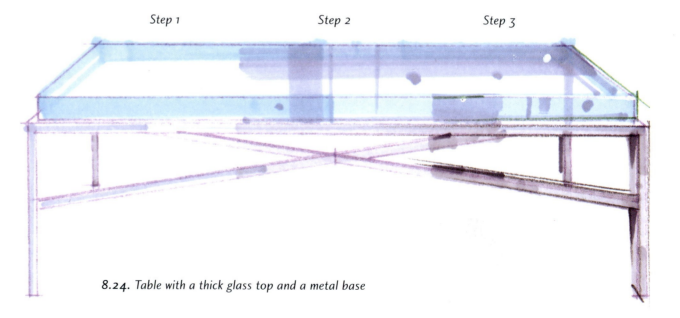

Step 1   Step 2   Step 3

8.24. Table with a thick glass top and a metal base

Glass-top table

Step 1:

- Mask the edges of the glass tabletop.

- Apply color (c429) to the glass top.

- Apply color (b118 and Ice Gray 07) to the base frame.

Step 2:

- Apply additional values (b118) to the glass top.

Step 3:

- Detail the glass (Prismacolor 2909 Grass Green watercolor pencil and white pen).

- Detail the base frame (Ice Gray 07 and Ice Gray 03).

Table with mirror, glass, or chrome

- Use the same techniques and base colors for surfaces finished in mirror, glass, or chrome. Remember that colors will vary slightly because the materials reflect the surrounding room elements.

- For mirrored surfaces, use nondescript reflections similar to those on the table legs here.

- For glass surfaces, use green pencil on the edges.

- For chrome surfaces, indicate more black in the dark areas.

8.25. *Table with mirror, glass, or chrome*

Plastic-laminate table

Step 1:

• Mask the top sections.

• Individually color each section, applying the colors (283T and 386T) evenly on the top surface.

• Apply the base color (Ice Gray 09) for the frame and the legs.

Step 2:

• Add values (Ice Gray 07 and Ice Gray 02) to the frame and the legs.

• Detail the top at the edges with pencil (black).

Cyclone table (Isamu Noguchi)

Step 1:

• Use frisket film to mask areas around the top and the base.

• Apply the base color (70% Cool Gray) to the tabletop and the base.

• Apply the darker value (90% Cool Gray) to the top and the base in the foreground.

• Apply the base color (155T) to the wood edge.

• Add the chrome (40% Cool Gray and 90% Cool Gray).

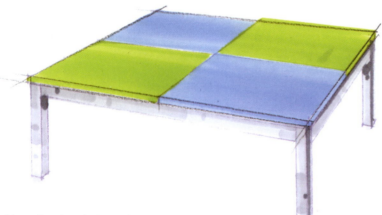

8.26. Table with colored plastic laminate

8.27. Cyclone table with black matte laminate, chrome, and wood (Noguchi)

Tripod side table (Hans Bellman)

Step 2:

- Detail the wood edge (155T, 466T, and O727), using an ellipse template.

- Detail the base (90% Cool Gray and black), again using an ellipse template.

- Detail the chrome (white gouache).

- Detail the base highlights (white gouache).

Step 1:

- Evenly apply the base color (Ice Gray 10) to the top.

- Apply a single stroke (Ice Gray 01) to the middle of each leg.

- Dab color (Ice Gray 01) on the top to indicate the three wood details.

Step 2:

- Apply color (black) to the legs, leaving a small line of Ice Gray 01 untouched.

- Apply a middle value (Ice Gray 05) to the top edges.

- Detail the top edge (black pencil), using an ellipse template.

Tip! Plastic laminate with a matte finish has a flat-looking coloration. Blend colors well with soft variations in the values.

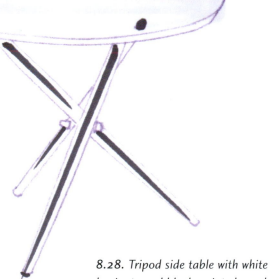

8.28. *Tripod side table with white plastic laminate and black-painted wood (Bellman)*

Crochet table

Step 1:

- Choose values from the ice gray or cool gray marker sets.
- Apply the floor color under the table, rendering it through the table.
- Apply any other colors that may occur behind the table.

Step 2:

- Place ice gray values on all table surfaces except the top and the front. For the inner right side, use the lightest value. For the inner back side, use a middle value. For the outer left side, use the darkest value.

Step 3:

- Dab the darker values on the top and the front.
- Detail the crochet pattern (white gouache).
- Define the edges (white gouache).

8.29. *Crochet table*

8.30. *Black granite table*

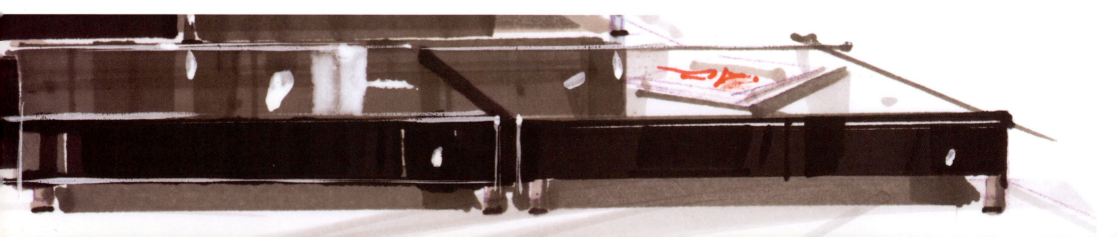

Black granite table

Step 1:

- This technique can be used for most black or dark reflective surfaces (see also figure 8.31).
- Apply the middle values (gray) to the tabletop and the front left edge of the side.
- Apply the light values (gray) to the legs.

Step 2:

- Apply the middle values (gray) to the tabletop in a vertical direction.
- Apply the dark values (gray) to the sides in a vertical direction.

Step 3:

- Detail the legs.
- Add reflections to the tabletop (white gouache).
- Define the table edges (white pen).

Tip! High-gloss black laminate or dark glass reflects adjacent surfaces.

Black laminate desk

Step 1:

- Use the same techniques as described in figure 8.30. Color values are from the ice gray marker set.
- Apply light gray to the desktop surface, which will help the darker edges pop out. Because the desk reflects the surrounding walls, use a vertical application technique to reinforce the nature of a reflective surface.

Step 2:

- Detail the aluminum base (light, cool grays and white).

8.31. Desk in high-gloss black laminate with an aluminum base

Storage

Techniques learned for wood can be applied to casework elements of storage units, such as office file systems and kitchen cabinets. Storage units with either a lacquered or a metallic finish have a moderately reflective quality and depth because of the gloss finish coats applied to the surface.

8.32. Red lacquered credenza

Lacquered and metal storage units

Step 1:

- Use similar techniques to illustrate lacquered and painted metal surfaces.

- Flood the base marker color onto the paper's surface, applying the color wet into wet. This softens the marker strokes and achieves some of the material's color depth.

Step 2:

- Detail the hardware (white pen, colored pencil, or fine-point marker).

- See figures 3.8, 4.8, and 4.9 for more examples.

8.33. Painted metal storage units

Wood kitchen cabinets

Step 1:

- Apply the base color (Y119) for the wood casework, using overlapping strokes.

- Add the darker values (Y217, Y216, and Y717) to define the cabinet doors and the drawers, under the drawer pulls, and in the shaded areas near the ovens.

Step 2:

- Indicate the stainless steel with scribbled strokes (Ice Gray 06, 05, 04, and 03), adding some of the wood color to the steel to represent reflections.

- Add shadows inside the ovens, sink, and stainless-steel cabinet.

- Detail the glassware, dishes, reflections, and hardware (white gouache).

Wood
Y119
Y217
Y216
Y717

Metal
Ice gray 06-03

8.34. Wood kitchen cabinets

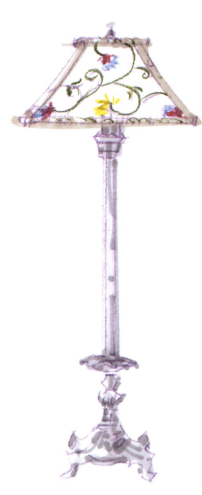

8.35a. *Table lamp with a silk embroidered shade and a silver-metal base*

For the lamp base, use 20% Cool Gray and 40% Cool Gray to simulate the metallic material. Use neutral colors (Warm Gray 03 and colored pencils) for the lamp shade.

8.35b. *Table lamp with a colored plastic shade and an aluminum base*

Apply metallic colors of 20% Cool Gray and 40% Cool Gray for the lamp base and green (365T) for the lamp shade.

8.35c. *Table lamp with a white linen shade and a glass base*

Begin with a neutral color (20% Cool Gray) for the lamp shade and then detail the colored base in red marker and pencil.

Lighting

In a full room illustration, add lighting of any type last. The secret is perfect technique, where skill in placing a marker or brush stroke does the job for you. You may find that a simple gesture to define the fixture shape is all that is needed. Nothing beats adding a brush stroke of white gouache to help indicate the sparkle for a light source, but note that illuminated fixtures do not have a completely dark area. Artistic license permits gradual color application from light to dark. Recall what you have learned about rendering basic forms as you place color for figures 8.37a to 8.37c.

Do not get bogged down in the details. Be daring and relaxed in your technique, and consider the lighting in relationship to the whole illustration. Study the renderings by Julian LaTrobe and other professionals in chapters 2 and 3. They have much to illuminate about color placement, especially for difficult subjects such as crystal chandeliers (see figures 8.39a and 8.39b).

Ceiling lights

Step 1:

- Indicate the light fixture with a marker color that is darker than the ceiling color (if they are of the same color). Use Ice Gray 02 and Ice Gray 05 if the lights are a silver-color metal.

Step 2:

- Place a dab of white (gouache or white pen) at the light source and around the fixture ring.
- Add reflections (white gouache) on the wall from the ceiling lights, keeping the placement in proper perspective lines.

8.36. Ceiling lights

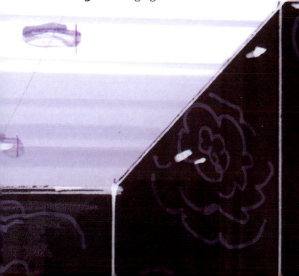

Pendant lights

8.37a. *Frosted-glass and chrome pendant light*

For this simple glass pendant, the colors (20% Cool Gray and 40% Cool Gray) are gradually applied from light to dark.

8.37b. *Pendant light with a silk shade*

Layers of marker (Cool Gray 20%) are used to capture this translucent shade and light, with details added in black pencil.

8.37c. *Gloss-painted metal and chrome pendant light*

Markers used for this golden pendant are Cool Gray 20%, Cool Gray 40%, 120T, 123T, and 141T.

Akari Light Sculpture L1 (Isamu Noguchi)

Step 1:

- Leave the middle sections of the lamp white, because most of the light radiates from there. Keep detail to a minimum.

- Indicate the shade's wrinkled surface by scribbling marker lines (gray) in many directions.

Step 2:

- Add values to help the form read, using very light marker strokes.

Crystal chandeliers

Step 1:

- Add value and shade to the chandelier and around it to help define the form. Use this technique for any chandelier where the ceiling and walls are very light.

Step 2:

- Leave the white of the paper to indicate reflections, or add white gouache on top of the color.

*8.38. Akari Light Sculpture L1
floor or pendant lamp (Noguchi)*

8.39a. Crystal chandelier

Apply 2707T for the light fixture and 5507T for the background.

8.39b. *Crystal chandelier*

Apply 134T, 5425T, and 535T for the light fixture and 5445T and 5425T for the background.

Watercolor

The need to keep your eye focused on an object, and not its outline, applies to watercolor as well as to marker techniques. Let's try a warm-up exercise similar to the one you did for markers earlier in this chapter, with a few modifications. The goal is to focus on an object as a whole, without rendering any lines. You will learn to look keenly at a subject and synthesize what you see, translating this into gestures on the paper. Revisit what you learned in chapter 3 about rendering basic forms.

First choose three objects around you to illustrate, such as a chair, lamp, vase, table, or sofa. Reduce each object to its dominant forms: cylinder, square, rectangle, cone. Squint your eyes to see the highlights, shades, and shadows. Now illustrate each object as a combination of three-dimensional forms with one color, keeping your eyes focused on the whole object, not on the paper. Work big, using your whole arm for brush strokes. It does not matter that you cannot see where your brush is going. Try to complete the warm-up in three minutes.

Seating

Use restraint in developing the forms of upholstered furniture. If you excessively model the shapes and the forms, spontaneity is lost—and we do not want furniture to look like mounds of rising pasta dough! A chair's essence is often the frame detail and the color, while the upholstery is secondary.

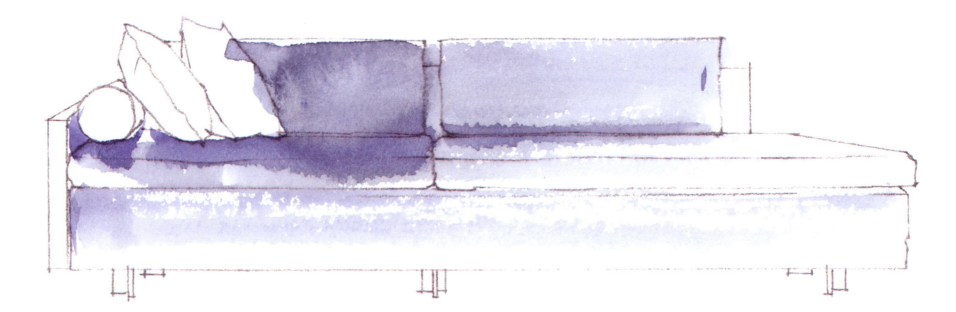

8.40. Sofa with solid-color upholstery

Solid-color sofa

Step 1:

- Apply the base-color wash (Cobalt Blue) on all surfaces, excluding the pillows. Use a flat, wide brush.

- Apply the middle value (Cobalt Blue) on all surfaces, excluding the pillows and the top of the seat (right side).

Step 2:

- Apply the dark values (Cobalt Blue) at pillows, cushions, and sofa back, using a round brush.

- Detail the pillows (Burnt Siena) and the sofa legs (Neutral Tint).

Raw-silk sofa

Step 1:

- Apply the base color wash (Burnt Umber + Cobalt Violet), using a flat brush.

- For highlights, leave white at the front edge of the seat cushion and in the skirt.

- Apply the middle values (Burnt Umber + Cobalt Violet), building up the values in layers.

Step 2:

- Apply the dark values (Burnt Umber + Cobalt Violet), using a round brush.

- Detail the pillow fringe (Burnt Umber + Cobalt Violet), using a round brush.

8.41. *Sofa with raw-silk upholstery*

Bottoni sofa (Marcel Wanders)

Step 1:

• Apply the base color (Aureolin), using a flat brush.

Step 2:

• Define the forms and the values (Aureolin + Raw Umber).

• Define the leg and the values (Neutral Tint), using a round brush.

Step 3:

• Develop the pattern (Neutral Tint), using a round brush.

8.42. Bottoni sofa with solid and patterned upholstery (Wanders)

Lorenzo le Magnifique sofa (Philippe Starck)

Step 1:

- Place the base color wash (Neutral Tint + Cobalt Blue) on the sofa back and the front of the slipcover, using a flat brush. Let it dry.

Step 2:

- Add the values (Neutral Tint + Cobalt Blue) and the slipcover folds, using a flat brush. Let it dry.

Step 3:

- Detail the piping (Neutral Tint), using a round brush.

- Detail the base color of the medalion and ribbon design on the sofa back (Aureolin), using a round brush.

- Detail the values of the same design on the sofa back (Raw Sienna), using a round brush.

Skirted stool

Step 1:

- Apply the base color (Aureolin + Raw Umber), using a flat brush.

Step 2:

- Apply the middle value (Aureolin + Raw Umber), using a flat brush.

- Apply the stripe pattern (Aureolin + Raw Umber), using a round brush.

- Darken the stripe pattern (Neutral Tint), using a round brush.

Step 3:

- Detail the cording and the cord knots (Neutral Tint), using a round brush.

8.44. *Skirted stool with horizontal-stripe upholstery*

8.43. *Lorenzo le Magnifique sofa (Starck)*

Elgin chair

Step 1:

- Leave the chair's front surface very light.

- Apply the base color (Aureolin + Raw Umber) for the wood and the seat, using a flat brush.

Step 2:

- Add shadows (Aureolin + Raw Umber) to the wood and the fabric.

- Detail the gold trim (Aureolin), using a very small, round brush.

- Define the stripe pattern (Aureolin + Raw Umber), using a very small, round brush. Keep it light at the front edge, dark in other areas.

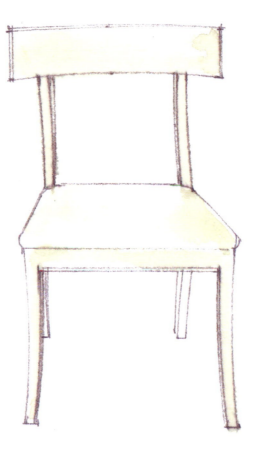

8.45. *Elgin chair in painted wood*

Zigzag chair (Gerrit Rietveld)

Step 1:

- Mask the edges.

- Apply the base color (Burnt Umber), using a flat brush.

Step 2:

- Using a dry-brush technique, detail the wood grain with a middle value (Burnt Umber).

- If you wish to emphasize the wood grain, add deeper values (Burnt Sienna) to the chair base and indicate grain with a black fine-line or colored pencil (Nougat or Sepia). If not, move to step 3.

Step 3:

- Develop the wood grain with a darker value (Burnt Sienna), using the dry-brush technique again.

- Add definition (Nougat or Sepia pencil).

8.46. Zigzag chair in wood (Gerrit Rietveld)

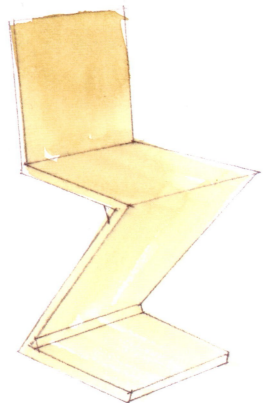

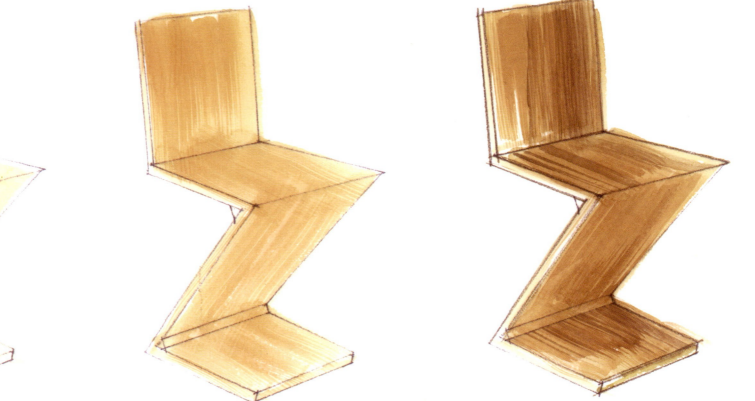

English chair

Step 1:

- Apply a light base color (Raw Sienna) to the chair seat, using a flat brush. Let it dry.
- Apply a light base color (Raw Sienna, Burnt Sienna, and Olive Green) to the chair frame, using a round brush.

Step 2:

- Apply the diagonal pattern to the seat (Raw Sienna). While wet, add the same color to the seat back.
- Add the darker values (Raw Sienna, Burnt Sienna, Olive Green, and black) to the chair frame.

Marie Antoinette boudoir chair

Step 1:

- Leave most of the frame white, without detail, to allow contrast and definition in the composition. Mask the parts of the chair frame to preserve white areas.
- First apply the lightest value and then the dark values (Neutral Tint + Cobalt Blue). Let it dry.

Step 2:

- Add the textile pattern (white gouache or white pen). Small patterns with curvilinear shapes are easier to indicate with a colored pencil if the pattern color is darker than the base color. If the pattern color is lighter than the base color, use paint to indicate the pattern.

8.47. Painted and gilded English dining chair

8.48. Marie Antoinette boudoir chair in painted wood and upholstery

Solid-color chair

Step 1:

- Apply the base color wash (Raw Sienna + Cadmium Yellow) for the upholstery, using a flat brush or an angular brush. Let it dry.

- Apply the base color (Raw Umber) for the wood frame, using a round brush.

Step 2:

- Develop the values (Raw Sienna + Cadmium Yellow) in the upholstery. Let it dry. Detail the piping with the same color.

- Detail the wood frame with dark values (Raw Umber), using a round brush.

Tip! Choose a different brush if you are having difficulty with a particular subject. We do not all produce the same results with the same tool.

8.49. Chair with solid-color upholstery

Louis Ghost chair (Philippe Starck)

Step 1:

- Leave white areas to show the reflective quality of the material.

- Apply the base color (Ultramarine Blue). Let it dry.

Step 2:

- Define the form by applying glaze (Ultramarine Blue) on top of the base color.

- Dab additional color (Cerulean Blue) on the chair back and the top edge.

Conference chair

Step 1:

- Tape the top of the chair back and the seat's front edge.

- Apply the base color (Neutral Tint) to the seat and the back with one continuous stroke, using a wide, flat brush. Let it dry.

- Add the shade area (Neutral Tint) to the back and the seat, using a wide, flat brush. Begin where the chair back curves in, and leave the upholstery's side edge in the lighter base color. Let it dry.

Step 2:

- Suggest the chair base (Neutral Tint), using a wide, flat brush.

8.50. Louis Ghost chair in transparent, colored polycarbonate (Starck)

8.51. Conference chair

Tables

Dining and conference tabletops are best rendered in a minimal technique to keep their large shapes from overpowering the composition; for example, a few vertical washes are sufficient to indicate a gloss-laminated surface (see figure 8.58). Balance can be achieved with architectural elements that provide symmetry (see figure 4.1), as well as a contrasting emphasis on chairs, tabletop arrangements, or overhead chandeliers.

Dark wood table

Step 1:

- Apply the base color wash (Cobalt Violet + Neutral Tint) for the wood top, using a flat brush. Let it dry.

- Apply the base color wash (Cobalt Violet + Neutral Tint) for the table base, using flat and round brushes. Let it dry.

- Apply a pale blue wash (Cobalt Blue) for the glass, using a flat brush. Let it dry.

Step 2:

- Add deeper values (Burnt Sienna) to the wood top, using a flat brush.

- Add deeper values (Burnt Sienna) to the table base. Let it dry.

- Apply darker reflections (Cobalt Blue + Neutral Tint) to the glass.

Step 3:

- Lightly detail the table base (black pencil stick) to achieve the antique pewter color.

- Add highlights (white gouache), using a small, flat brush and a small round brush.

8.52a. Dark wood table with pewter and glass

Antique gold-leaf table

Step 1:

- Apply a light wash of the base color (Naples Yellow) for the frame, using a small, flat brush. Let it dry.

- Apply the base color (Raw Sienna) for the tinted glass top, leaving some white. Use a small, flat brush. Let it dry.

Step 2:

- Add the deeper values of the base color (Raw Sienna + Burnt Umber) to the frame, using a small, round brush. Let it dry.

Step 3:

- Apply the dark cool values (Neutral Tint) to the glass top, using a small, flat brush. Let it dry.

- Apply the dark values (Raw Sienna + Burnt Umber) to the frame, producing a strong contrast. Use a small round brush. Let it dry.

- Add reflections (white gouache), using a small, flat brush.

8.52b. Antique gold-leaf table with glass

Gold-leaf table

Step 1:

- Apply a base color wash (pale yellow). Let it dry.

- Apply another wash (light brown or beige) to the glass surface. Let it dry.

- Apply a glaze (deeper yellow) to shaded surfaces, using a small, flat brush.

Step 2:

- Detail the values with glazes of deeper tones (yellow).

- Apply a glaze (blue) to the glass.

- Add glass reflections (white gouache).

Tip! Use a brighter yellow for a gold-leaf material. Use a darker, greener yellow for an antiqued gold or brass material.

8.53. *Gold-leaf table with smoked glass*

Pewter and iron table

Step 1:

- Mask the tabletop to save the white surface, while painting around it (the typical way of adding in furniture).

- Apply the base color (Neutral Tint + Cobalt Violet) to the top, using a flat brush. Let it dry.

- Shape the tabletop (Neutral Tint + Cobalt Violet) by painting scallop strokes around the sides of the top, using a small, round brush.

Step 2:

- Paint or detail the black iron legs (black pencil).

8.54. Pewter and iron table

Sculptered-brass table

Step 1:

- Apply the base color wash (pale yellow) for the decorative brass, using a flat brush. Let it dry.

- Apply the base color wash (pale blue) for the glass surface, using a flat brush. Let it dry.

- Apply a browner glaze to define the values of the brass, using a small, flat brush. Let it dry.

- Paint the leaf pattern, using a round brush.

Step 2:

- Detail the darkest values at the core of the table frame's edges and where shadows occur. Let it dry.

- Apply a glaze (gray) to the glass, using a flat brush. Let it dry.

- Add the glass reflections and the frame details (white gouache), using a round brush.

8.55. Sculptured-brass table

Cyclone table (Isamu Noguchi)

Step 1:

- Use frisket film to mask the areas around the tabletop and the base. Cut a very small V shape from a piece of tape or frisket to save a white area at the base of the chrome legs.

- Apply the base color (Neutral Tint) to the tabletop and the base, using a flat brush. Let it dry.

Step 2:

- Apply the darker value (Neutral Tint) to the top and the base.

- Apply the base color (Light Sepia) for the wood edge, using a small, round brush.

- Remove the tape or frisket.

- Detail the chrome legs (black and Neutral Tint), using a small, round brush.

8.56. Cyclone table with black matte laminate, chrome, and wood (Noguchi)

Tripod side table (Hans Bellman)

Step 1:

- Apply a small amount of color (Neutral Tint) to the tabletop, using a small, flat brush.

- Apply a single stroke (Neutral Tint) to the middle of each table leg, using a small, round brush.

Step 2:

- Dab color (Neutral Tint) on top for the three wood details, using a small, round brush.

- Apply color (Neutral Tint) to the legs, using a small, round brush. Leave a small line of light value untouched.

- Apply value (Neutral Tint) to the top edges, using a small, round brush.

Step 3:

- Detail the top, using an ellipse template. Use a small, round brush or, if you are a beginner, a black pencil.

8.57. Tripod side table with white plastic laminate and black-painted wood (Bellman)

White laminate conference table

Step 1:

- At the same time that the walls and floor are indicated, apply a few vertical washes for the gloss-laminate tabletop with a wide, flat brush in order to achieve the same color.

Step 2:

- Add the middle values, small gray reflections, and white dabs.

- Add lines with a colored pencil (black or gray) to define the tabletop edges.

Tip! *To avoid backwash paint puddles where the brush hits the paper, start and end brush strokes over tape, masking, or a paper overlay.*

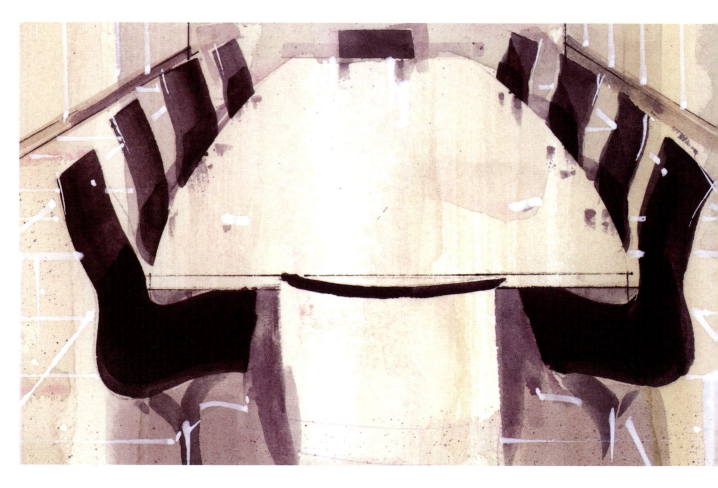

8.58. Conference table in white gloss laminate

Crochet table

Step 1:

- Draw the detail with a "painter's" calligraphy opaque paint marker. Let it dry.

- Add the color washes on top of the detail, using quick, light strokes of a wide, flat brush. Let it dry.

Step 2:

- Add more white detail or other definition if necessary. Use masking fluid if desired for this detail work.

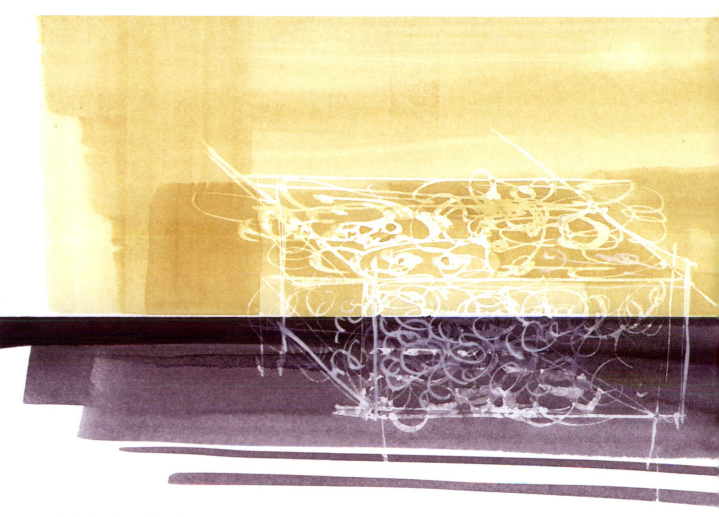

8.59. Crochet table

Storage

Items within or on top of storage units will typically provide the melody while the storage unit itself fades away to showcase the contents or to simply harmonize with the room. You can sublimate the casework and emphasize its functional or decorative elements, such as books, artwork, accessories, or special collections of objects.

Modular wood casework

Step 1:

• Tape sections as you work.

• Apply the wall base color wash (Ultramarine Deep), using a large, flat brush. Let it dry.

• Apply the base color wash (Purple Madder and Peach Black) for the wood surfaces. Let it dry.

Step 2:

• Apply the grain indication (Purple Madder and Peach Black), using a fan brush. Let it dry.

• Detail the grain (Peach Black), using a fan brush.

Step 3:

• Detail the base legs (Peach Black).

• Detail the accessories (Gambouge + Neutral Tint).

• Detail the artwork (Raw Sienna + Neutral Tint).

8.60. Modular wood casework

Lighting

The architectural lighting illustrations that follow represent simple techniques that can be applied to most ceiling illumination. Figure 8.61 is illustrated with a white pen, which works well because there is sufficient contrast with the ceiling color. Figures 8.62 and 8.63 are indicated with simple gestures to define the light fixtures' shapes; white gouache can be added at the light sources. For table lamps, the goal is to complete an illustration in four to six brush strokes, or fewer if possible.

Adding pale yellow at a light source is not the best technique to use. It looks like yellow spots on the illustration (one begins to wonder if Tinker Bell is hiding in the lamp). In addition, yellow or amber colors are used to warn, sending a psychological message of danger, caution, stay away. You certainly do not want to communicate that message.

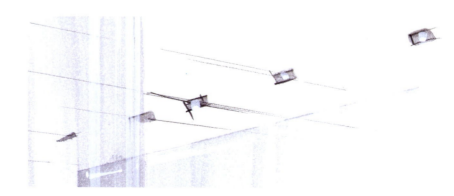

8.63. Track lighting

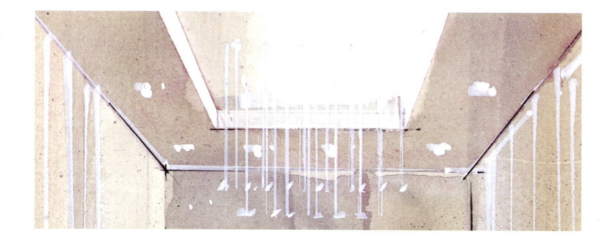

8.61. Recessed and teardrop lighting

Consider these lighting illustrations as line work, regardless of the color. Use an artist's bridge to steady the lines as you paint them with whichever tool feels most comfortable to you: a rigger brush; a small, round brush; or a small, flat brush.

8.62. Track lighting

Chandeliers

Crystal chandelier:

- Use this technique when the ceiling and the walls are very light, adding value and shade (Raw Sienna and Blue Violet) to the chandelier to help the form read.

- Leave the white of the paper for reflections, or add white gouache on top of the color.

Colored crystal chandelier:

- Use this technique when the ceiling or the wall color provides enough contrast for the chandelier. This is much quicker and easier than painting on a white background.

- Use a thin, round brush and white gouache or a white pen; a brush can create more believable crystal shapes.

- Add the black lines on the wall and the ceiling for drama.

8.65. *Colored crystal chandelier*

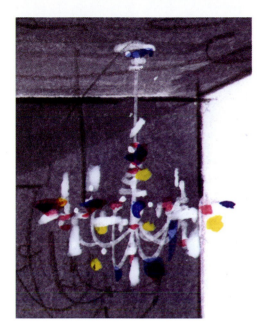

8.64. *Crystal chandelier*

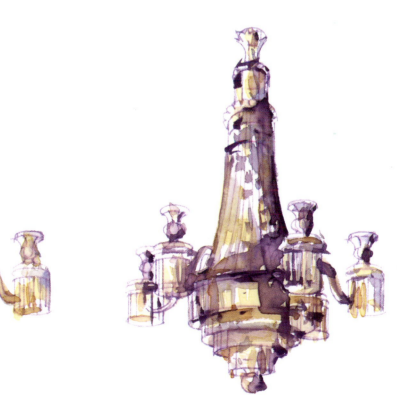

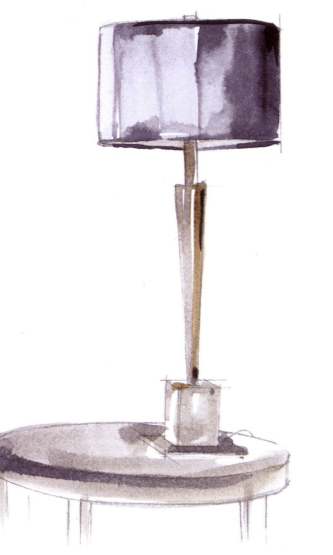

8.66. *Table lamp with an aluminum base and a black shade*

Place values to help the surfaces and the overall color read, using only a few strokes.

Crushed-silk lighting sculptures (Aqua Creations)

Step 1:

- Apply the base color wash (Raw Sienna), using a flat brush. Let it dry.

- Apply the wrinkled-pleat texture (Raw Sienna + Quinacridone Violet), using a fan brush.

Step 2:

- Detail the wavy yellow line at the top of the illustration with the same color.

8.68. *Morning Glory and Happy Days crushed-silk lighting sculptures (Aqua Creations)*

8.67. *Table lamp with a glass base and a silver paper shade*

When a lamp has a glass base, the simplest approach is to render what is beyond the glass surface. Apply a value to one edge of the base, and then add detail or textures with a colored pencil or white gouache.

Assignments

1. Musical chairs. Render any chair in this chapter. Place it in an envelope, saving it until you are later instructed to open it again.

2. Variety. For this exercise, use figures 8.6 (or A.11 in the appendix) and 8.42. Trace several copies of the drawings with a nonphoto or nonprint pencil. Render them using a different technique, color, light placement, and brush or marker.

3. Pieces of eight. Chose any two to four furniture illustrations in this chapter. Trace each drawing, and make numerous copies. Create eight modifications of each; for example, render a trendy or classic material, alter the frame finish, add or rearrange pillows, and so forth.

4. Light exercise. Trace any chandelier, drawing only the main structure with guidelines for the crystal locations (using elliptical lines at the top and the bottom and straight lines for the drops); later you can draw the shape of each crystal and the decorative details with paint or marker, using dots, dabs, or blots. Lay in a medium to dark base color. Indicate the crystals with quick, minimal gestures of white gouache (in both an opaque and a transparent consistency).

Repeat the exercise, this time using a white gel pen or a "painter's" calligraphy opaque paint marker to scribble the lines shown in figure 8.65.

5. Minimalism. Draw or trace a furniture item, and then fully render it. Now that you understand the subject, you will be able to decide what you could leave out. Start with a new drawing of the same subject, but this time reduce its size. Render it with minimal gestures. Remember this exercise when illustrating subjects far back in a drawing.

6. Earning your stripes. Use figure 8.7 for this exercise, which is challenging because it requires more control when placing the stripes with quick, fluid gestures. Changes occur in perspective, spacing, direction of lines, and shapes that go from straight to curved. Practice the gestures for indicating the stripes, finding a comfortable drawing position ahead of time. Photocopy the illustration and repeatedly trace over the marks, at a faster pace each time, until you feel comfortable to begin the next part. If you illustrate the stripes too slowly or firmly, you will have unwanted blobs of color on the paper. (A line with blobs in it could be used for some other pattern or texture—that's a keeper.)

Now trace or draw figure 8.7. Render it using a different-colored stripe, such as deep gray and pale yellow or a rich brown and a robin's egg blue. Study, test, and adjust the base colors to work with your new stripe colors. Render the drawing again with a wider, white-on-white stripe.

"When I examine myself and my methods of thought, I come to the conclusion that the gift of fantasy has meant more to me than any talent for abstract, positive thinking."

Albert Einstein (1879–1955)

By now you have an inclination toward a free or tight illustration technique— your own distinctive personal style is budding. Release your spirit by practicing without an attachment to any specific outcome. Simply trust what you have learned, and know that every day you are making steady progress. Let the exercises here alter your mind, bringing you closer to your own true style and ability.

Enhancements

Decorative items such as artwork, accessories, and plants
add a special sizzle to an illustration, imparting a unique persona.
I have even named a ficus or a palm tree a "brooch"—because
no illustration left the office without one! By now you will be able to
mimic the design enhancements you see in most of this chapter's
illustrations. The appendix also includes many drawings from this
chapter to use as practice and in your own professional illustrations.

A residence enhanced with people and artwork (marker)

Artwork

Start creating a file of artwork you like. Print a contact sheet of the art to refer to when rendering a space, and practice beforehand how you would illustrate the art. This process will become second nature to you and then reside in your memory theater. Modern and contemporary artists such as Joan Miró, Alexander Calder, Jean Dubuffet, Cy Twombly, Frank Stella, Robert Rauschenberg, and Jasper Johns, as shown in a few of the illustrations here, are a good place to start, especially for commercial spaces.

Use paint and a brush to illustrate artwork, unless you have a highly developed skill with markers. Quick strokes and dabs should be enough to suggest the art's subject matter. Paint only the dominant elements and colors, but do not allow them to overpower the room elements unless the art is an important part of the center of interest. Look at the illustrations here and be a copycat. Keep in mind two words—*interpret* and *reduce*—when you apply your marker or brush strokes, using a loose, quick, and spontaneous technique. Scribble gray strokes into the background of white artwork, and add a few strong diagonals with a guide. Place dark values at the side edges of the canvas or the frame, and place a vertical shadow line on the wall as well as a horizontal one underneath the art.

9.1a. *Large abstract art (marker and pencil)*

9.1b. Large abstract art (marker)

9.1c. Large abstract art (watercolor)

9.1d. Art by Guy Romagna (marker)

9.1e. Art by Guy Romagna (watercolor)

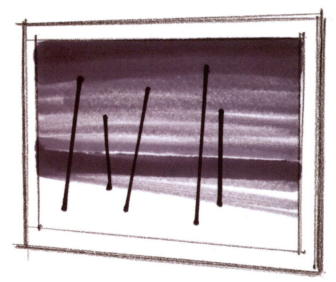

9.2. *Two-dimensional framed production art (marker and white gouache)*

Tip! If a color seen here mystifies you, match it to the watercolor or marker color matrix that you made previously. This will help you learn quickly about color.

9.3a. *Group of etchings (marker, pencil, and white gouache)*

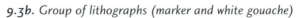

9.3b. *Group of lithographs (marker and white gouache)*

9.4a. *Sculpture and three-dimensional art (marker and pencil)*

9.4b. *Mobile (marker and pencil)*

Plants

Plants and floral arrangements are fun to draw and can work in your favor to create interest in a rendering. When used to the side or in the foreground, they help keep the viewer's eye inside the illustration, rather than floating off the composition. Each flowering plant has something distinctive about it; illustrate that primary quality, its uniqueness.

Plants require a free and loose approach. Express these images through flow, color, and the movement of your brush or marker stroke. Get yourself into an automatic style of painting. When their basic elements are merely suggested without being literally portrayed, plants and flowers become more abstract and less dominant.

Illustrate based on the techniques you have already learned and what you know about plants. The primary quick techniques to use include (1) dot, blot, and dab; (2) spatter, scrape, and scribble; and (3) bounce, drop, and roll. To help you loosen up and approach your subjects in a free-spirited manner, spend some time warming up and practicing with your left hand, if you are right handed, or vice versa. As an exercise, complete figures 2.19 and 2.25 once again.

Marker Colors

The marker colors used for the trees, plants, and floral arrangements in this chapter's illustrations are:

Greens	Blues	Violets	Browns
G149	B418	V518	O727
G139	B118	V127	O535
G159	B128	M128	168T
G178	C618		
G346		Reds	Yellows
G136			
Y923		R738	134T
		R228	Y417

9.5. Floral arrangement (watercolor)

Watercolor Colors

The key paint colors to use for the trees, plants, and floral arrangements in the illustrations here are as follows (in addition to white gouache):

Greens

Sap Green
Olive Green
Sap Green +
   Payne's Gray
Sap Green + Yellow
   Ochre + Black

Blues

Cerulean Blue
Cobalt Blue

Violets

Cobalt Violet
Quinacridone Magenta

Reds and orange

Alizarin Crimson
Rose Madder
Cadmium Red
Cadmium Orange

Browns

Raw Sienna
Raw Umber
Raw Umber +
   Payne's Gray

Yellows

Aureolin
Lemon Yellow
Cadmium Yellow

Techniques for Plants

If you can illustrate one tree (see figures 9.6 to 9.11) or floral arrangement (see figures 9.12 to 9.18), you can do any. I do not recommend using a sponge to paint trees, because this often looks contrived and mechanical. For palm-tree trunks, scribble marks and cross-hatched lines are good techniques.

Imprinting (using paint and the edge of a ruler) is a quick way to illustrate straight dried sticks and branches (see figure 9.18). Apply paint to the ruler's edge, place it on the paper, and lift it off. This leaves a thin, painterly line of color that is also useful for grout lines in tile.

The following is a basic technique usable for both marker and watercolor:

Step 1:

• Apply the colors from light to dark, with the lightest values at the outer edges and the dark values in the interior of the foliage or the flower. Use a brush-tip marker or a round brush.

• Apply the lightest-value base color on the shape of the tree, tree trunk, branches, plant, or flower.

9.6. *Lacy ficus tree (marker and pencil)*

Tip! A line drawing of a plant is a good way to frame an illustration.

290

Step 2:

• Apply a layer of middle-value colors, which can be eliminated on very small subjects.

Step 3:

• Apply a layer of darker-value colors.

• When using watercolor, you can eliminate steps 1 and 2. Place the dark-value color on damp paper (dampen only the shape), and let the color bleed from dark to light. Or on dry paper, using firm pressure, place the dark value, gradually releasing pressure with the brush stroke as you draw near the light-value areas.

Step 4:

• Add the details to indicate branches or flowers.

• Use a rigger brush to define smaller branches at the edges, leaving gaps within the branches so the tree or the greenery does not look too heavy.

• Add flower colors with dabs, blobs, and spatter. These simple gestures will look remarkably lifelike when viewed from a distance.

9.7. Tree in full foliage (marker and pencil)

9.9. *Plant foliage and areca palm (marker)*

9.8. *Bamboo, royal palm, and date palm (marker)*

A painted silhouette of a leafy tree or plant achieves a weighty effect.

9.10. *Plant foliage and areca palm (watercolor)*

9.11. *Bamboo (watercolor)*

9.12. *Arrangements of papyrus, orchids, ornamental grass and birds of paradise, pom-poms, tulips, and Queen Anne's lace (marker)*

9.13. *Flower arrangements, including papyrus, yarrow, orchids, and Queen Anne's lace (watercolor)*

9.14. *Lilac bouquets and lemon leaves in vases (marker and watercolor)*

9.15. Modern assortment with color, leaf assortment, birds of paradise, and corkscrew branch arrangements (watercolor)

9.16. *Wildflower arrangements (watercolor)*

9.17. *Minimal bamboo arrangement and coconut (watercolor)*

9.18. *Dried sticks, branches, and bamboo stalks (watercolor)*

9.19a. Table setting (watercolor)

Tabletops

Choose tabletop arrangements that support your design concept, create harmony in the illustration, and help create a focal point in an interior. Test your color choices by illustrating the subject first on a different piece of paper, cut it out, place it in the illustration, step back from it, and determine if the colors work. Ask yourself if a complementary color, analogous color, or white may be a better choice. If you are unsure, try the same test again.

Remember to reserve white areas of your paper for tabletop linens, china, and glassware. Gouache works well in previously applied, dark color areas where watercolor pigment does not provide enough coverage. Cobalt Blue, Titanium White, Payne's Gray, and black are the only colors needed to paint white dinnerware, silver, and glassware, as shown in figure 9.19a. Simply indicate a few shadows and values to help the shape read, and then finish with white highlights. Do not blend colors. For glass surfaces, add dabs of color from the space that may reflect in the glass. Apply these same principles to glassware and bottles in a back bar (see figures 9.37a and 9.37b).

9.19b. Table arrangement with a carnation (marker and watercolor)

Tip! Work with light staining pigments to mix your colors, because they are easier to lift out if corrections are needed.

Bedding

Your presentation can fall apart if the fabric samples for bedding and pillows are too dominant, and the same is true when illustrating these room elements. Yet they should have some visual interest. A sleeping space looks best when the bed is neatly made or the bedding is turned down slightly. An unmade bed in an illustration looks messy, cluttered, and gives the wrong impression for even a casual setting. Turned-down linens are more difficult to illustrate because of the numerous folds and changing pattern directions. They can also be distracting, so instead let accent pillows add the interest.

The trick to illustrating pillows, linens, and bedding is simply a little exaggeration of the light values and the shadows. Revisit what you learned in chapter 3 about surface shapes, and simplify it. Study the bedding and pillows illustrated here. You will see that the dominance and placement of the dark values and the shadows are what makes the folds and shapes read, with no muddling of too many values.

Follow the method here for both marker and watercolor (see figures 9.20 to 9.26).

Basic technique for bedding

Step 1:

• Study the subject to observe how the light will fall on the forms (remember squinting). Pick out the lightest and the darkest values. Look at the shadows. Draw the outline of those shapes on the pillow or the fold.

• Apply the base color, leaving the lightest value almost white (unless it is a very dark fabric).

Step 2:

• Apply a layer of darker-value colors and shadows.

• If you do not want a hard edge when using marker, keep working the marker into the paper wet on wet (see figure 9.20).

• If you do not want a hard edge when using watercolor, dampen the area of the paper with clear water before applying the paint and let it bleed to a lighter area (see figure 9.21).

9.20. Damask-style pillows (marker and watercolor)

Step 3:

- Apply the details, including pattern, trim, piping, and buttons. (See chapter 11 for more instruction on patterns.)

- A directional pattern will naturally define folds and turns, because the pattern changes direction if it is turned at any angle by being draped or folded (see figures 11.2, 11.11, and 11.12). After such a pattern is defined, add more dark values in the shadow areas if needed.

9.21. Turned-down bedding with a patterned, upholstered headboard in Aureolin and Raw Umber (watercolor)

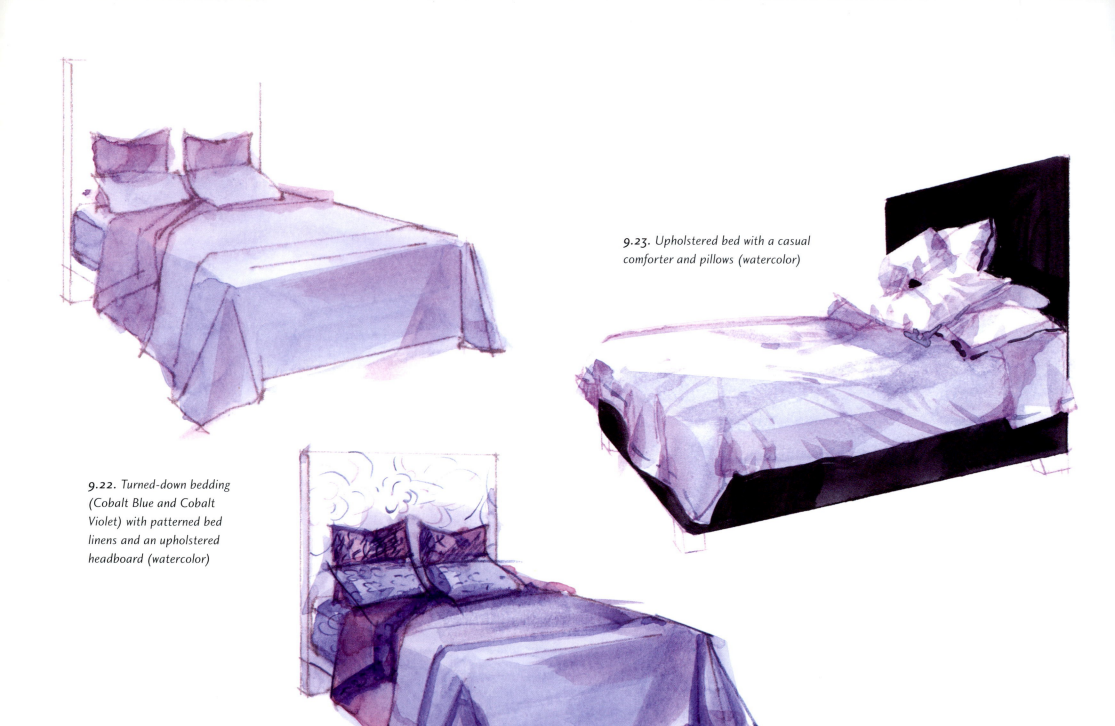

9.23. Upholstered bed with a casual comforter and pillows (watercolor)

9.22. Turned-down bedding (Cobalt Blue and Cobalt Violet) with patterned bed linens and an upholstered headboard (watercolor)

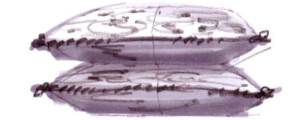

9.24. *Pillows of various sizes and shapes and a throw (marker)*

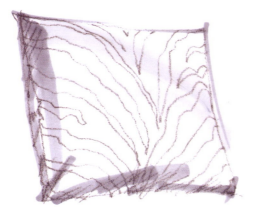

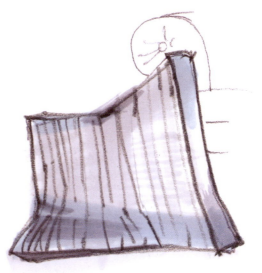

9.25. *Patterned pillows (marker)*

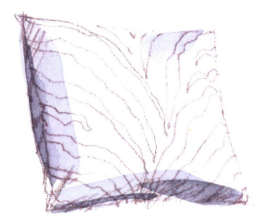

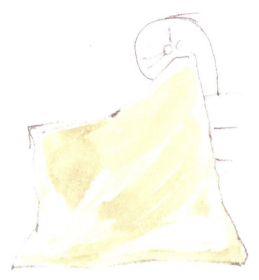

9.26. Pillows with print covers (watercolor)

9.27. People (marker)

People

People, such as seated figures in hotel interiors, add a human relationship and scale to a drawing. Many illustrators, however, do not place figures in their work, believing that their use detracts from the interior or dates an illustration. Other illustrators include ghost figures that are not as fully rendered as the interior space—a good compromise. With less detail, figures will blend into a space. Whatever your choice, consider its appropriateness and effectiveness for the illustration, the presentation, and the client.

Figures are a good foreground device in renderings of retail as well as public spaces. In most retail illustrations, figures are needed as shoppers and mannequins. In this instance, you must carefully research the merchandise and correctly illustrate the displays.

For retail renderings, select fashionable figures, including women, men, and children. (I like the proportions of a longer leg for public spaces.) It is best to restrict clothing to a subtle color or pattern, possibly using colors from the interior, other than those used in the retail displays. Figures must be at the proper scale in relationship to their placement in the space. Place the eyes of figures on or just above the horizon line (eye level) if that line is approximately five feet high; of course, children should be placed at a lower eye level appropriate for the age and height.

Research and study figures in drawings and fashion magazines, and continue to update your creation files. Many books include tracing files of people of all genders, ages, and sizes and in various activities. A recommended book on fashion figures is *Marker Rendering for Fashion, Accessories, and Home Fashions* by Bina Abling (Fairchild Books, 2005).

Tip! I sometimes render a figure that bears a resemblance to my client. Feeling good goes a long way in a design presentation.

9.28. Small-scale people (for distance) and ghost figures (marker)

Sizzle

Furnishings and accessories draw one into an illustration and help the viewer make a connection. Carefully choose your subjects and situate them within the rendering's focal point. Instruction is provided here for some of the more difficult subjects.

9.29. Baby grand piano
(marker and white gouache)

Residences

Most of the sizzle in a residential setting centers around an architectural element, emphasizes a primary function, or features a specific decorative element. Today's lifestyles focus on home entertainment, while traditional home design more often relies on fireplaces and perhaps custom bookcases or wall units. Either way, books on a coffee table, a vase collection on a shelf, a baby grand piano, or flames in a fireplace make an illustration more inviting.

The piano in figure 9.29 is illustrated with just two gray marker values plus black and white; you may choose to add a dark yellow for the hardware, but this is necessary only for a close-up view. Compare it to the piano in figure 4.11. But surely you can see this on your own now—you have learned many techniques thus far, so test your skills here. Be a copycat again, and trace figures 9.29 to 9.31, applying the colors and the values as you see them and adding details and highlights.

9.30. Bookshelves and a home theater
(marker and white gouache)

9.31. Books on a shelf (watercolor)

Rough stone-slab fireplace

Step 1:

- For the stone surround and hearth, apply the base color (10% Cool Gray).

- Apply the medium value (30% Cool Gray).

- Apply the dark value (50% Cool Gray).

Step 2:

- For the interior floor, use a dark value (90% Cool Gray).

- For the sides, use a brush tip (80% Cool Gray) and work from the top to the bottom, leaving white areas for the flame.

- Detail the frame around the opening and the grate (black).

- For the face of the surround, add rough texture (40% Cool Gray) (see also figure 10.28).

Step 3:

- Detail the flame (Y417), using a brush tip.

- Add values to the flame (V518), using a brush tip.

- Paint a rough texture over the surround and the hearth (white gouache), using a flat brush in the dry-brush technique.

9.32. Rough stone-slab fireplace (marker and watercolor)

Neoclassical fireplace (marker)

Step 1:

- Leave most of the surfaces white.

- Apply the base color (427T).

Step 2:

- Detail the shaded areas (420T).

- Detail the veining in the same color (420T).

- Apply the design details (Prismacolor Raw Umber, Dark Gray, and Dark Sepia pencils).

9.33a. Neoclassical fireplace (marker)

9.33b. Neoclassical fireplace (watercolor)

Neoclassical fireplace (watercolor)

Step 1:

- Plan the white areas.

- Apply the base color (Raw Sienna + Neutral Tint).

- Apply the darker values (Raw Sienna + Neutral Tint).

Step 2:

- Apply the darker values to the hearth.

- Add details (Raw Sienna, black, and white).

Offices

A business client certainly wants to see what its lobby or waiting room will look like, because this space makes a statement about what the company is. This is one of the most important business images presented to the community, clients, and guests. The lobby is usually the place where the company brand name and logo are clearly evident. For crisp and accurate line work in indicating letters, use drafting tools and circle and ellipse templates. It is much easier to draw letter forms and fill them in with color when a pencil is sanded to a chisel point or if a chisel-point marker is used. A small, flat brush works best with paint.

In an individual office illustration, it is good to show enough of the desk and file components to establish a basis for dialogue in your design presentation. Romance it a bit more with indications of the electronics and incorporate the equipment used. Why not also place a pear on the desk, as Teknion does in its product brochures?

9.34. *Brand sign (marker and white pen)*

9.35. *Graphics (colored pencil)*

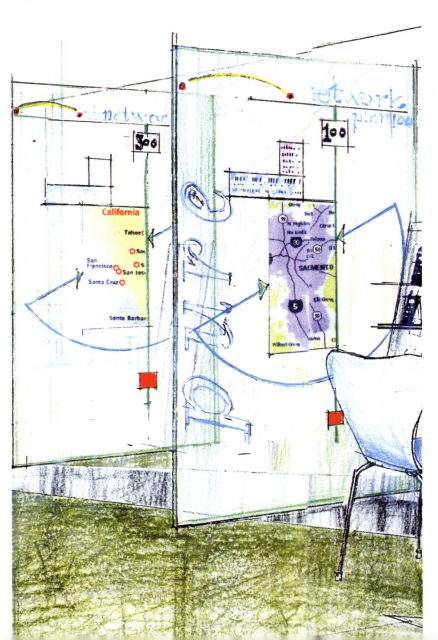

9.36. *Laptop and desktop computers (marker and white pen)*

Hospitality Spaces

The lobby, guest rooms, restaurant, ballrooms, and meeting rooms all may make an appearance in a hospitality presentation. An illustration may show a functional element, such as the registration seating group, and a dynamic design feature, such as elevator doors, a dramatic staircase, ceiling details, or perhaps a water feature. Also to be considered are people, plants, and tabletop items.

Here are a few techniques to use if you are illustrating a water feature or a back bar in a lounge. Figure 9.38 is a quick and easy technique to add gently falling water on top of any base illustration.

9.37b. Back bar (marker)

9.37a. Back bar (watercolor)

Light glazes in groups of color suggest glass and bottles on shelving.

Water wall

Step 1:

• Apply paint (white gouache) to indicate the falling water. Let it dry.

• Apply shade and definition, using the wall color; blues can signify a white background wall.

Step 2:

• Apply additional highlights (white pen).

9.38. Water wall (watercolor)

Still-water feature

Step 1:

- Apply the base color markers (c429T, 317T, 3105T, and 292T), using strokes with a gentle movement and fluidity in a horizontal direction. Do not be stiff.

- Because water gets its color from the setting, adjust the colors accordingly. This illustration represents a clear sky or blue color as in the sur-roundings. Use brown, green, and ochre if natural habitation is in the water.

- Allow the white paper to show in the areas of lightest reflection.

Step 2:

- Add the dark reflections (535T), making sure that they go straight down. Wavy vertical lines are used to show dark reflections in gently moving water. They may gradually fade out.

- Add the middle reflections (292T and 3105T), using the same techniques as above.

- Apply the light reflections (white gouache). The reflections begin on the water's surface and gradually diminish into the water.

9.39. *Still-water feature (marker)*

Multilevel water feature

Step 1:

- Apply the base colors for the falling water, allowing the white of the paper to show.

- Use loose, fading vertical strokes to express movement in the falling water.

Step 2:

- In the pool at the base of the waterfall, use scribbled marker strokes to express the water's movement. Allow a few loose scribbles to move up to the falling water.

- Make ripples in the distance closer together and smaller.

Step 3:

- If the water is falling fast, spatter paint (white gouache) across the base of the waterfall to indicate water spray or foam.

9.40. Multilevel water feature (marker)

Fountain

Step 1:

- This subject matter and technique work best on a rough-surface paper (Strathmore® Imperial watercolor paper was used here).

- Apply the first wash (Cobalt Blue) to the basic shapes of the water elements, using a large, round brush. Make swift, horizontal strokes, applying the paint in a back-and-forth motion for the pool of water.

- Using a dry-brush technique, apply vertical strokes for the high center water spray and strokes that curve outward from the center for the arched water sprays.

Step 2:

- Add blobs and sprays of white, following the direction of the water. Use a loose, dry-brush technique. Let it dry.

- Add the dark values (Cerulean Blue). Let it dry.

- If needed, repeat the step of blobs and sprays of white.

Step 3:

- Add spatter (white gouache and Cerulean Blue).

- For a fountain lit with colored lighting, use color in the white gouache.

9.41. Fountain (watercolor)

Merchandise must appear throughout a retail illustration, but special displays are a primary focal point. They are illustrated more prominently, as are any featured wall merchandise presentations. Clothing is indicated in groups of color, because it is often displayed in that manner and groupings keep the illustration from appearing too choppy. Suggest merchandise displays on tables. For fixture hardware, use a minimum amount of line detail, drawn in color and gouache lines and dabs; remember to use guides for straight lines.

To indicate glass case displays (see figure 9.44), render the values on the inside of the case to define surfaces and display forms; suggest merchandise with a small amount of detail; and add white gouache to the glass. Figures 9.45a, 9.45b, and 9.45c are representative of the amount of line detail to indicate for various types of merchandise displays.

The following are a few examples of retail displays for various types of merchandise, incorporating all of the relevant techniques—straight strokes, curved strokes, dabs, dots, and scribbles.

9.43a. Women's dresses, face-out bar, and accessory displays (watercolor)

9.42. Distant retail display (watercolor)

9.43b. Women's sportswear straight hang-bar display and electronic fashion show at a table (watercolor)

9.44. Storefront window jewelry display (marker and watercolor)

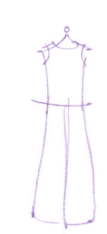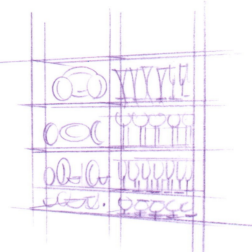

9.45b. *Display of dinnerware, glassware, folded towels, and women's shoes (nonprint pencil)*

9.45a. *Hanging and folded clothing (nonprint pencil)*

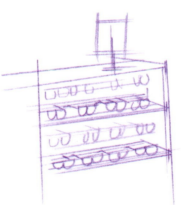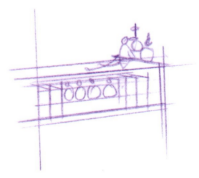

9.45c. *Eyeglass and cosmetics showcases (nonprint pencil)*

Assignments

1. Creation files. Research this chapter's topics for your creation files. Do not limit your sources to books and magazines, but also visit museums, galleries, public spaces (indoor and outdoor), shops, restaurants, and even a botanical conservatory. Take photographs where permissible, or sketch the subjects if photography is not allowed.

2. Picture hanging. Select a large painting and a sculpture from your creation files. Consider how each of these pieces of art would look if placed in a large office lobby. Study where you would place them, taking into account the surrounding materials. Illustrate the scenarios. (If you are a beginner without perspective drawing skills, trace the walls and floor in figure A.18, in the appendix.) Prepare simple vignettes presenting the wall, the floor, and the art. Remember to consider each vignette's outline in relation to its content, its surfaces, and its materials. Compose!

3. Contour drawing. Select four plant and flower illustrations from the appendix, and photocopy them. Chose a planter or a vase, and lightly draw it on the same photocopy. Place a sheet of vellum or drawing tissue on top. Working very quickly, draw the outline with a soft pencil or a marker. Trace it again on another tissue, drawing the contours and some detail, but leave out the lines on one side of the plant. Do this for all four subjects.

Using a photocopier, now make a few reductions and enlargements of the drawings on acetate or translucent paper. Lay each over one of your large room illustrations from a previous project (or over one in chapter 4). Move it around, considering where it might be placed to enhance the illustration. Keep these new drawings in your files for future use.

4. Line work. Look at the vase in the illustration on page 74. Its shapes include a triangle and a group of circles in an oval. This is a quick, minimal drawing technique often used as base line work for plants. Use the drawings in figure A.14 (in the appendix). Draw them again with shapes and arcs where the top of the arrangement ends. Illustrate the drawings, using only these shapes as your guideline.

5. Tabletop details. Mimic the details on top of the tables in figures 8.48 and 8.55. Add a bottle of wine to the vessel in figure 8.48 and wine in the glass in figure 8.55. Use paint, gouache, and white pen.

6. Darks and lights. Take several photographs of one pillow and a group of pillows, using several arrangements in different lighting conditions. (Turn the general lighting and the table lamps on and off in various combinations.) Convert the photographs to black and white or make photocopies. Look at the darks and the lights. In using them in an illustration, a simple gesture at the dark area will usually be enough to make the pillow read as a pillow. This situation research gives you more general information to refer to and then refine with particular design details in your future illustrations.

7. Human figures. Use any three figures in this chapter or those in A.15 (in the appendix). Trace them, and then resize a copy, as described in assignment 3 above. Study the colors to use for flesh tones and clothing, matching the colors to your own color matrix. Practice your illustration technique for the figures, using a loose, partial-color technique as well as a tight, full-color technique. Now try to illustrate the figures without line work.

8. Merchandise. Visit a specialty boutique and a mass-merchandise retail space. Notice the differences in merchandise presentation, and make notes in your sketchbook. Use figures 9.45a to 9.45c. Trace several copies of the drawings with a nonphoto or nonprint pencil. Practice your illustration technique.

"Enthusiasm is excitement with inspiration, motivation, and a pinch of creativity."

Bo Bennett (businessman, b. 1972)

By the end of your studies, your inner creativity and intuition will flow through you quite naturally. Trust it, let it challenge you, and let yourself be surprised by what it may suggest to you.

Materials and Textures

Special materials and textures—reflective glass and shiny metal, veined stone and grained wood, rough textures and woven textiles—call for special illustration techniques. The possibilities for success are endless when you experiment as well with different papers, media, and tools to fashion a distinctive material or texture. You will become a better illustrator if you tackle challenging assignments—such tests will ultimately increase your competitive edge in the job market.

Artistic interpretation of the Barcelona Pavilion (1928–29, Ludwig Mies van der Rohe) (watercolor)

Materials

Architectural and decorative materials are the building blocks of any interior design. Glass, wood, and stone as well as shimmering wall coverings, metallic bath fixtures, and painted surfaces likewise form the essence of any illustration. Shiny materials such as mirrors and silvery metals tend to reflect their surroundings, while pitted or veined marble requires an understanding of the material's basic structure. Granite can be rendered quickly with little more than paint spatters; wood grain is best indicated with markers. More techniques follow for materials you may want to specify.

Tip! The thickness of traditional glass block gives it a green appearance. Newer materials, however, eliminate that color factor. Adjust your base marker color by considering the color in the room and the colors behind the glass.

10.1. Glass block and art glass (marker)

Glass and Mirrors

Glass and mirrors, as well as clear plastic, are illustrated with similar colors and techniques (as is white metal, discussed later in this chapter); the amount of white paper, gouache consistency, and highlights will vary, however. Leaving white—to represent translucency and reflections—is key to rendering glass and mirrors. Plan white shapes in advance by masking areas to leave some white paper surface. If you lose the white space while applying color, you can go over it later with white gouache. Add more or less gray or blue to indicate pattern and values.

Glass block and textured glass have a moderate to heavy amount of refraction. Figure 10.1 shows several types of textures and surfaces. Study each, noting where the colors and values are applied. Marker colors include gray (427T), blues (290T and 317T), and green (351T); details were added in green or blue pencil.

Mirrored walls, a cliché of the 1970s, are a big challenge—but mirror is back, this time in furniture. Study figures 2.3, 2.5, 3.20, 3.24, and 3.25, noting the techniques used and the amount of reflection indicated. See also the mirror in figure 10.2a, where marker colors used include 552T, 317T, and B418; in 10.2b, the paint colors are Cerulean Blue and Neutral Tint. Add or use more gray if the blue is too dominant in the color composition.

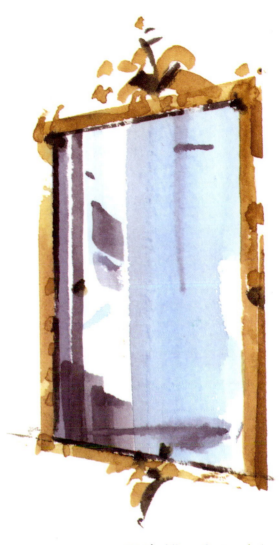

10.2a. Mirror (marker)

10.2b. Mirror (watercolor)

Traditional glass block

Step 1:

- Apply clear water to paper.

- Brush in the base colors (Ultramarine Blue, Sap Green, and Cerulean Blue), allowing them to blend into the wet paper and bleed into one another. Use a #24 flat brush. Let it dry.

Step 2:

- Brush in vertical strokes (Ultramarine Blue + Sap Green) to indicate the glass-block thickness, using a #12 flat brush.

- Repeat the above for the horizontal strokes.

- Sweep in a glaze (Sap Green + Cerulean Blue), using a ¾" flat brush. Let it dry.

Step 3:

- Add the grout lines (white pen or white gouache). Alternatively, you can add color lines with paint while the wash is still damp; the lines will be softer. Another approach is to paint the edge of a ruler, press it firmly onto the paper, and then lift it off quickly.

- Add line work (Grass Green pencil) for more definition of the grout and the glass thickness.

Glass and mirror shower enclosure

Step 1:

- Use the same techniques described for glass doors and windows (see figure 5.21).

- Plan the white areas, masking them if necessary.

- Achieve the glass effect with a series of blue and gray glazes (such as Cobalt Blue, Cerulean Blue, or Ultramarine Blue and Cobalt Violet + Neutral Tint).

- Remember to let the paper dry between each color glaze.

Step 2:

- Add reflection details and define the edges of the glass (white gouache).

10.3. Traditional glass block (watercolor)

10.4. Glass and mirror shower enclosure (watercolor)

Glass vanity basins

Green basin:

- Apply a series of pale green glazes for this thick, smooth glass, using simple gestures of color.

- Dab in some blue before the paint dries.

- Define the top edge.

- Dab in white gouache.

Blue basin:

- Apply a blue wash for this colored, textured glass.

- Spatter darker blue before the wash dries.

- Add dark blues to the top edge and the shaded areas.

- Spatter with white gouache.

- Dab in white paint, using a toothbrush.

10.5a. Vanity basin of thick, smooth glass (watercolor)

10.5b. Vanity basin of colored, textured glass (watercolor)

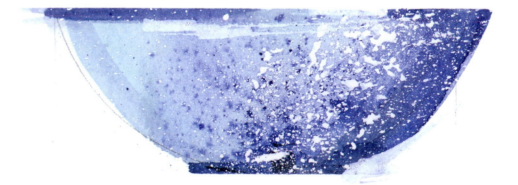

White Metals

Do not automatically pick up a gray marker to indicate a white-looking metal, such as aluminum, chrome, pewter, steel, or silver. Instead have some multicolor base colors at hand, and choose neutrals with blue or green tints, depending on the metal's warm or cool quality. Use a scribble technique, working markers wet into wet for a softer look. Think scribble, flood, and float.

10.6a. *White metal marker colors*

Blend white metal markers as shown below, including 1205T, 250T, 649T, 430T, 431T, Ice Gray 07, Ice Gray 06, B418, Ice Gray 03, process black, Cool Gray 11, 5425T, 5507T, 5545T, and 365T (left to right).

10.6b. *White metal paint colors*

Blend white metal paint colors as shown above, including Neutral Tint, Cerulean Blue, Cobalt Blue, and Cobalt Violet (left to right).

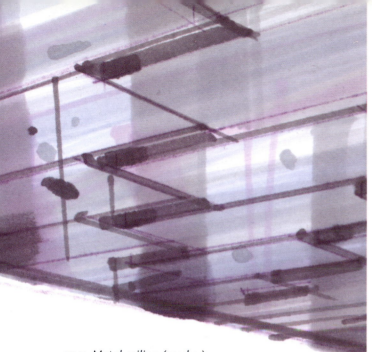

10.7. *Metal ceiling (marker)*

Metal ceiling

Step 1:

- Use a horizontal scribble technique, working markers wet into wet. Use colors 2707T, 427T, 5445T, and 430T.

Step 2:

- For the reflections, use vertical strokes (Pale Lilac or Mauve).

- For a satin finish (see figure 10.8), use a soft and blended color application (gradation of color to white). Leave the paper white for highlights.

Silver-leaf wall covering

Step 1:

- Flood in the base color (420T), using a scribble technique. Allow the colors to mingle together to create a shiny-looking surface.

- Scribble and flood in the next color (2706T) on top. Leave some yellow peeking through.

Step 2:

- Add square patches of the third color layer (649T).

- Apply a solid color (5445T) in the upper left section (in shade). Allow more base colors to show as you move toward the lower right section (in light).

Step 3:

- Add detail (Red and Indian Red pencils).

10.8. *Satin-finish aluminum surfaces (watercolor)*

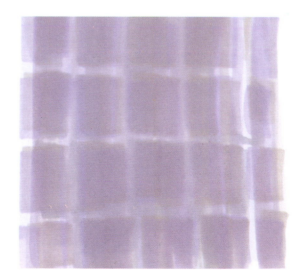

10.9. *Silver-leaf wall covering (marker)*

Warm Metals

Like silvery surfaces, warm metals reflect adjacent colors and have highlights, but they also have a strong tint of the metal color. Imagine illustrating this subject looking through golden- or bronze- tinted sunglasses. It is not a good idea to use metallic markers or paint for warm metals, because they actually reflect light and will pop out too much in the illustration.

10.10. Warm metal marker colors

Warm metal marker colors include Y919, Y217, Y417, 1205T, 141T, 468T, 4525T, 466Tt, 1205T, 4655T, 466T, and 2707T.

10.11a, b, and c. Warm metal paint colors

Warm metal paint colors can include (a) brass developed with Naples Yellow, Burnt Umber, and Raw Sienna; (b) more Burnt Sienna added to the previous colors; and (c) copper developed with Alizarin Crimson added to Naples Yellow, Burnt Sienna, and Burnt Umber (for the highlights, color can be lifted out with a damp, clean brush or a sponge).

Gold-leaf wall covering (marker)

Step 1:

- Scribble and flood in the base color (1205T).

- Scribble and flood in the next color (468T) on top. Leave some yellow peeking through.

Step 2:

- Add square patches of the third color layer (141T).

- Apply the solid color (141T) in the upper left section (in shade). Allow more base colors to show as you move toward the lower right section (in light).

Step 3:

- Add detail (Red and Indian Red pencils).

Gold-leaf wall covering (watercolor)

Step 1:

- Brush on the base color (Naples Yellow), using a flat brush.

- Brush in color for the square definitions (Burnt Umber), letting the base color peek through. Use a flat brush.

Step 2:

- While the paint is still wet, float in the medium and dark values (Burnt Umber and Raw Sienna), using a flat brush. Maintain the definition of a square grid when placing the brush strokes. Allow some of the base color to show at the edges.

- Apply a light violet glaze if necessary to key down the color.

- If there is a contrasting, darker color between or behind the gold-leaf squares, add it after the paint is dry (paint or colored pencil).

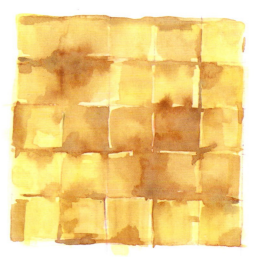

10.13. Gold-leaf wall covering (watercolor)

10.12. Gold-leaf wall covering (marker)

Marble and Granite

The pitted texture of any type of stone is typically illustrated with a series of watercolor glazes and spatter. Marbles include a wide range of veins, which look best as an overall pattern. Vary marker or brush strokes by rotating and turning the marker or the brush tip as the line is extended on the paper surface. Also vary the pressure, and allow strokes to fade away. By stopping midway through a stroke, you achieve nice dab puddles caused by changing direction. Granite is much easier and more fun: simply spatter various colors on top of the base colors.

Detailed marble

Step 1:

- First apply a base wash (Raw Sienna).

- Spatter Cobalt Violet before the wash is dry.

Step 2:

- Sponge out sections with a slightly damp sea sponge, which will leave water marks and lighter spots when dry.

- Spatter again.

- Scrape out some paint, using a palette knife dipped in the veining color.

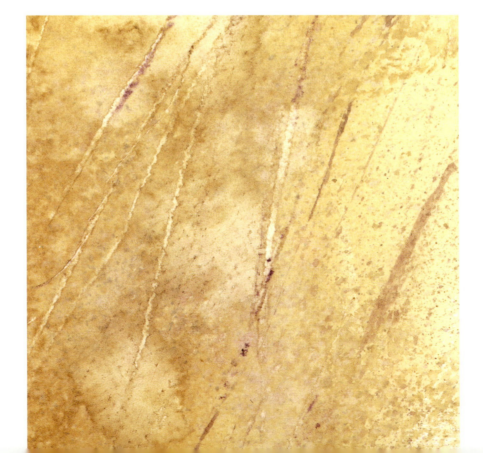

10.14. Detailed marble (foreground technique) (watercolor)

To detail marble with this technique is a time-consuming process to be used only in an illustration's foreground.

Quick marble and granite

Step 1:

- Apply the base color wash.

- Apply the value color glazes.

Step 2:

- Spatter.

- Apply grout lines (white pen). (See also figure 2.29, which shows a grout option detailed with a black pigment liner pen.) For a painterly grout line, use the imprint method: paint the edge of a ruler, press it firmly onto the paper on top of the grout lines, and lift it off quickly.

10.15. Quick marble and granite (basic technique) (watercolor)

Wood

Experimentation with color is the best way to study and develop a file of wood tones. Pencil, paint, and marker can be used to indicate wood grain. Try not to make the grain too fussy, because the illustration will look overworked. Wood is much easier to achieve with marker; the range of brown paints from the tube can look quite dull if not mixed with some violets. When trying to match a wood sample, you may have several studies that are not a match. Note the colors used, but do not toss these out because they may be useful in the future.

The following are some basic colors for wood, from which you can create variations.

Light wood

Markers

2706T
155T
134T
168T
263T
473T
492T
4655T
464T
469T
Warm Gray 03

Watercolors

Raw Sienna
Raw Umber
Neutral Tint
Cerulean Blue
Cobalt Violet

Dark wood

Markers

4655T
479T
4505T
168T
440T
469T

Watercolors

Burnt Umber
Payne's Gray
Quinacridone Violet

Pencils

Nougat
Burnt Ochre
Terra Cotta
Sepia
Dark Sepia
Gray
Black

10.16a. Color variations for wood (marker)

10.16b. Zigzag chair in basic light wood colors (marker)

This chair uses 162T, 155T, 263T, 468T, and 482T. Variations are Light Sand (AD Marker) and 527T; Y217 and 0727; Mauve or Lilac and 527T; and Light Sand and Cool Gray.

Wood grain indication

Step 1:

- To indicate grain using paint and pencil over marker, begin by applying the base color (Light Sand AD Marker).

Step 2:

- Scribble gray (Warm Gray 08) on top of the base color.

Step 3:

- For the grain, apply darker values (Dark Sepia and Nougat pencil), and blend with a marker blender.

- Apply the paint (Neutral Tint), using a fan brush.

10.17a. Wood grain indication (watercolor and pencil over marker)

10.17b. Wood grain indication (watercolor and pencil over marker)

Exotic woods

Zebra wood:

- Use a fan brush dipped in the colors to match the desired wood tones. Figure 10.18a illustrates a dry-brush technique, while figure 10.18b illustrates a wet-into-wet technique.

Burl wood:

- Use spatter or a large, dry brush to indicate the burl pattern. Figure 10.18c shows burl with a dry brush dabbed on the dry base color, while figure 10.18d shows spatter on a wet base color.

Satin wood:

- Apply wavy glazes on top of the dry base color.

Lace wood:

- Develop a burl surface, as described above. While it is wet, pull out the color with a damp brush or a cotton swab. Apply vertical strokes of a darker value in small sections, using a fan brush.

10.18a. Zebra wood (watercolor, dry brush)

10.18b. Zebra wood (watercolor, wet into wet)

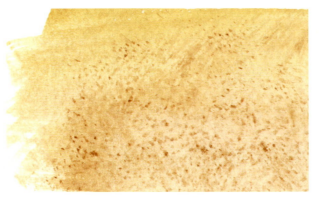

10.18c. Burl wood (watercolor, dry brush)

10.18d. Burl wood (watercolor, spatter into wet)

10.18e. Satin wood (watercolor)

10.18f. Lace wood (watercolor)

Additional Materials

Techniques such as spattering, scraping, sponging, and even rubbing a painted surface with sandpaper open paths to discovery. Caran d'Ache, for example, is a medium that allows you to simulate the brush strokes of oil paint like those in Julian LaTrobe's illustrations. Caran d'Ache and marker are used in figure 10.19 to achieve a soft effect for latticework around a panel door; in the study, rendered in a loose technique, the white and dark brown marks are Caran d'Ache. Be encouraged to try and experiment this way, practicing the materials that follow.

10.19. Lattice (marker and Caran d'Ache)

Rice paper wall covering

- Apply the base color wash.

- Before this wash is dry, immediately begin a scrape technique. Scraping creates dark marks first and then white strokes as the wash begins to dry.

10.20a. *Rice paper wall covering (watercolor)*

Corian surface

- Produce the Corian surface pattern with multiple layers of spatter, beginning with a fine application (white gouache).

- Next apply a color wash, but do not press too hard with the brush. The result is a milky-white spatter.

- Before the wash is dry, spatter again (white gouache).

10.20b. *Corian surface (watercolor)*

Sponge pattern

- Apply a base color wash.

- To create a sponge pattern for painted surfaces, apply paint to a sea sponge.

- Dab it on top of the base color wash to achieve the sponge pattern.

- Limit this technique, as it has a tendency to look contrived.

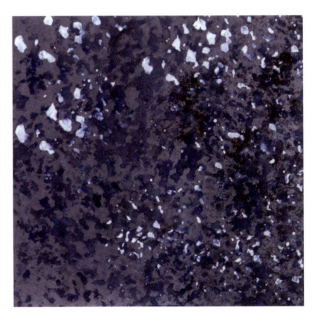

10.20c. *Sponge pattern for painted surfaces (watercolor)*

Fabric scrim

Step 1:

- Use layers of translucent watercolor glazes and the texture of the paper to create the effect of scrim panels. Do not place too much pressure on the brush while layering the paint, because it may lift up the previously applied colors.

Step 2:

- Paint the wall in the background. Let it dry.
- Next paint the middle-ground scrims. Let it dry.
- Finally paint the foreground scrim.

10.21. Fabric scrim (watercolor)

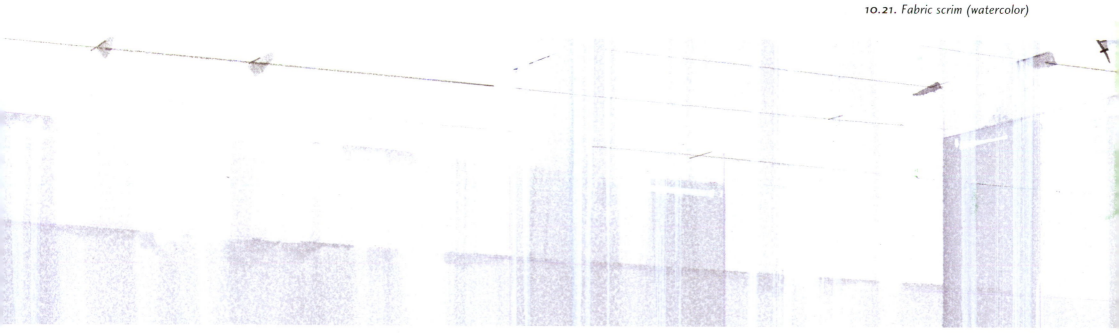

Textures

A highly textured surface is one of the most difficult features to render, yet such surfaces are often used in interior features and furnishings. Capturing shade and shadow will help make deep surface textures read. Designers often use direct light sources to emphasize textures. Rendering a texture's essence requires little detail. The difficulty is determining how to indicate it, what symbols to use, and how much detail to include.

Texture Techniques

Here is a simple warm-up to help develop your skills in seeing texture. You already know that squinting your eyes helps focus a subject's form, but squinting also helps highlight a texture's light and dark areas. How you see it in the lights and the darks is how you render it. Illustrate texture in a simplified manner within the light areas of your illustration and at the edges of the dark areas. This technique depends on where the light source is.

We do not want you to go around squinting all the time—it is not a lovely facial expression. Instead try changing or dimming the light to a level at which you cannot see all the detail; then look at your textured material sample to see the essential details. It helps to place the light source at a location similar to the light source in your illustration. A textured fabric may have no visible details at a very low or very high light level, excluding some texture definition at the edges. Do likewise in the illustration, placing the detail at the edge of a surface. Remember that it is easier to go back into the illustration to add more, but it is far more difficult to take it out later. Ludwig Mies van der Rohe's aphorism "Less is more" definitely applies here. Keep that in mind as you work on the following examples and when you develop illustrations for your own design projects.

10.22a. Cracked paint surface (wax crayon and watercolor)

Various aged paint surfaces with cracked, distressed, and pitted surfaces are often used on furnishings and interior surfaces.

Cracked painted surface

Step 1:

• Apply scribble strokes on the paper (white wax crayon or candle or a colored crayon to match your materials). The wax will resist the paint and reserve the white paper or color underneath.

Step 2:

• Apply a color wash (Raw Sienna) on top. Let it dry.

Step 3:

• Scrape the entire surface with a palette knife.

• To completely remove the wax residue, place an absorbent paper on top and press with an iron to absorb the wax.

Distressed or cracked surface

Step 1:

- Apply a light base wash (Raw Sienna). Let it dry.

Step 2:

- Use a scribble technique to apply masking fluid with a stylus (or a quill pen or a palette knife). Masking fluid is the preferred method for preserving a perfectly clean base color or a white paper surface. Let it dry.

Step 3:

- Apply another wash (Raw Sienna) on top. Let it dry.

- Lightly rub the masking fluid to peel it away.

Pitted surface

Step 1:

- Apply a color wash (Raw Sienna).

Step 2:

- Sprinkle sea salt on the surface while the wash is wet but not too shiny. Allow this to dry for at least ten minutes before removing the salt. Use table salt for a fine pattern or coarse salt for a larger-scale pattern. The salt absorbs the pigment and leaves a pattern on the paper. This is messy, so you may want to do it outside or over a sink or a towel.

Alternative:

- If you do not have salt on hand, press an even-textured paper towel on top of a wet wash and lift it off quickly. The result is a softer-looking pitted surface. (See this technique on the walls in the page 134 illustration.)

Tip! Your brush is ruined if the smallest amount of masking fluid is left on it. You can wrap your brush in a paper towel to paint over the masking fluid areas just in case a spot of masking fluid on the paper is not quite dry. Use a nylon-bristle brush to apply masking fluid, because it is easier to clean.

10.22c. Pitted surface (watercolor)

Use this technique for travertine and rough stone as well as textured glass and wall coverings.

10.22b. Distressed or cracked surface (watercolor)

Grass cloth

Step 1:

- Apply a light layer of dry wash (Raw Sienna).

Step 2:

- Apply a darker, dry-brush glaze (Raw Sienna) over the first layer to achieve the texture of grass cloth.

- Overlap the glazes, using a stroke applied in vertical and horizontal directions. Use a wide, flat brush or a fan brush. Use less moisture in the brush for a rougher-looking surface.

Alternative:

- Drag a comb filled with paint across the top of the first wash. (See this technique in the white areas of the center wall in the page 134 illustration.)

10.23. Grass cloth (watercolor)

Textured plaster or Silk Dynasty wall covering (Palazzo)

Step 1:

- Apply a beige base color (P137).

- Add the darker value and the burlap texture to indicate the wall covering's base material (466T).

Step 2:

- Add spatters and smudges (466T). Use uncontrolled marks, applied by bouncing the side of the nib on the paper.

- Create a dirty smudge by rubbing the marker or marker blender on a black area and then dabbing it on the sketch. This is sometimes called "pick-up" color.

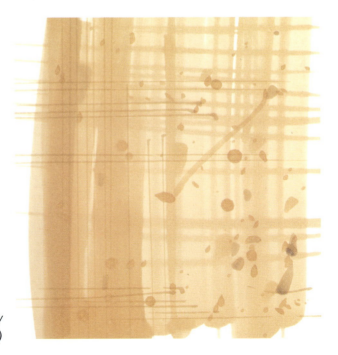

10.24a. Textured plaster or Silk Dynasty wall covering (Palazzo) (marker)

Raised surface textures

Step 1:

- Quickly scribble in the base color to indicate the desired surface, blending the marker while wet to achieve a gradual value change.

Step 2:

- Apply two more layers of dabs, waiting between layers. This will define the pattern and give the appearance of a raised surface.

- Add a dark shadow line to define the shape in some areas.

Alternative:

- Adjust the marker application to a patch-into-patch technique to achieve the texture in figure 10.24c, using wet base layers and dry final layers.

10.24b. Raised surface textures such as stamped metal, rubber flooring, or pebble stone (marker)

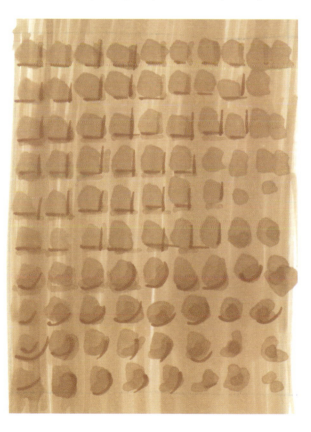

10.24c. Overlapping plaster surfaces (marker)

Marker resist techniques

Marker over pencil stick :

• Apply vertical and horizontal lines to the paper (white colored pencil or white pencil stick).

• Scribble a layer of marker color on top. The penciled areas will resist most of the marker, while the marker blends and softens the white lines underneath. This results in a fine, soft-looking, lighter texture.

Marker over wax candle :

• Use the same technique, but use a candle instead of a pencil. The candle creates a thicker line and results in a larger-scale texture with more dominance.

• Use textured paper to achieve interesting sparkling textures.

Marker over Caran d'Ache crayon :

• Use the same technique, but use Caran d'Ache crayon (white) instead of a pencil. Caran d'Ache crayon creates a varied texture, because the crayon marks resist the marker where the white lines have been applied with heavy pressure and blends where the crayon marks are applied using less pressure.

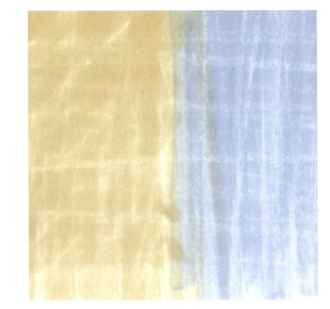

10.25c. Marker over white Caran d'Ache crayon

10.25a. Marker over white pencil stick

10.25b. Marker over wax candle

Resin panel with twigs

10.26. *Resin panel with twigs (marker)*

Step 1:

- Apply the base color (Y119).

Step 2:

- Add the next colors (Y217, Y216, and Y717), using a fine-point nib. Varying the pressure, start and stop the marker midway in the stroke to achieve dabs.

Watercolor alternative:

- Apply a base color wash. Let it dry.

- Apply some light strokes of clear water in one or two areas.

- Apply lines with the brush, varying the pressure. The result is a combination of sharp lines and soft feathered lines.

- For an even softer-looking subject, try painting with a palette knife.

Handpainted wallpaper

Step 1:

- Lightly flood in the marker (155T).

Step 2:

- While still wet, flood in another color (466T).

Step 3:

- Place strips of card stock underneath your paper, lining it up with the pattern direction. Do this so that the paper surface will be uneven when you apply the next step (a rubbing technique).

- Scribble lines with a water-soluble painting crayon (brown). Serrate the tip with a metal file, or use four pencils at a time. Apply the lines in vertical and horizontal directions. Use more pressure where the lines begin.

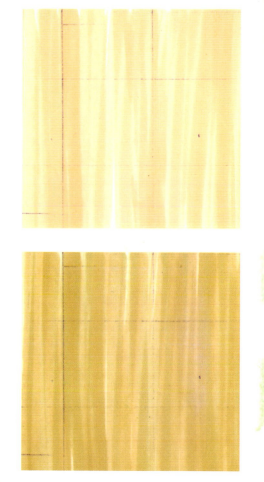

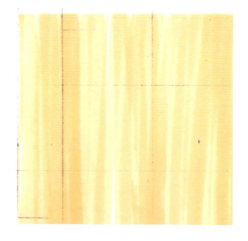

10.27. *Handpainted wallpaper (marker)*

Rough textures

10.28. *Rough bleed-through texture for stone, concrete, and numerous other materials (marker)*

Step 1:

• Apply the base color.

Step 2:

• Place a sticky note or a thin, uncoated paper on top.

• Scribble a marker on the sticky note, allowing the marker color to bleed through onto the paper below. The result looks like a rough texture.

Alternative:

• Recall the scumble strokes you painted with as a child to create the look of rough stone. Select an old brush because this technique can ruin a brush.

• Apply a base color wash.

• Load the brush with fairly dry paint, and then push it down on the paper until the ferule hits the surface (bristles are bent at a ninety-degree angle to the ferule). Twist and turn the brush in circular motions.

Fine texture

Step 1:

• This spatter technique uses markers over a multicolor base.

• Use Letraset or a similar marker paper. Uncoated paper will produce much more color bleed-through.

• Apply the base colors.

Step 2:

• Scribble a black marker on the back of the paper, which will produce a bleed-through that looks like spattered paint.

10.29. *Fine bleed-through texture (marker)*

Striations

Step 1:

- Select a fan brush or split the hairs on another brush.

- Put different paint colors on the brush all at once, or layer the colors one at a time on the paper.

Step 2:

- Apply a dry-brush technique to indicate tiny vertical, parallel grooves or multicolor fibers on walls or floors.

10.30. *Striations (watercolor)*

Metal Textures

Shiny surfaces reflect light and attract a viewer's eye, creating subtle color and pattern changes. Stainless steel, for example, will reflect surrounding colors from floors, ceilings, and walls. Metal textures are not prominent in an atmosphere of soft, diffused light. The metal colors will be the same as used for smooth surfaces, and base color applications are similar as well. The key is the final indication of detail to capture the texture to be illustrated.

Smooth and hammered-metal surfaces

Smooth metal basin:

- Paint the basin with light and dark glazes (Blue and Neutral Tint).

- Define the edge.

- Dab in white gouache.

- Detail the base (black).

Hammered-metal basin:

- Paint the basin with light and dark glazes (Blue and Neutral Tint).

- Define the top and the side edge.

- Use a spatter technique (Blue and Neutral Tint), applied while the base color is still wet.

- Detail the base with a dark value or black.

- Dab the surface, using a toothbrush dipped in a watery paint (white gouache), to soften some of the hard-edge spatters.

10.31a. Smooth metal basin (watercolor)

10.31b. Hammered-metal basin (watercolor)

Embossed stainless-steel elevator door

Step 1:

- For the base color marker application (290T), use the reflected colors from the surrounding walls, floors, and ceiling.

Step 2:

- Use grays (Ice Gray 10, Ice Gray 08, and Ice Gray 04) to indicate the stainless steel, working wet into wet or using a marker blender. The colors should have soft transitions between values.

- Choose a marker direction depending on the subject. Study actual materials or photographs of stainless steel for the selection.

Step 3:

- Add dabs of paint (white gouache) to indicate highlights.

- Indicate the dimples on the surface (gray, black, and white gouache).

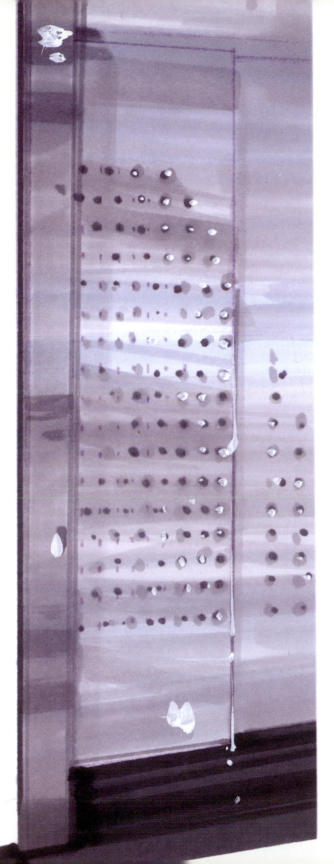

10.31c. Embossed stainless-steel elevator door (marker)

Stone Textures

Rough textures such as stone generally have a high visual weight and will appear to be closer to the viewer. The stronger the texture, the more it will influence a room's qualities. Impact also comes from the direction of the texture, as found in raw silk, brushed metals, marble veining, and wood grain.

10.32. Mosaic pebble tiles (watercolor)

Mosaic pebble tiles

Step 1:

• Concentrate the detail within an area that is part of a center of interest, so it has the most detail.

Step 2:

• Fade out the detail by painting wet-into-wet dabs that gradually fade into a value wash.

• Paint the soft-looking section wet into wet. Let it dry.

Step 3:

• Define the pebbles with dabs of color glaze at the center of interest

Concrete floor (marker)

Step 1:

- Plan the shadow and reflection areas.

- Use a scribble marker technique, working wet into wet. Scribble in the light yellow base color (Y919) at the reflection area adjacent to the shadow reflection.

- Add multiple layers of the second base color (Y217).

Step 2:

- Add texture (Y217), as described in figure 10.28.

- Define the joints, and detail the surface cracks (Y616).

10.33. Concrete floor (marker)

Concrete floor (watercolor)

Step 1:

- Use a series of color glazes to create the floor. The more color glaze applied to the paper for the concrete floor surface, the richer the texture created by this particular paper (Strathmore™ 500 Series illustration board, heavyweight plate).

- Drag, scrub, or smear the brush strokes on the paper as you work.

Step 2:

- Define the joints with fine lines (paint, pencil, or marker), using any line technique you have learned.

10.34. Concrete floor (watercolor)

Grainy textures

Painted concrete floor:

• To create a painted concrete floor as shown here, use Caran d'Ache over a marker base color. Somewhat opaque when applied over marker, Caran d'Ache can be used like a crayon to scribble and blend. It creates an interesting mood for a textured illustration.

• Vary the pressure or use multiple layers to achieve a wide range in appearance, from smooth to grainy.

Other textures:

• Use this medium over marker or paint base colors to achieve the look of broadloom carpet, suede, bouclé, or chenille textiles. Consider its use for wall textures as well.

10.35. Grainy textures (Caran d'Ache and marker)

Woven Fibers and Textiles

You will have a much cleaner illustration if you can capture the essence of a woven fiber or a textile by choosing the right paper, medium, and technique. With these in place, it will not be necessary to add too many layers of indication marks or media, which would result in an overworked or a muddy illustration. This is where your previous experimentation with paper and media techniques becomes a gold mine of reference material.

Rattan and cane

Basket-weave pattern:

• In the first of three slightly different methods for illustrating natural woven fibers, apply a base color (Cadmium Yellow + Raw Sienna + Raw Umber).

• Scrape out the paint (on the left) and add detail with a glaze of paint in the same color (on the right).

Twill pattern:

• Apply a base color (Cadmium Yellow + Raw Sienna + Raw Umber).

• Scrape out the paint in a twill-weave pattern.

10.36b. Twill pattern (watercolor)

Natural cane pattern:

• Apply several glazes (Cadmium Yellow + Raw Sienna + Raw Umber) in vertical, horizontal, and diagonal directions.

Marker alternative:

• To achieve the same textures with marker, add dabs and lines for texture instead of scraping it out.

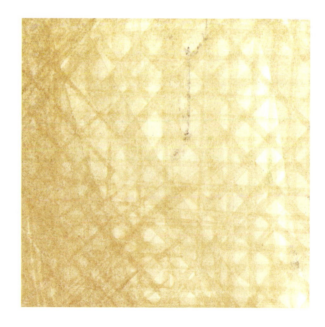

10.36c. Natural cane pattern (watercolor)

10.36a. Basket-weave pattern (watercolor)

Mesh, cane, and heavy woven fibers

Brush handles:

- Using a loose technique, scrape out the paint with either a brush handle or with the end of a brush handle (below left). An alternative is to scrape the paint onto the paper, using the end of a brush handle (below right).

10.37. Mesh, cane, and heavy woven fibers (watercolor)

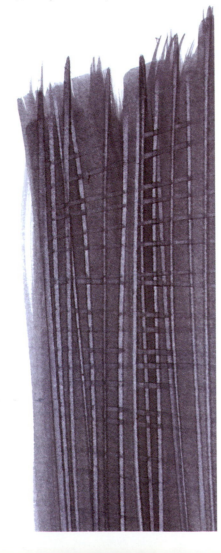

Alternatives:

- Experiment with other scraping tools, such as a trowel-shaped palette knife, a Popsicle stick, or your thumbnail.

- Create different patterns, for example, cross-hatching, hatching with parallel lines, wavy lines, and curly lines.

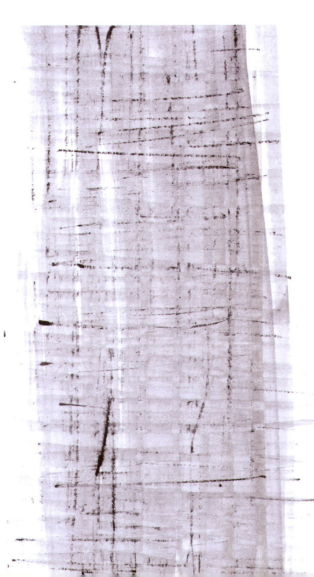

Raw-silk chairs

Step 1:

- Apply the base color and the deeper value layers for the upholstery.

- For the light chair, use marker colors 4535T, 4525T, and Cool Gray 09.

- For the dark chair, use Cool Gray 09, black, and black Caran d'Ache.

10.38. Raw-silk chairs (marker)

Raw-silk sofa

Step 2:

• Detail the horizontal weave and the slugs with a fine-point marker nib. Do not forget to leave white paper peeking through the lightest areas.

Step 1:

• Build up the values in marker layers (Cool Gray 01 and Cool Gray 04).

• Leave white at the top front edge of the seat cushion.

Step 2:

• Apply horizontal texture with a fine-point nib.

Tip! Do not toss out dried-up markers. A dry marker leaves white texture showing through the marker color, so it can be used to achieve material surface qualities.

10.39. Raw-silk sofa (marker)

Suede, mohair, velvet, velour, corduroy, chenille, and bouclé chairs

Suede, mohair, velvet, or velour:

- Use a slightly dried-out marker, keeping the color application (R566 and 180T) the lightest where the surface turns into the light source.

- If you do not have dry markers, try removing some of the color with sandpaper to create the highlights. Use sandpaper only on heavy paper or board.

Corduroy:

- Use the same technique.

- Add darker lines in the direction of the pattern. Allow them to go slightly beyond the edges to help the surface depth read.

Chenille or bouclé:

- Use the same technique.

- Add stipples and fine curly lines.

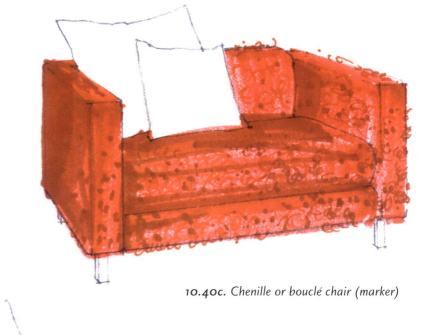

10.40c. Chenille or bouclé chair (marker)

10.40a. Suede, mohair, velvet, or velour chair (marker)

10.40b. Corduroy chair (marker)

Satin-upholstered chair

Shiny materials usually have contrasts between
highlights and dark values. Here bright whites
and sharp dark values (Raw Sienna, Burnt Umber,
and Burnt Sienna) create a convincing shiny
satin surface.

10.41. *Satin-upholstered chair (watercolor)*

Assignments

1. Take a bow. Render the same chair you illustrated in chapter 8, assignment 1. Retrieve the envelope containing this previous rendering, and then ask a friend to come by. Open the envelope, and compare the two chairs. You worked hard— you deserve to show off your work to your friends.

2. Materials. Study the colors of glass, mirror, metal, stone, and wood. Test colors in marker and watercolor, along with appropriate techniques. Experiment with colors and strokes to see which gives you the greatest feeling for the material.

Begin with reflective materials. Choose two subjects with shiny or highly reflective qualities, such as polished dark granite, a mirrored table, or a glass surface. Study them in different lighting conditions. Very shiny materials usually have contrasts between highlights and dark values. Highly reflective surfaces are appropriate to illustrate with more white, but remember that including too many reflections breaks up the shape or the surface too much, so the rendering will not read well.

Next practice your techniques for the remainder of the materials.

3. Involve your viewer. The tactile and visual textures of materials engage curiosity. Experiment with ways to illustrate a material to get the greatest feeling for it. Choose three materials that may have solids and voids, lines from straight to curved, or coexisting vertical and horizontal directions or that may be smooth, rough, fine, coarse, even, uneven, matte, glossy, light, dark, brilliant, dull, warm, or cool. Practice your techniques for these materials, experimenting with colors and strokes to see which creates engagement and curiosity for a viewer.

4. Plant a seed. Be a self-initiator to observe, experiment, and learn. Research classes or workshops that can make you a better designer and illustrator, such as studio art courses in drawing, painting, sculpture, experimental textiles, and so forth. You are not required to enroll in a class for this assignment, but you are encouraged to do so as soon as it is possible.

5. Spatter. Try new tools to create spatter. Use Bristol board or a rigid paper. Test different brush sizes, and experiment with varying the amount of water and paint in your brush. Try a quick and forceful brush motion in applying the paint to create a splash line. Test the same techniques on wet paper. Try different papers, including those with smooth and textured surfaces. Try different media, and develop soft gesture marks on each paper surface. Charcoal pencils, watercolor, water-soluble pencils, and soft pastel chalk give you soft effects, merging with the paper surface to create atmospheric qualities. Experiment further by mixing these media with marker and watercolor base colors.

6. Textures. Select four textured materials that can be illustrated with the techniques described in assignment 5 above, including at least two furniture items. Determine the color and the value to use. Manipulate the color and value patterns, using the techniques learned. Illustrate the materials by tracing any three drawings from this book, or create your own.

7. Architectural elements. Illustrate three architectural surfaces—such as a wall, a ceiling, or a floor—made of three different textured materials. Trace any three drawings from this book, or create your own.

8. Inspiration. Do you have some thoughts about a new technique that is not covered in this book? Illustrate your inspiration. There it is—your personal style. Illustration is no longer elusive for you; instead it is your advantage. Great work.

"There are painters who transform the sun to a yellow spot, but there are others who with the help of their art and their intelligence, transform a yellow spot into the sun."

Pablo Picasso (1881–1973)

By now you must see marked changes in your illustration ability, achieved through metamorphosis and transformation. Perhaps you don't quite feel like a butterfly yet. If not, look at your early illustrations, before you started the studies in this book, and compare them to your latest. Now think again about your butterfly state— because you no doubt have remarkable proof of the changes.

Patterns

The work of Jeremiah Goodman, Julian LaTrobe, and Robert Martin shows a talent for suggesting just enough of a pattern to communicate a space's personality. With pattern, the goal should be credible indication, rather than total accuracy. You are creating illustrations to use as a sales tool, not a construction document. Keep pattern suggestions believable, make them resemble the actual color sample, and be sure that the pattern scale is correct.

Upholstered side chair with a large-scale floral pattern (watercolor)

Pattern Repeats

Knowing the repeat dimensions of your textile or carpet will help you illustrate your pattern in perspective. To correctly indicate a pattern, lay out a grid on your line drawing similar to that of your selected design. The grid lines must follow the vanishing points of the perspective and be measured according to the repeat dimensions. Take your time to make the drawing correct. In the case of furniture or drapery, it is helpful to have a large memo sample to drape in folds or to wrap on the arm and the seat of a chair.

All-over Patterns

A popular trend in pattern is the very large-scale, highly stylized all-over patterns that are arranged in a random match. Most often you will see a tossed layout, in which flowers or other design elements are scattered randomly across the pattern repeat, as shown in figure 11.1. Because large-scale patterns create a dramatic statement, it is important to determine the pattern placement in advance. A beautifully illustrated chair such as the one in the illustration on page 362 is best placed in the foreground of a rendering or as part of its center of interest.

11.1. Drapery with a tossed layout (watercolor)

Spaced Patterns

A spaced pattern repeat has an ordered placement and usually follows a basic grid. Traditional layouts of spaced patterns include square (basic or block), brick, half-drop, diamond, ogee, and scale:

- **Square:** stripes or a gridlike pattern

- **Brick:** every second row shifts halfway horizontally

- **Half-drop:** a design repeated halfway down the side in a vertical direction

- **Diamond:** a pattern arranged along diagonal lines

- **Ogee:** an onion-shaped grid pattern motif

- **Scale:** a fish-scale pattern of alternating rows in a scalloplike design

Always look closely at the direction of a pattern repeat, because not all are right side up. Some can go both up and down, up and down and left and right, or in all directions. Spaced grids of the basic repeats form invisible lines for the placement of repeat units. The backs of fabric tags indicate the dimension of the repeat in inches. Use it to place your lines on a wall, drape, or furniture item.

Perspective foreshortening occurs on the seat top, arm top, and sides of the chair in figure 11.2. The grid lines follow the perspective lines. It is not typical to illustrate as much detail as is shown in this plaid pattern. A more appropriate solution is to fade the pattern as it recedes, as in figure 11.3.

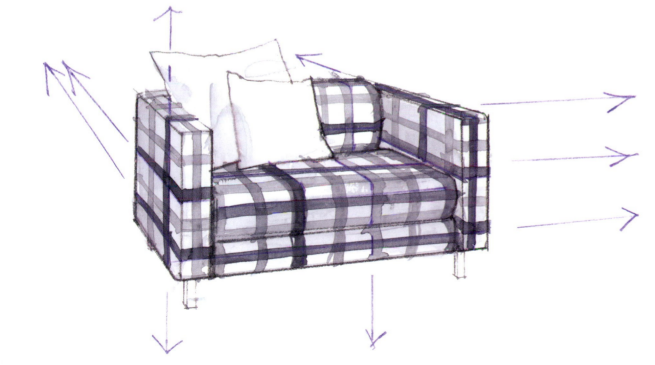

11.2. Chair with a spaced pattern repeat, showing a basic grid layout in perspective (watercolor)

11.3. Chair with a large ogee-pattern repeat, representing the amount of pattern detail to illustrate (marker)

Textiles

Remember that high and low levels of light will have the effect of washing out a pattern. Try lighting your textile samples in reduced light so you cannot see all of the detail. This will help you determine how to simplify the amount of detail in the illustration. Another modifier is to light one side of the sample with bright light. As you did in the warm-up suggestions in chapter 10, decide what is most important to include in an illustration.

Upholstery

"Colors have their own distinctive beauty that you have to preserve, just as in music you try to preserve sounds," said Henri Matisse. "It is a question of organization, of finding the arrangement that will keep the beauty and freshness of the color." Keep this in mind when choosing colors for patterns.

When illustrating chairs with curved arms, such as those in figure 11.4, note that the arm pattern should be rendered with minimal to no pattern detail; the pattern fades as it meets the curve of the arm.

11.4a. Upholstered armchair with an all-over, tossed pattern repeat (watercolor)

11.4b, 11.4c, and 11.4d. Upholstered armchairs with plaid and gingham patterns with a basic grid repeat (watercolor)

Bottoni sofa with a patterned seat and a plush back (Marcel Wanders)

Step 1:

• Apply the base color (Neutral Tint + Raw Umber) to define the values and the form, using a flat brush.

Step 2:

• Develop the back of the sofa (Yellow Ochre + Sap Green), using a flat brush.

Step 3:

• Add the pattern definition (Neutral Tint + Raw Umber), using a small, round brush.

• Add the darker pattern areas (black or Neutral Tint).

11.5. Bottoni sofa with a patterned seat and a plush back (Wanders) (watercolor)

Side chair with floral upholstery and a painted wood frame

Step 1:

• Apply the fabric's base color (Naples Yellow).

• Develop the values (Raw Umber).

• Add the highlights (Aureolin).

• Apply the base color of the frame and the legs (Neutral Tint), leaving some white.

Step 2:

• Develop the flower pattern (Quinacridone Rose + muddy palette color).

• Develop the leaves and the stem patterns (Green and Yellow).

Step 3:

• Develop the values of the flowers (Dark Red).

• Develop the values of the greens (Dark Green).

• Develop the frame and leg forms with darker values (Red and Neutral Tint).

11.6. *Side chair with floral upholstery and a painted wood frame (watercolor)*

Armchair with printed animal-hide upholstery and a light wood frame

Step 1:

- Apply the Brick Beige base color layer (9181) for the chair frame.

- Develop the values (2706T).

Step 2:

- Apply the base color (430T) for the pattern.

Step 3:

- Define the pattern (black). Do not cover the pattern's base color at the top front edge of the seat.

11.7. *Armchair with printed animal-hide upholstery and a light wood frame (marker)*

11.8. *Armchair with animal-hide upholstery and a light wood frame (watercolor)*

Watercolor achieves good texture quality and color blending for animal hides.

11.9. *LC1 chair with animal-hide upholstery (Le Corbusier) (watercolor)*

For hide patterns, a large spatter technique, wet into wet, helps blend the irregular shapes. Simple spatter works best for small-scale hide patterns and looks less overworked.

Linens and Drapery

Linen and drapery patterns are simple to illustrate as long as you plan ahead with a sketch of the pattern before you apply color. The sketch can be placed under the paper or traced onto the paper. Either way it will help you follow the basic pattern of the textile repeat. Often a simple shape such as a circle or a square (as seen in figures 11.10a and 11.12) is enough to help you place the pattern with your marker or brush within it.

11.10a. Random-match pattern repeat (Summertime by Brunschwig & Fils) (mixed media)

A random-match pattern such as this is fairly easy to illustrate if it is sketched in before color is applied. More of the pattern is illustrated in the forward sections, while it fades into the ground cloth as it recedes. The top surface pattern has minimal indication because of the foreshortening.

11.10b. Striped pattern repeats (marker)

A pattern with direction, such as a stripe, will curve around draped folds and change direction or will become offset to the adjacent fold. This principle applies to bed linens as well as tieback drapes and swag drops.

Like upholstery, these patterns follow the same perspective principles as to light, fading into shadows and folds, and dissipation when changing direction. There is no hard and fast rule concerning which media to use, because the choice has more to do with your skill level in handling each. Pattern indication is achieved with many combinations of blots, dots, dabs, and scribbles. Do not forget that you can also scrape or brush away a painted surface for the desired effect.

11.11. Bedding with a striped repeat (marker)

The stripes are vertical at the front and turn on the top edge, following the direction to the vanishing point, from front to back, of the head of the bed.

11.12b. *Drapery folds with a tossed pattern (watercolor)*

This random pattern has a tossed, small-leaf design. Focus on scale and fading the pattern design indication.

Tip! *If you do not have a light box for tracing, tape the illustration to a window in daylight.*

11.12a. *Drapery folds with a leaf pattern in a diamond pattern repeat (mixed media)*

When rendering patterned drapery with folds, the pattern should skew slightly and dissipate as it turns toward the inside folds.

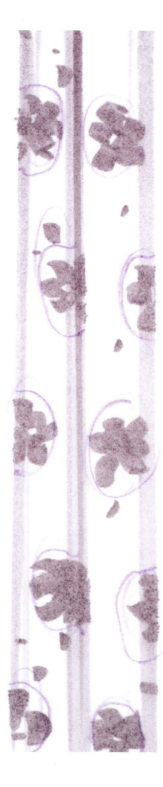

11.12c. *Drapery folds with a floral pattern (marker)*

To indicate the patterns on the drapery folds, loosely draw a circle, a square, a diamond, or an ogee where the dominant shapes occur. Some will show only partially. Mask each side of the fold with a piece of tape before you indicate the pattern. The tape helps keep a hard edge where the pattern disappears into the fold.

11.13. *Drapery with a striped pattern (watercolor)*

This horizontal-stripe pattern has a vertical repeat dimension. Draw it in the correct scale with light lines before adding the color. The stripe changes perspective as it returns into the inside fold. Because folds do not always fall perfectly from top to bottom, it is best to fade out the pattern in those areas.

11.14. *Drapery with a geometric pattern (marker)*

Here a gridlike square repeat with alternating color is placed offset to the adjacent fold of the drapes.

11.15. Drapery with a loose pattern (watercolor)

In this quick technique, the folds and the pattern do not have well-defined pattern indications or boundaries, but the values are placed to create overall shade and shadow.

Walls

Henri Matisse used decorative patterns and motifs to dissolve spatial boundaries in his art, lending his work a balance between areas of line drawing and areas of paint. We do not normally go that far with our illustrations, but Matisse's color and technique are splendid examples for learning how to indicate pattern. In his painting *Odalisque in Red Trousers* (1922), the wall patterns are reduced to glorious brush strokes of color. Use a little bit of the Matisse in you.

Tossed-pattern wall and upholstery

Step 1:

• Apply the base color (Naples Yellow).

• Apply the values (Naples Yellow + Quinacridone Rose).

Step 2:

• Detail the design (Rose pencil). Although a tossed layout has a random match, it is still important to locate the elements as you want them to be.

• Detail the wood (Faber-Castell Albrecht Dürer 8200-178 Nougat pencil).

11.16. *Tossed-pattern wall and upholstery (watercolor)*

Patterned wall covering

Step 1:

- Flood in the base wall color (c919), working wet into wet, and apply gradation from dark to light.

Step 2:

- Plan the pattern detail on a tissue overlay.

- Place the tissue under the illustration. If it helps you see the lines better, use a light box under the tissue and the drawing.

Step 3:

- Detail the pattern (white gouache) in an area with the medium-value background, using a round brush. Fade the pattern in the dark and light background areas.

11.17a. Patterned wall covering in a contemporary damask style, including a lighter gradation on the right side that could be used to represent a sheer-pattern textile (marker)

11.17b. Matching patterned pillows in a contemporary damask style, featuring white pigment on linen (marker and watercolor)

Tip! Loosely indicate intricate patterns of walls and textiles. Allow them to fade in and out so they do not dominate an illustration.

11.18. Patterned wall covering and matching drapes (watercolor)

Keep in mind that in room backgrounds, overall color is more important than detailed pattern.

11.19. *Random all-over naturalistic pattern (watercolor)*

Naturalistic fantasy patterns such as this wall and chair fabric by Tord Boontje can be reinterpreted freely with dots, dabs, and scrolling lines. The floral area carpet design by Emma Gardner has planned perspective foreshortening but is also illlustrated freely.

Floors

For floor patterns, concentrate on illustrating the beautiful detail in an illustration's foreground, showing more detail and larger pattern there. Remember that furniture will cast shadows and that the pattern detail diminishes as the floor covering recedes. Know beforehand where you are going to place the pattern detail in a way that is representative of the design. How the pattern is placed in the overall room shape is important both as visual information for the client and as a technical aid for the designer in the construction-document phase.

Carpet

Adding a touch of artistic interpretation to a carpet pattern will enhance an illustration. When you make slight modifications to the color, mix beautiful darks to place by whites, and cast a dramatic shadow silhouette of a chair, your work will encourage people to explore and imagine what is inside such a beautiful interior.

Broadloom carpet with a loop pile in a linear geometric pattern

Step 1:

• Apply the base color (Y919).

• Layer the color (Y417) on the background.

Step 2:

• Define the foreground pattern (Y217).

• Define the background pattern (Y717).

Step 3:

• Deepen the values (Y717), and blend the pattern into the background.

11.20. Broadloom carpet with a loop pile in a linear geometric pattern (marker)

Broadloom carpet with a loop texture in a geometric pattern

Step 1:

• Apply the base color (Cool Gray 02).

Step 2:

• Apply the medium value (Cool Gray 03).

• Dab in the yellow accent color (Y919).

Step 3:

• Dab in gray colors (Ice Gray 06, Ice Gray 03, and Cool Gray 03).

• Blend in the background (Cool Gray 03).

11.21. Broadloom carpet with a loop texture in a geometric pattern (marker)

Patterned wool Berber carpet

Step 1:

- Apply the base color (Y119).

- Apply the medium value (O729).

- Apply the dark value (Y217).

Step 2:

- Define the plaid pattern grid (Y119 and Y217).

Step 3:

- Define the plaid pattern grid with the second set of plaid colors (155T and 134T).

11.22. *Patterned wool Berber carpet (marker)*

Tweed broadloom carpet

Step 1:

• Scribble back and forth with a very broad nib for the base color (20% Cool Gray).

• Apply the tweed pattern with the same stroke (20% Cool Gray), using the tip of the broad nib. This creates a finer line with interesting variation.

Step 2:

• Apply the tweed pattern with the same stroke (30% Cool Gray), using the tip of the broad nib.

• Repeat the above (40% Cool Gray).

• Repeat the above (50% Cool Gray).

11.23. Tweed broadloom carpet (marker)

Ribbon-pattern printed or sculptured carpet

Step 1:

- Apply the base color (30% Cool Gray), using a scribble technique.

- Apply colorless masking fluid to the ribbons, which will appear as the lightest value. Let it dry. (Remember that masking fluid may yellow coated bond paper within a few days.)

- Apply deeper values (30% Cool Gray), using the scribble technique.

- Remove the masking fluid by rubbing it with your finger. The result will be light gray ribbons on a medium gray base color.

Step 2:

- Draw darker ribbons (40% Cool Gray) with the tip of a broad nib.

- Add the deeper, overall value at the back (40% Cool Gray).

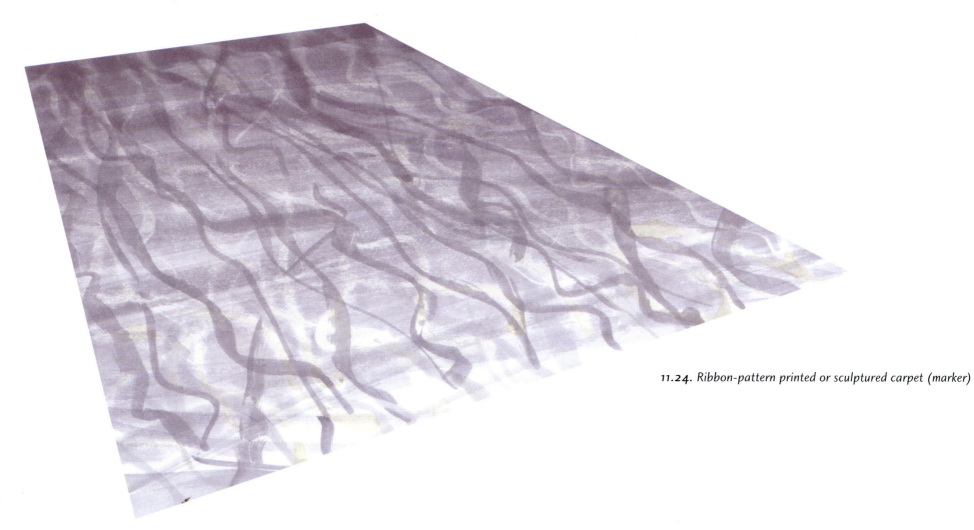

11.24. Ribbon-pattern printed or sculptured carpet (marker)

Circular-pattern printed or sculptured corridor carpet with a border

Step 1:

- This is a good subject with which to practice circular patterns in perspective.

- Apply the base color washes (Payne's Gray + Peach Black), using a large, flat brush.

- Apply the deeper values, suggesting circular forms with a deeper value.

- Paint long, curved lines with a damp angular brush to pull out the color. Let it dry.

Step 2:

- Lightly draw the grid lines. Then lightly draw circular forms in each square. Finally draw light guidelines of the patterns with an ellipse guide.

- Paint in the circular and leaf patterns (Payne's Gray + Peach Black), using a small, round brush.

Step 3:

- Tape the edges. Apply the border (Peach Black), using an angular brush.

- Spatter for more texture. Let it dry.

11.25. Circular-pattern printed or sculptured corridor carpet with a border (watercolor)

Wood

Concentration and a steady hand are a must for illustrating highly detailed wood flooring in a tight technique. Straight lines and crisp edges are achieved through masking. An artist's bridge is your best friend to guide and steady your hand or brush. When rendering a dark floor, the base color may cover up all of your pattern line work. Plan ahead. Use white or colored transfer paper and trace the line work on top of the base color.

There are several ways to achieve the desired effect of a patterned wood floor; one is shown in the illustrations that follow. Another way, as can be seen in the page 134 illustration, is by applying a vertical base color and then applying the pattern detail line work on top. Study the pattern indications in figures 3.30 and 3.31, which present a minimal technique for suggesting wood patterns in a beautiful way.

Wood parquet pattern with inlays

Step 1:

• Apply the base colors (Y119 and Buff).

• Apply the light grid color (O527), reducing the lines as they recede in perspective.

Step 2:

• Apply the dark grid color (168T) in the center of the previous grid lines. Add small squares of color where they intersect.

• Tape each section as you apply the wood color variation (Light Sand AD Marker and Buff) and the parquet direction.

Step 3:

• Add detail (Nougat pencil and white pen).

11.26. Wood parquet pattern with inlays (marker)

Intricate wood parquet floor

Step 1:

- Apply the base colors (O819 and Y119).

- Add the medium value (Y217).

Tip! Skip the step of indicaing wood grain on a parquet floor with highly intricate wood inlay detail.

Step 2:

- Lightly draw the pattern grid lines.

- Indicate the dark geometric inlays (O727). Fade the detail in the background.

- Detail the geometric inlays in the foreground (Dark Sepia pencil).

- Lightly draw the intricate curvilinear design and add the details (Nougat pencil).

11.27. *Intricate wood parquet floor (Palace Pallavicini, Vienna) (marker)*

Black herringbone-pattern wood floor

Step 1:

- Mask each section on the left and the right, individually rendering each. Sections should follow two different 45-degree vanishing points.

- Apply the base colors (Cool Gray 07, Cool Gray 09, and Cool Gray 11). (See figure 6.0 for an alternative watercolor technique.)

Step 2:

- Apply the dark values (black) to the distant wood planks.

- Apply horizontal strokes (Cool Gray 09) to the background to make the floor look level.

Step 3:

- Define the wood grain in the foreground and add lines where the planks meet (black pencil).

- Add highlight lines (white pencil).

11.28. Black herringbone-pattern wood floor (marker)

1. Freedom. With a medium of your choosing, mimic the area carpet in figure 3.20, the flooring and area carpet in figure 3.30, and the window drape and the furniture in figure 3.31.

2. Inspiration. Using a gray brush-tip marker, trace a few pattern designs on furniture, walls, and drapery images found in design magazines. This will help you see, develop the technique gestures, and use your own imaginative interpretation. Save these studies for your creation files.

3. Perspective. Render figure 11.2 to help understand the pattern's perspective direction. Trace several copies of figure A.11 (in the appendix) with a nonphoto or nonprint pencil. Select a stripe and a floral textile sample. Study the textile to determine the repeat size. On the chair draw guidelines for the repeat dimensions in perspective. Illustrate the chair's pattern.

4. Windows. Illustrate three window coverings in three different patterned textiles. Trace any three drawings from this book, or create your own. This exercise will help you see, develop appropriate gestures, and use your own imaginative interpretation.

5. Walls. Illustrate three walls in three different patterned materials. Trace any three drawings from this book, or create your own.

6. Floors. Illustrate three floor surfaces in three different patterned materials. Trace any three drawings from this book, or create your own.

7. Furniture. Illustrate three pieces of furniture covered with three different patterned textiles. Trace any three drawings from this book, or create your own.

"Do not quench your inspiration and your imagination; do not become the slave of your model."

Vincent van Gogh (1853–90)

Patterns do not have to be overly precise in their amount of detail—you do not have to become the slave of your pattern. Instead use your own creative interpretation. Have you noticed a personality in your illustrations that reveals your unique rendering style? It is exciting to see your passion and your illustration ability take you to the pinnacle of your interior design imaginings. Really great work!

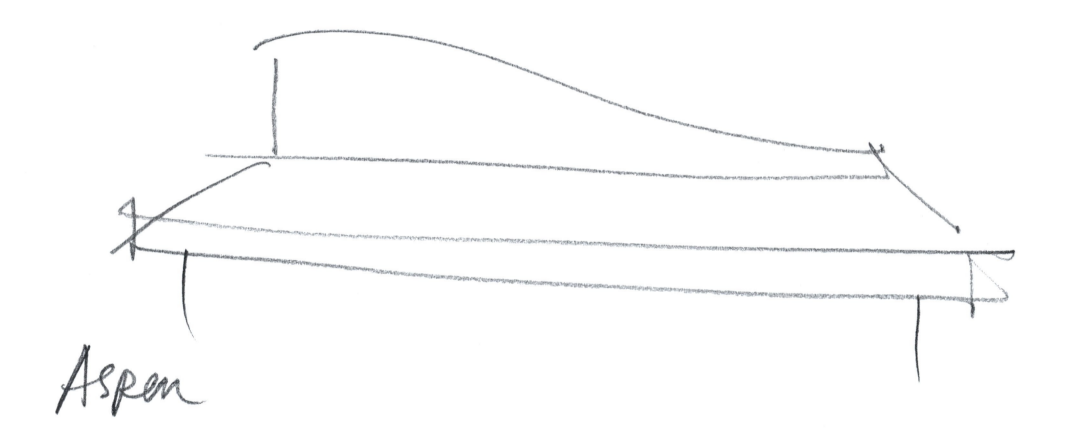

Aspen

Minimal line drawing of Aspen Sofa (Jean Marie Massaud) (pencil)

Tracing File

This tracing file is a collection of drawings to trace or copy for practice exercises or to use for reference. It is best to trace these items with your own drawing hand so you can develop a technique of your own and hone your drawing skills. When tracing the drawings, try a lively and light technique if it reflects the design's spirit, as seen in the line drawing on the opposite page. If you prefer to use a photocopier, reproduce the drawings on paper suitable for either marker or watercolor. You will achieve much better results, and the markers will not dry out prematurely. The enhancement elements included here will bring your illustrations to life and give your presentations more impact.

"Matisse said that when he drew something, he had to be able to do it with his eyes closed. For example, he drew Saint Dominic, over and over with his eyes closed, until he felt he possessed his subject."

Sister Jacques-Marie (Monique Bourgeois)
(1921–2005)

Walls

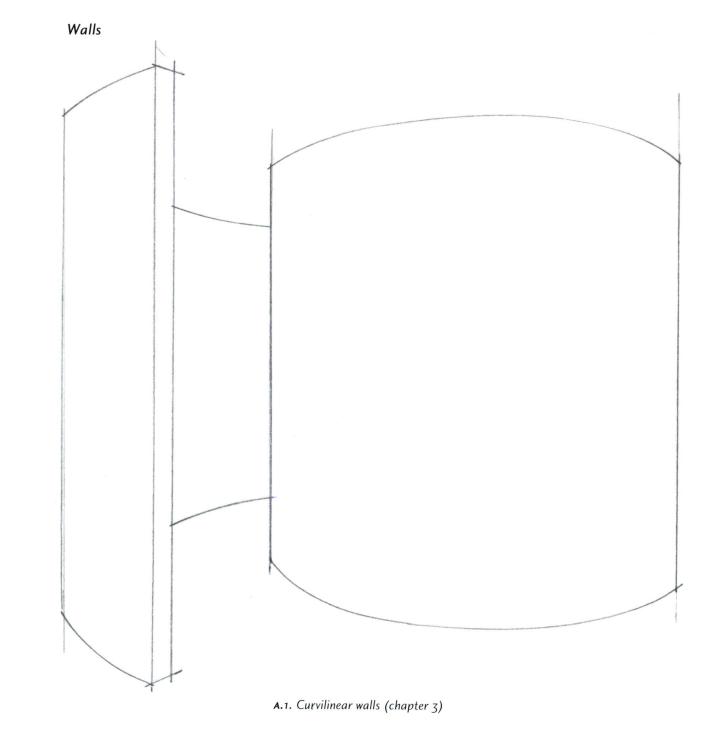

A.1. *Curvilinear walls (chapter 3)*

A.2. *Marble wall (chapter 6)*

A.3. *Wall mural (chapter 6)*

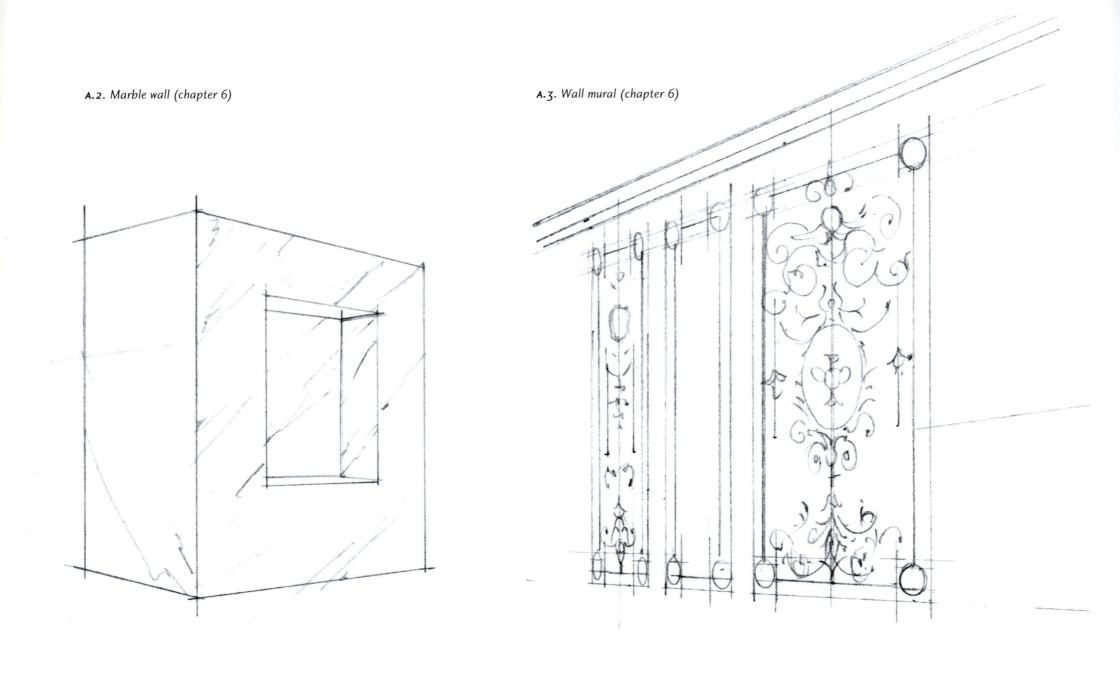

A.4. *Tieback drapes (chapter 6)*

A.5. *Drapery (chapter 6)*

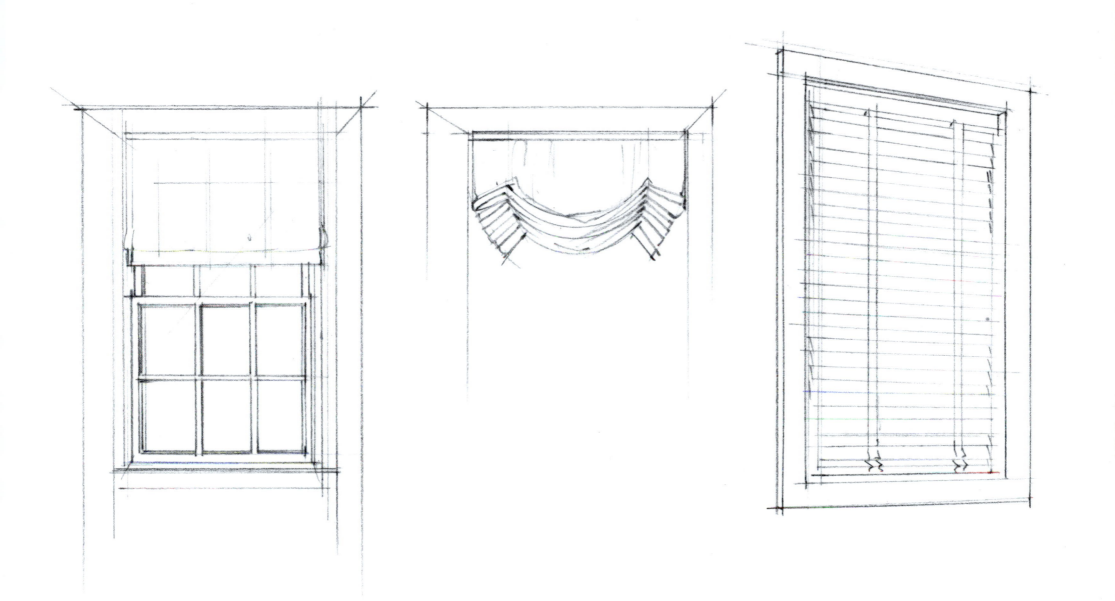

A.6. *Shades and blinds (chapter 6)*

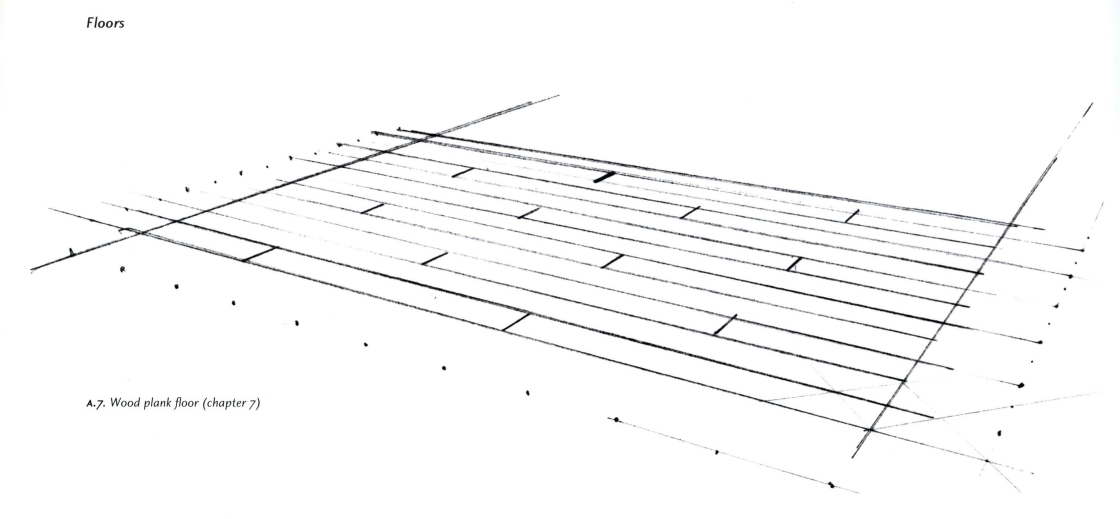

A.7. *Wood plank floor (chapter 7)*

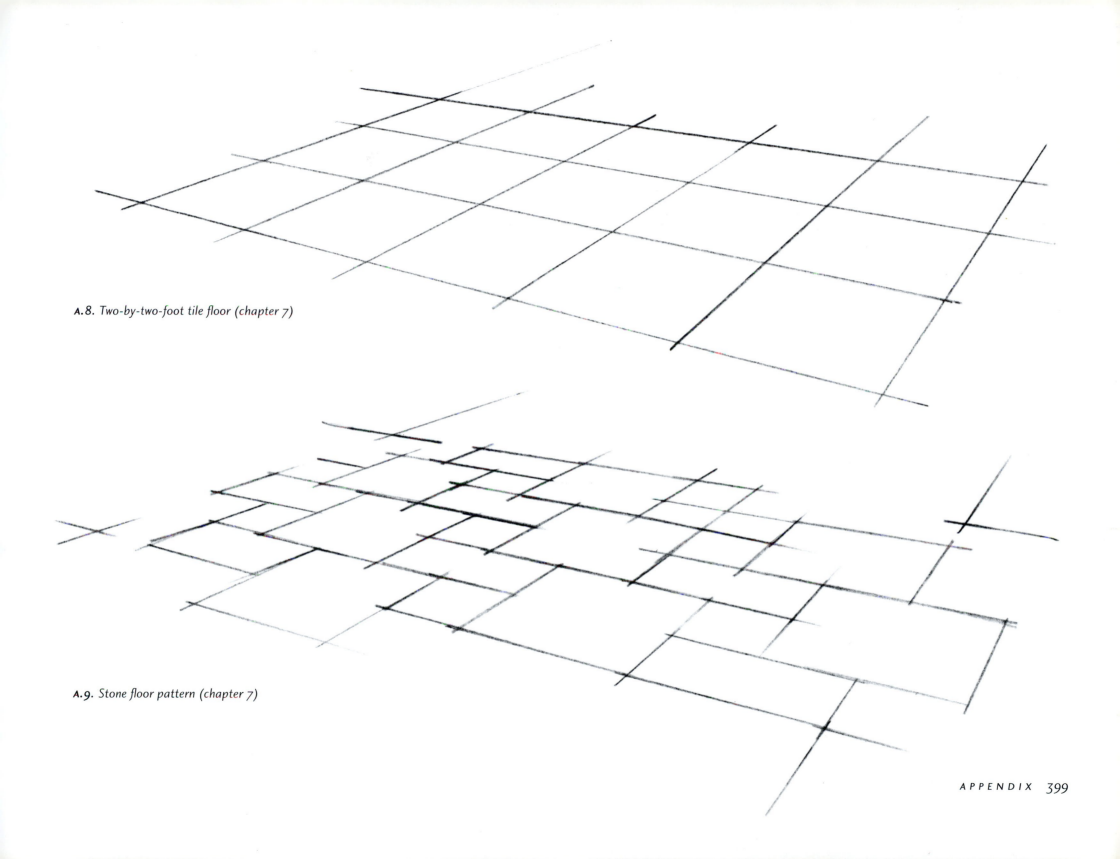

A.8. *Two-by-two-foot tile floor (chapter 7)*

A.9. *Stone floor pattern (chapter 7)*

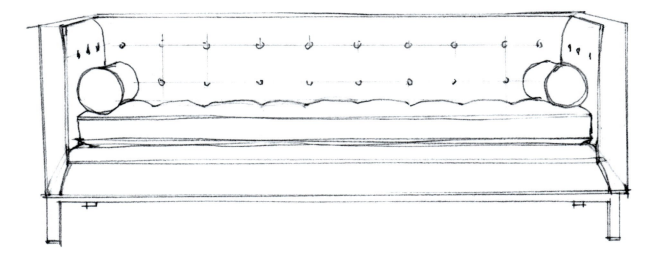

A.11. *Chairs and a skirted stool (chapter 8)*

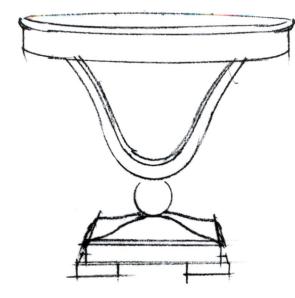

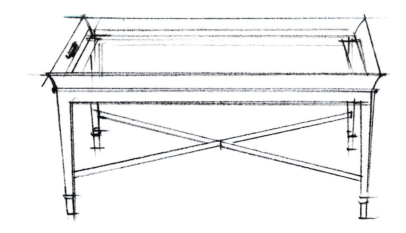

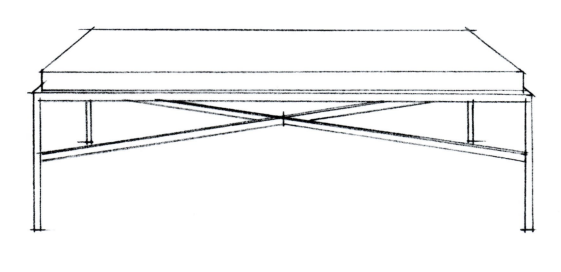

A.12. *Tables (chapter 8)*

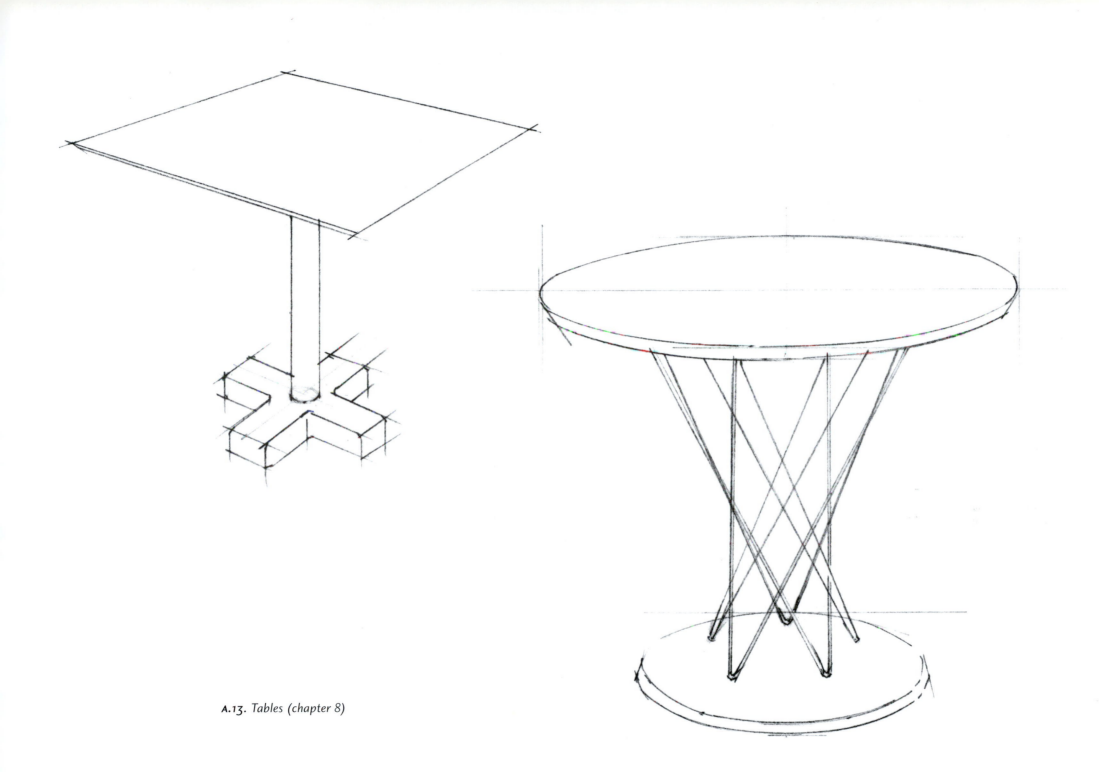

A.13. *Tables (chapter 8)*

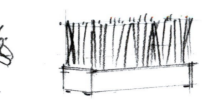

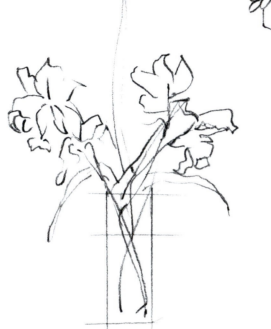

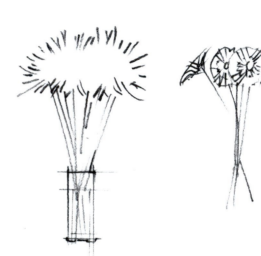

A.14. *Floral
arrangements
(chapter 9)*

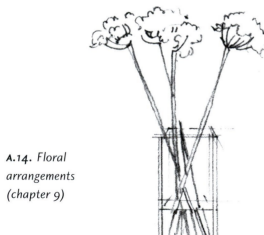

Tip! Copy the people and the plants onto acetate sheets (one actual size, one reduced, and one enlarged). To help determine the placement and the scale, position the acetate on top of the line drawing of your room.

A.15. *People (chapter 9)*

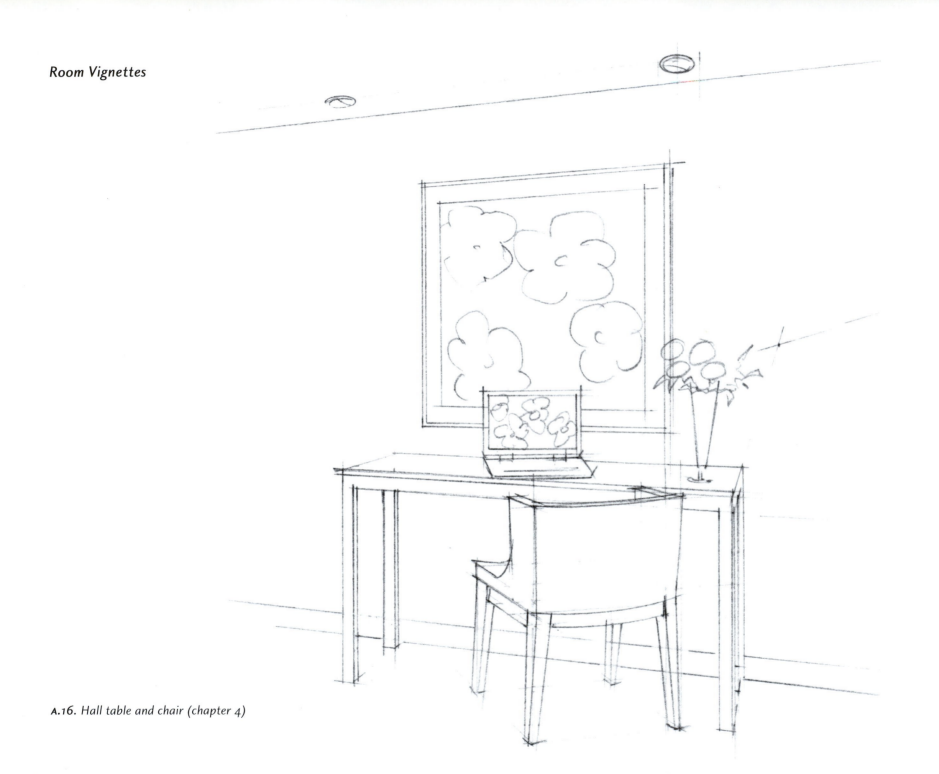

A.16. Hall table and chair (chapter 4)

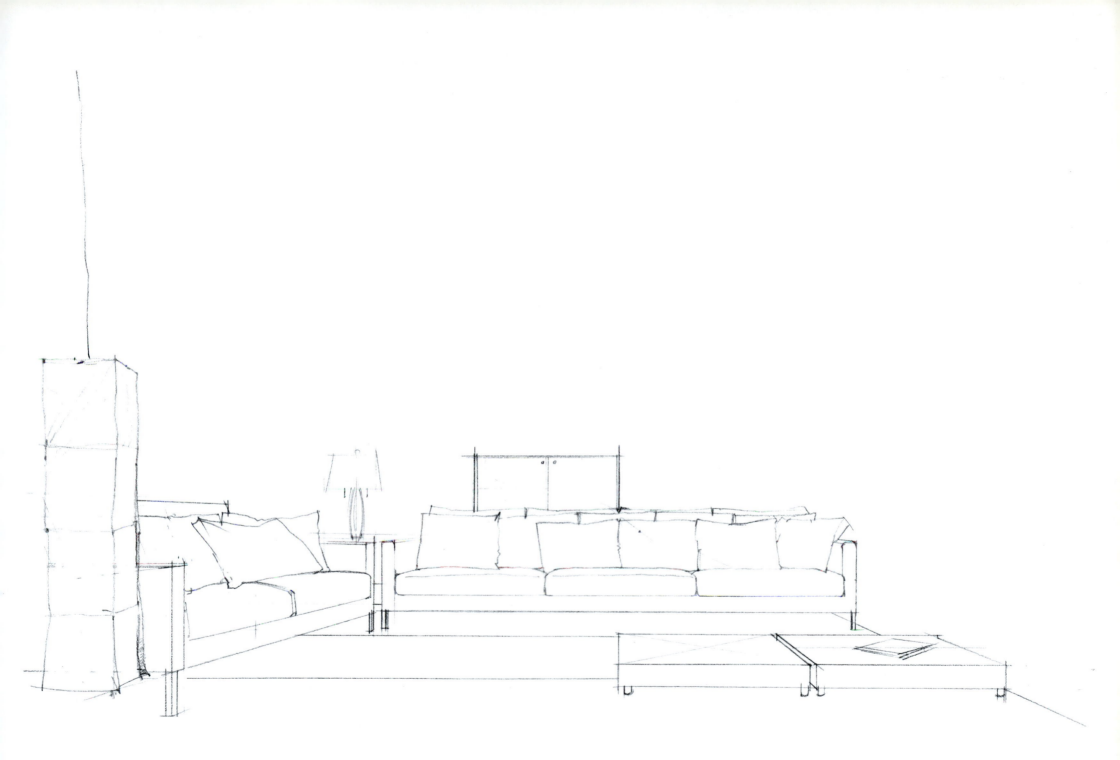

A.17. *Loft living room (chapter 4)*

A.18. *Conference room (chapter 4)*

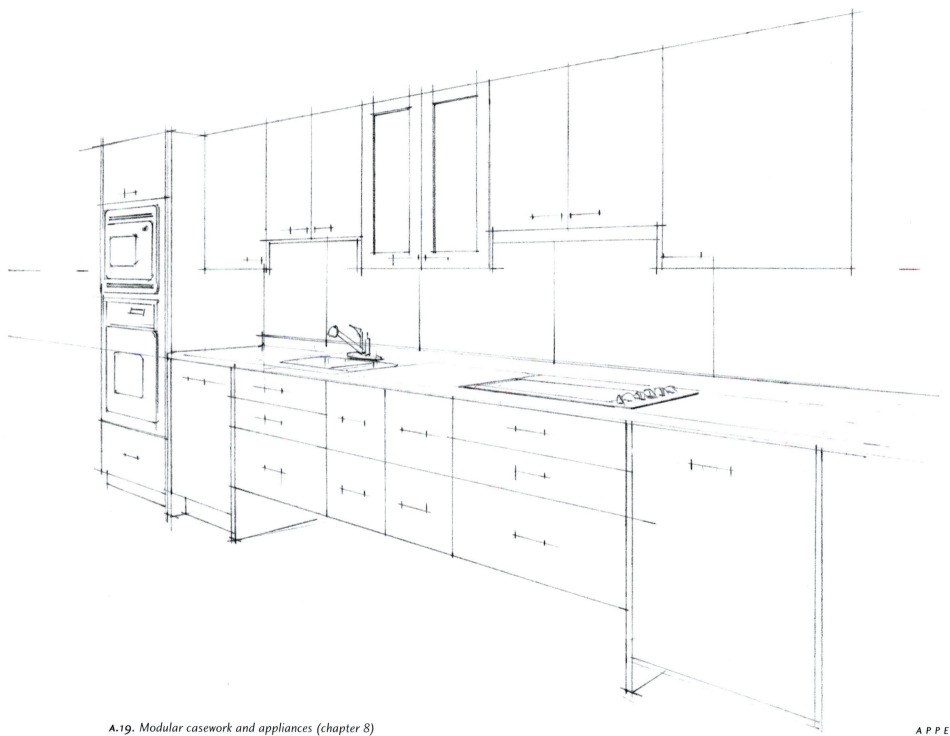

A.19. *Modular casework and appliances (chapter 8)*

The Critique

Who hasn't left a critique—or even worse, a design presentation—devastated, mad, or teary eyed? These feelings are natural, but you can get over them by often initiating feedback from your fellow students, instructors, clients, and design associates. A basic premise of the design process is continuous analysis and feedback. Don't wait for comments. Ask for them.

The worst part of facing a critique is anxiety, because presenting to a group of individuals is not easy. Don't fall to pieces. Be confident. If you can master a studio critique with grace and dignity, you will be ready for anything that members of a board of directors may say. Strengthen your resolve to learn and improve. Assimilate the comments made, and be pleased about the feedback so you do not respond in resentment. Be open. Critical reviews from colleagues and clients—and yourself— are part of the design process. A critique is your opportunity for discussion, a chance to improve your skills and your designs. Record the feedback. Be honest. Apply the recommendations.

Self-Analysis

It is difficult to analyze one's own work, yet it is important to develop this skill. Following are a few critique questions, from general to specific, to ask yourself. Many stem from elements and principles of design, which help you create a pleasing interior and, when used correctly, a pleasing composition. Approach the questions thinking about how to improve your subject. Ask what you can do differently to make it more successful—not what is wrong with it. Break it apart and analyze its parts.

1. What is successful in the illustration?

2. Are you looking at the illustration from the correct presentation viewing distance?

3. If there is a problematic part, are you looking at it in the context of the whole illustration?

4. Does it look like the subject or the material that you wish to portray? Where can it be improved? Is anything missing?

5. Does the illustration tell others what you want them to know? What could be done to explain this better?

6. Have you chosen the wrong material for the project? (It does happen.)

7. Would the illustration be more successful with a different paper, medium, or color? Would a different gesture or stroke work better?

8. Is the material detailed correctly? Or does it have too much or too little detail?

9. Is the medium application too heavy handed or too light?

10. Is a particular surface too dominant? If so, can you sublimate it by repeating the gesture in a small way somewhere else in the illustration for visual balance?

11. Does the illustration have the right contrast or value placement? Do the contrast and value help the rendering read, or is the illustration too broken up visually?

12. Does the line work interfere with the illustration or harmonize and support it? Is there too much line or too little? How is the line quality? Is it drawn correctly?

13. Does the illustration look muddy or fresh and inviting? Is there too much gray?

14. What is salvageable? Does the illustration require complete redoing, or can it be successfully modified?

15. Was enough time and effort devoted to the illustration?

Artist's Block

Sometimes looking at a digital photograph or a photocopy of an illustration makes it easier to see where improvement is needed. Turn it upside down or sideways to see if you can find any errors. Ask more questions centered around the principles of design and composition. Perhaps one of the questions was tough to answer—for example, Is there too much gray? Use comparative analysis. The answer can be found by redoing the illustration or part of it with less gray. Then compare the two versions.

Still no answers? Walk away, and come back to the illustration a few hours or even a day later. Don't think about it at all. You have already asked the questions. The answers may come to you while you are doing a totally unrelated activity, while at rest, or when you have a fresh eye and perspective. Immediately jot down your thoughts.

Try this brainstorming process for a class critique. The Design Council has developed a "scribble-say-slap" method to generate ideas from a group of people. In quick time, participants write down their ideas (scribble) on sticky notes before shouting them out (say) and sticking them up (slap).

All creative people sometimes get what is called a block. You know—running your hands through your hair, no words or ideas springing from your right brain to the paper, your head dropping to the desk as you let out a frustrating sigh. Staring at a piece of white paper for more than a minute without thought or motion is a sure sign of artist's block. It can happen when you are beginning a creative endeavor, illustrating a project, or encountering a blunder.

Suggestions given in the chapter warm-ups, drawing upside down or sideways, and even simply looking at a magazine or a book all help stimulate a designer's right-brain activity. Using analytical questions and feedback from others can also generate new ideas and bring you to new conclusions. Want to get out of a block? Use a critique to get unstuck.

One of my favorites is a "charade charette." This requires at least two persons. Render together very fast, imitating the style of a well-known professional, or use a photograph of an interior and duplicate the space shown. Learn from and inspire each other. It can be energizing when each person works on a different part of the same drawing. An alternative is to choose a difficult subject and encourage the other person along the way. This process is reminiscent of working in a design office and leads to improved team skills.

Resources

This compilation of books and resources will lead you to thousands of examples of images with which to develop and refine your skills. You will also find information on significant illustrators and artists, techniques, materials, how to draw people, entourage, and much more.

Abling, Bina. *Marker Rendering for Fashion, Accessories, and Home Fashions.* New York: Fairchild Books, 2005.

_____. *Model Drawing.* New York: Fairchild Books, 2003.

Barr, Vilma, and Dani Antman. *The Illustrated Room: 20th Century Interior Design Rendering.* New York: McGraw-Hill, 1997.

Burden, Ernest. *Entourage.* New York: McGraw Hill, 2002.

Campbell, Nina, and Caroline Seebohm. *Elsie de Wolf: A Decorative Life.* New York: Clarkson Potter, 1992.

Carbonetti, Jeanne. *The Yoga of Drawing.* New York: Watson-Guptil, 1999.

Design Council. www.design-council.org.

Drpic, Ivo D. *Sketching and Rendering Interior Space.* New York: Watson-Guptill, 1988.

Fisher, Richard, and Dorothy Wolfthal. *Textile Print Design.* New York: Fairchild Books, 1987.

Goodman, Jeremiah. *Jeremiah: A Romantic Vision.* New York: powerHouse Books, 2007.

Graphic-sha Editorial Staff. *Interiors: Perspectives in Architectural Design.* Tokyo: Graphic-sha Publishing, 1987.

Hampton, Mark, Mario Buatta, David Anthony Easton, and Mariette Himes Gomez. *Albert Hadley: Drawings and the Design Process.* New York: New York School of Interior Design, 2004.

Leach, Sid DelMar. *Techniques of Interior Design Rendering and Presentation.* New York: Architectural Record Books, 1978.

Lin, Mike W. *Architectural Rendering Techniques: A Color Reference.* New York: Van Nostrand Reinhold, 1985.

_____. *Drawing and Designing with Confidence.* New York: John Wiley, 1993.

McGarry, Richard M., and Greg Madsen. *Marker Magic: The Rendering Problem Solver for Designers.* New York: John Wiley, 1992.

Olendorf, Donna and William, and Robert W. Tolf. *Addison Mizner, Architect to the Affluent: A Sketchbook Raisonné of His Work.* Detroit: Gale Group, 1983.

Pable, Jill. *Sketching Interiors at the Speed of Thought.* New York: Fairchild Books, 2004.

Pike, John. *Watercolor.* New York: Watson-Guptil, 1966.

Tasma-Anargyros, Sophie. *Andrée Putman.* New York: Overlook Press, 1997.

Wang, Thomas C. *Sketching with Markers.* New York: Van Nostrand Reinhold, 1992.

Webb, Frank. *Strengthen Your Paintings with Dynamic Composition.* Cincinnati: North Light, 1994.

_____. *Watercolor Energies.* Cincinnati: North Light, 1983.

_____. *Webb on Watercolor.* Cincinnati: North Light, 1990.

Whitney, Edgar. *Complete Guide to Watercolor Painting.* New York: Dover, 2001.

"Somewhere, something incredible is waiting to be known."

Carl Sagan (1934–96)

Illustration Credits

Illustrations by Guy Romagna, contributing artist:

3.3, 3.4, 3.19, 6.40, 6.41, 6.47, 6.52, 7.29c, 7.29e, 7.29f, 8.40, 8.41, 8.44, 8.45 8.46, 8.47, 8.50, 8.52, 8.53, 8.56, 8.57, 8.64, 8.66, 9.1e, 9.10, 9.11, 9.13 (watercolor), 9.14 (watercolor), 9.15, 9.16, 9.17, 9.26, 10.13, 10.23, 10.41, page 362, 11.4, 11.5, 11.6, 11.8, 11.9, 11.15, 11.18

Figures:

1.3. All trademarks herein are the property of Letraset Limited. Copyright © 2008 Letraset Limited.

1.7. Color chart and Van Gogh paint courtesy of Canson, Inc., and Royal Talens

2.3. Nadim Racy. Courtesy of McCluskey Design Group/McGraw Hill

2.5. Julian LaTrobe. Courtesy of Random House

2.6. José M. Reinares Méndez. Courtesy of Random House

3.20. Julian LaTrobe. Courtesy of Random House

3.21. Andrée Putman. Courtesy of Overlook Press

3.22. Nadim Racy. Courtesy of McCluskey Design Group/McGraw Hill

3.24. Julian LaTrobe. Courtesy of Random House

3.25 Jeremiah Goodman. Courtesy of Jeremiah Goodman

3.27. Andrée Putman. Courtesy of Overlook Press

3.30. Robert Martin. Photographed by J. Karsten Moran. Courtesy of Yale R. Burge Antiques

3.31. Nadim Racy. Courtesy of McCluskey Design Group/McGraw Hill

3.32. Julian LaTrobe. Courtesy of McGraw-Hill

4.1. Paper courtesy of Strathmore™ Artist Papers

4.3. Paper courtesy of Strathmore™ Artist Papers

4.11. Illustration courtesy of Christian Lacroix

10.34. Paper courtesy of Strathmore™ Artist Papers

Index